Christian Mission
in Theological
Perspective

Christian Mission
in Theological
Perspective

An Inquiry by Methodists

Edited by Gerald H. Anderson

Prepared by the Board of Missions
of The Methodist Church
Published by Abingdon Press
Nashville—New York

CHRISTIAN MISSION IN THEOLOGICAL PERSPECTIVE

Copyright © 1967 by Abingdon Press

Library of Congress Catalog Card Number: 67-11709

Scripture quotations unless otherwise noted are from the Revised Standard
Version of the Bible, copyrighted 1946 and 1952 by the Division of Christian Education, National Council of Churches, and are used by permission.

Scripture quotations noted NEB are from The New English Bible, New
Testament. © the Delegates of the Oxford University Press and the Syndics
of the Cambridge University Press. 1961. Reprinted by permission.

Quotations from "Missions as the Test of Faith" by W. A. Visser 't Hooft
first appeared in Witness in Six Continents, edited by R. K. Orchard, Edinburgh House Press, London, 1964.

"The Work of the Holy Spirit in the World" is from Upon the Earth by
D. T. Niles, copyrighted 1962 by McGraw-Hill Book Company; used
by permission of McGraw-Hill and Lutterworth Press.

"The Issue: Ultimate Meaning in History" by Carl Michalson, copyrighted
© 1959 by Abingdon Press, Nashville.

SET UP, PRINTED, AND BOUND BY THE
PARTHENON   PRESS,   AT   NASHVILLE,
TENNESSEE, UNITED STATES OF AMERICA

To
Eugene L. Smith
Who inspired this inquiry
and
Carl Michalson (1915-1965)
Who contributed much to it

Contributors

Gerald H. Anderson, Professor of Church History and Ecumenics, Union Theological Seminary, Manila, Philippines.

L. Harold DeWolf, Dean and Professor of Systematic Theology, Wesley Theological Seminary, Washington, D.C.

A. Roy Eckardt, Professor of Religion and Chairman of the Department of Religion, Lehigh University, Bethlehem, Pennsylvania, and Editor of *The Journal of the American Academy of Religion.*

John D. Godsey, Professor of Systematic Theology, The Theological School, Drew University, Madison, New Jersey.

W. Richey Hogg, Professor of World Christianity, Perkins School of Theology, Southern Methodist University, Dallas, Texas.

7

Carl Michalson was Andrew V. Stout Professor of Systematic Theology, The Theological School, Drew University, Madison, New Jersey.

Walter G. Muelder, Dean and Professor of Social Ethics, Boston University School of Theology, Boston, Massachusetts.

J. Robert Nelson, Professor of Systematic Theology, Boston University School of Theology, Boston, Massachusetts.

D. T. Niles, General Secretary of the East Asia Christian Conference and Chairman of the North District of the Methodist Church, Ceylon.

S. Paul Schilling, Professor of Systematic Theology, Boston University School of Theology, Boston, Massachusetts.

Everett Tilson, Professor of Old Testament, The Methodist Theological School in Ohio, Delaware, Ohio.

Faith is tested in various ways, but there is no more decisive test than the one concerning the translation of faith into missionary witness.

———•———

It is in that witness that the Church proves or disproves . . . whether it believes in the "happenedness" of the great deeds of God in Christ, . . . whether it really believes in the universality of the Gospel, . . . whether it really believes that the Word of God is not bound.

———•———

The missionary witness is at all times a test of the faith of the Church. . . . And nearly all the signs in the realm of politics and of ideas point in the direction of increasing rather than decreasing unwillingness to recognize the *raison d'être* of missions. A new testing time for missions has arrived.

—W. A. Visser 't Hooft
Mexico City, 1963

Preface

The following news item appeared in *The New York Times* for January 20, 1966: "More than 500 Methodist leaders began today the delicate task of redefining the church's mission in theological terms that would be applicable to the modern world." Fortunately, these leaders did not have to begin empty-handed. Their work was based on more than ten years of study and discussion that was part of a larger ecumenical undertaking.

Ever since 1952, ecumenical leaders have recognized the urgent need for a major study of the theological questions raised by the present situation of the Christian world mission. The Willingen Meeting of the International Missionary Council in 1952 asked the churches to give continuing study to the following theological issues: (1) the theological significance of the foreign missionary enterprise within the total missionary obligation of the church; (2) the meaning of the Christian hope in relation to our missionary message and practice; (3) the relation between "history" and "salvation-history," between God's sovereignty in creation and his grace in redemption; and (4) the relation of the

11

doctrine of the Holy Spirit to the doctrine of the church and the ministry.

In 1956 the Central Committee of the World Council of Churches requested its Department of Missionary Studies to undertake a study of the theology of mission that would deal with the following questions:

1. What does it mean, theologically and practically, to discharge the Christian mission in an ecumenical era?

2. To what extent is there an inner tension between an interchurch perspective and a missionary perspective which looks beyond the church into the world?

3. In what way is the missionary imperative essentially linked with the kingdom of God? How does this call into question the autonomy of the church?

In response to this request for study, the Division of World Missions of the Board of Missions of The Methodist Church began in 1956 to hold annual consultations on "The Theology of Mission," as a contribution to the ecumenical discussion and for clarification of its own thinking on the subject. Through the initiative of the then General Secretary, Dr. Eugene L. Smith, these consultations brought together theologians and professors of missions from all the Methodist seminaries in the United States, to discuss with the mission board executives those theological questions put forward by the ecumenical study, especially as they were related to the problems and perspectives of The Methodist Church in mission.

From the outset there was an awareness of the danger of over-intellectualizing the mission, and a recognition that these studies should not be used as an escape from the hard reality of decision-making in mission administration. Instead, there has been an effort to see the theological issues in terms of the action facing the church in the unfinished missionary task; to provide a theological perspective for dealing with the problems of Christian world mission in this new era, and to understand what it means to be a responsible church in a revolutionary world.

All these essays were prepared originally for this series of consultations, except the one by Dr. D. T. Niles, and his thought as an Asian Methodist theologian has been so influential in all parts of the world that it seemed appropriate to include here his relevant study on the work of the Holy Spirit. The essays represent only a selection from the studies in this series, and as such there is no systematic development of a single theme, but rather a critical and sensitive probing of several areas of major concern in missionary thinking today. It is interesting to note that the greatest area of overlapping in these studies is in the attention given by several of the writers to the doctrine of the church, as it relates to the basis and aim of mission—and this in a theological tradition that has not been known for its concern with ecclesiology!

Two appendices are included that reveal something of the immensity and urgency of the Christian world mission in terms of the numbers of non-Christian peoples and the size of the Christian missionary task force, both Protestant and Roman Catholic, at work throughout the world. Despite the sacrificial effort and significant gains of the Christian mission through the centuries, there are still more non-Christians in the world today than on the day when Jesus was crucified. Two out of three people in the world today do not recognize him as Lord, and as many as one billion people have never even heard the name of Jesus. Our conviction is that he alone can bring healing and wholeness to men and nations. To this end we dedicate our efforts and seek for a radical renewal of Christian mission in our time.

GERALD H. ANDERSON

Manila, Philippines

Contents

15

The Church and Its Ministry

S. Paul Schilling

In 1949-50 The Methodist Church published for study by its members a series of booklets on "Our Faith." The eight essays deal with our faith in God, Christ, the Bible, love, prayer, immortality, the Holy Spirit, and the kingdom; but they omit the church. The omission exemplifies the marginal consideration customarily given by Methodists in the past to the doctrine of the church. We have made much of the church as an institution and developed a high degree of organizational efficiency, but we have seldom bothered to inquire what we mean by the church.

For this neglect American Methodists are paying a high price in individual confusion and denominational ambiguity. In a nationwide survey of the beliefs of Methodists in 1959, 30.4 percent of the 5,020 respondents conceived the church primarily as "a society of those who have joined together in their quest for the religious life"—a definition lacking any distinctively Christian orientation. [1] In various ecumenical discussions Methodists have created an impres-

[1] S. Paul Schilling, *Methodism and Society in Theological Perspective* (Nashville: Abingdon Press, 1960), pp. 161, 281.

17

sion of theological imprecision, denominational rigidity, and inordinate concern for structure and polity which have jeopardized understanding and which might have been partially averted by deeper grounding in doctrinal issues. Fortunately, this situation has recently begun to change. Within the past two decades individual Methodist theologians have devoted increasing attention to the church's nature and mission. Most seminary students are now learning to see the church in biblical and theological perspective. The 1962 Oxford Institute on Methodist Theological Studies, sponsored by the World Methodist Council, produced an important symposium on *The Doctrine of the Church*, the theme of the meeting. [2] In 1937, after two years of committee work, the Methodist Conference of Great Britain adopted a careful statement on *The Nature of the Christian Church According to the Teaching of the Methodists*. [3] Representatives of the same body joined a committee of the Church of England in issuing in 1963, after seven years of study, a report which includes chapters on Scripture and tradition; gospel, church order, and ministry; and the sacraments. These theological considerations then became the basis for proposals looking toward reconciliation and full communion of the two bodies. [4] In The Methodist Church in the United States several biblical and theological studies of the church have recently been carried out under the auspices of particular boards as bases for their work. The creation by the General Conference of 1964 of the Commission on Ecumenical Affairs holds much promise for the future.

Fundamental and systematic thinking on the church and its ministry is urgently needed if Methodism is to participate

---

[2] Dow Kirkpatrick, ed., *The Doctrine of the Church* (Nashville: Abingdon Press, 1964).

[3] (London: The Methodist Publishing House, 1937).

[4] *Conversations between the Church of England and the Methodist Church* (Westminster: Church Information Office, 1963; London: The Epworth Press, 1963).

responsibly in the ecumenical conversations now going on, both contributing to and learning from other Christian traditions. This need is especially apparent in connection with the Christian world mission. Questions related to possible mergers, the issue of regionalism versus confessionalism, and the encounter of Christianity with resurgent non-Christian religions admit of no constructive solutions apart from clear understanding of agreements and differences concerning the nature and purpose of the church. Inseparably related to this is the question of the nature and validity of the ministry.

The Thought and Practice of John Wesley

Methodist teaching concerning the church and the ministry, while not determined by the thought of John Wesley, is certainly profoundly influenced by him. We accordingly begin with an effort to interpret his often puzzling if not contradictory views.

THE CHURCH

Throughout his life Wesley was a staunch churchman. He was convinced that the holiness of heart and life which he sought could be adequately nurtured only within the fellowship of the church. "The gospel of Christ knows no religion but social: no holiness but social holiness." [5] He observed acutely that the perseverance of his converts in their new life was in direct proportion to their participation in societies of like-minded people. Beyond this, he did his utmost to relate them directly to the life of the organized church, particularly the Anglican—"the best constituted national church in the world." He regarded himself as a loyal member and priest of the Church of England. With few exceptions, he required his societies to meet at hours which did not conflict with church services, and to the last he refused to

---

[5] George Osborn, ed., *The Poetical Works of John and Charles Wesley* (London: Wesleyan Methodist Conference Office, 1868-72), I, xxii.

countenance the "separation" of the societies from the Anglican Church.

In his *Earnest Appeal* (1743), Wesley concurs with the Nineteenth Article of Religion in defining the visible church as " a congregation of faithful men, in which the pure Word of God is preached, and the Sacraments be duly administered according to Christ's ordinance." Writing his brother Charles on August 19, 1785, he describes this as "a true logical definition, containing both the essence and properties of a Church." He interprets the whole article in accord with its opening emphasis on faith, finding three essentials in a visible church: "living faith, without which, indeed, there can be no church at all"; "preaching, and consequently hearing, the pure Word of God, else that faith would languish and die"; and "a due administration of the sacraments—the ordinary means whereby God increaseth faith."

This typically Anglican—and Protestant—view of both "the essence and properties" of the church seems uppermost when on September 24, 1755, Wesley writes to Samuel Walker opposing the separation of the Methodist societies from the Church of England. Here he distinguishes carefully between the worship and doctrines of the church and her orders and laws, insisting that only the former constitute the essence of the church. Separation would be indicated only if Methodists either renounced her doctrines or repudiated her worship; actually they do neither, accepting her fundamental doctrines as sound and her worship as in the main "pure and scriptural."

Yet in 1788, in his sermon "Of the Church," he strongly emphasizes the faith which is the "essence" of the church and raises serious questions about the "properties," even though this entails direct criticism of the validity of Article XIX and, indirectly, a modification of his earlier stress on doctrine and worship as essential. Preaching on Ephesians 4:1-6, he defines the church as all the persons in the universe who through God's call have become " 'one body,' united by 'one Spirit'; having 'one faith, one hope, one baptism; one God and Father of all.' " This definition, he asserts, is "exactly agreeable" to Article XIX. But clearly he felt the agreement to be less than exact. Parenthetically he adds, "Only the Article includes a little more than the Apostle has expressed"; and a few paragraphs later he describes the article as including "Much more," through "that remarkable addition" of the clauses concerning the preaching of the pure word of God and the due administration of the sacraments. By these words the article implies that congregations in which these conditions are not met are not really parts of the true church. Hence Wesley declares,

I will not undertake to defend the accuracy of this definition. I dare not exclude from the Church catholic all those congregations in which any unscriptural doctrines, which cannot be affirmed to be the "pure word of God," are sometimes, yea, frequently preached; neither all those congregations, in which the sacraments are not "duly administered."

On such a basis even the Roman Church must be excluded from the catholic church, since it meets neither condition. On the contrary, those who have "one Spirit, one hope, one Lord, one faith, one God and Father of all," however wrong their opinions or superstitious their ways of worship, qualify for membership in the true church. [6]

Inseparable from the manifold oneness of such a church, however, is its mission. It is a "body of people, united together in the service of God." Its members are to let their light shine before all men, evidencing their faith and their empowerment by the Spirit in works of love. [7] In similar vein Wesley elsewhere commends the primitive church at

[6] "Of the Church," pars. 14, 16, 18, 19; *The Works of the Rev. John Wesley, A.M.*, ed. Thomas Jackson. (3rd ed.; London: Wesleyan-Methodist Book-Room, 1829-31; Grand Rapids: Zondervan Publishing House, n.d.), VI, 396-97.

[7] *Ibid.*, pars. 1, 30; pp. 392, 400-401.

Jerusalem as "a native specimen of a New Testament church; which is, a company of men, called by the gospel, grafted into Christ by baptism, animated by love, united by all kind of fellowship, and disciplined by the death of Ananias and Sapphira." [8] Christians thus united are summoned to bear witness to the love of God who has given them his Son, and to strive to restore "the image of God, pure love, in every child of man." [9]

THE MINISTRY

Wesley's view of the church, influenced as it was by his relations with the Church of England, came to a focus in his changing conceptions of the ministry. In his Oxford and Georgia period his beliefs largely agreed with those of the *Apostolic Constitutions,* a fourth-century manual of Christian discipline, doctrine, and worship, purporting to be a compilation by Clement of Rome of the instructions of the apostles. He apparently accepted three ministerial orders—bishops, presbyters, and deacons—along with the restriction to bishops of the power of ordination, and a high conception of apostolic succession.

There is no evidence that this basic orientation was immediately changed by his Aldersgate experience of firsthand communion with God. The deepened emphasis on personal faith gradually lessened his zeal for institutional requirements, and his increasing associations with nonchurchmen made him less exclusive. But as late as December 30, 1745, he wrote to his brother-in-law Westley Hall: "We believe that it would not be right for us to administer either baptism or the Lord's supper unless we had a commission so to do from those bishops whom we apprehend to be in a succession from the Apostles. . . . We believe that the three-

---

[8] *Explanatory Notes upon the New Testament,* Acts 5:11.
[9] Sermon on Num. 23:23, Sec. II, pars. 1, 2, 4, 17; *Works,* VII, 423-25, 430.

fold order of ministers . . . is not only authorized by its apostolical institution, but also by the written Word."

Two influences combined to produce a marked, if gradual, change in Wesley's doctrine of the ministry: the growing practical needs of the societies which multiplied as the result of Methodist evangelistic endeavor; and Wesley's restudy of the nature of the ministry in the New Testament and the "primitive church."

Methodist preaching brought about the spiritual rebirth of thousands of people, many of whom had never been related to the Church of England. Because Wesley and his preachers were, through the opposition of bishops and clergy, excluded from Anglican pulpits and driven to preaching in the open air and in meetinghouses, their converts were formed into religious societies with no organized relation to the parish churches. Though these people evidenced a powerful experience of the Holy Spirit, many of them were unconfirmed, hence denied the right of participation in the Lord's Supper. They needed a total religious ministry, but did not receive it from the parish clergy, who often manifested either indifference or hostility.

Particularly urgent was the missionary situation in America following the achievement of independence by the colonies, where Wesley was convinced there were not enough clergymen to carry forward the work of God. The Anglican bishops peremptorily refused to act to remedy matters by ordaining his preachers. Circumstances like these led him, after much searching of heart, to "set apart" Richard Whatcoat and Thomas Vasey as elders and Thomas Coke as superintendent for the American Methodists; and later to ordain several other men for Scotland and three for England.

Wesley recognized that these acts violated the regular procedures of the Church of England, but insisted that they were required by his commission to spread the gospel and "save souls." His sole aim was "to promote, so far as

23

I am able, vital, practical religion; and by the grace of God to beget, preserve, and increase the life of God in the souls of men." [10] This he regarded also as the central task of the church itself.

No doubt goaded by the practical demands of the expanding evangelical movement, Wesley reexamined the New Testament and other writings for light on the true nature and meaning of the Christian ministry, and became convinced that his earlier views had been partially in error. In 1746, through reading Peter King's *Enquiry into the Constitution, Discipline, Unity, and Worship of the Primitive Church,* he became convinced that bishops and presbyters (or elders) are essentially one order rather than two. Both have the same spiritual power, including the power to preach, administer the sacraments, and ordain. In support of the presbyter's right to ordain Wesley cites Jerome's testimony that such presbyterian ordination, even of bishops, was practiced in the ancient church at Alexandria. The *episcopos* (overseer) is a presbyter who has been given special administrative leadership and authority, but no new spiritual authority. Hence there is no sound basis for reserving to the bishops a divine right of ordination. Presbyters are of the same order, and have the same authority to ordain.

Later Wesley read Edward Stillingfleet's *Irenicon*, and gave up his belief that the episcopal form of church government is prescribed in the Scriptures, though he continued to regard episcopacy as "both Scriptural and apostolical." In a letter to James Clark, dated July 3, 1756, Wesley writes that in his judgment Stillingfleet "has unanswerably proved that neither Christ or His Apostles prescribed any particular form of Church government, and that the plea for the divine right of Episcopacy was never heard of in the primitive Church."

[10] Letter to Samuel Walker, September 3, 1756.

It is strong testimony to the genuineness of Wesley's personal commitment to Anglican polity and his desire for harmony that, in spite of his broadened views of the ministry, he declined for so many years to exercise the right of ordination which he believed he possessed, even though he was urged repeatedly to do so. When he finally exercised the power to ordain, it was at first not for England, where there were "bishops who have a legal jurisdiction," as well as large numbers of parish ministers, but for America, where in vast regions there were no persons authorized to baptize or administer the Lord's Supper. This was to him the most "rational and scriptural way of feeding and guiding those poor sheep in the wilderness." [11]

In response to criticism, Wesley was emphatic in claiming for himself the ordaining authority which he had previously acknowledged in general to belong to presbyters no less than bishops. "I know myself," he wrote to Barnabas Thomas on March 25, 1785, "to be as real a Christian bishop as the Archbishop of Canterbury." To his brother Charles he wrote on August 19 of the same year, "I firmly believe I am a scriptural *Episcopos* as much as any man in England or in Europe; for the *uninterrupted succession* I know to be a fable, which no man ever did or can prove." Yet in the former letter he asserts his resolution never to act as a bishop "except in case of necessity," which he feels may never arise in England. The fact that on several later occasions he deemed it necessary even in Great Britain to exercise the power to ordain involves no departure from this principle.

What, then, may we say concerning Wesley's view of the ministry? Several conclusions may be drawn:

1. He regarded the episcopal polity of the Church of England as biblical, apostolic, and normally practical, but not as prescribed by the Scriptures or necessary for a true church.

[11] Letter to "Our Brethren in America," September 10, 1784.

25

2. He rejected the threefold ministry in favor of two orders: deacons and presbyters or elders. In the primitive church, he was convinced, bishops were simply elders who as superintendents exercised administrative oversight as well as spiritual leadership. This interpretation of early church practice became his norm, and on this basis he affirmed that presbyters have the power to ordain not only deacons and presbyters but also bishops. In this framework, Coke, Whatcoat, and Vasey were in spiritual powers *pares*, while from the standpoint of Coke's administrative function he was *primus inter pares*.

3. He rejected the doctrine that ordination is valid only if performed by a bishop whose power has been handed down by apostolic succession from Christ himself.

4. He insisted on the validity of lay preaching. In support of the right and duty of qualified laymen to preach, Wesley cites: a. the practice of the apostolic age, when many who preached the gospel were not ordained (Acts 8:1, 4), and when some preaching was required as a demonstration of ability prior to ordination (I Tim. 3:10); b. the important part played by Calvin and other laymen in the Reformation; c. the utilization of lay evangelists by Catholic religious orders; and d. the proven ability of Methodist lay preachers to "save souls" ignored by ordained priests. It is desirable, he believed, for the preacher to have an outward as well as inward call, but not *"absolutely necessary."* [12] "If one of the two be supposed wanting, I had rather want the outward than the inward call. I rejoice that I am called to preach the gospel both by God and man. Yet I acknowledge I had rather have the divine without the human than the human without the divine call." [13]

5. To the end Wesley distinguished carefully—if artificially

---

[12] Sermon, "A Caution Against Bigotry" (1749), sec. III, par. 7; *Works*, V, 488.

[13] Letter to Samuel Walker, September 3, 1756.

—between the offices of evangelist-preacher and pastor-priest, regarding only the latter as authorized to administer the sacraments and refusing to permit his lay preachers to exercise the priestly role. This prohibition was no doubt motivated partly by his desire to avoid separation from the Church of England, but it also reveals Wesley as a churchman who took ordination seriously.[14] His ordinations themselves demonstrate his concern for an orderly rather than a haphazard ministry.

Seen in perspective, Wesley's utterances and his practice alike show him living and working in uneasy but creative tension between two concerns: his deep loyalty to the Church of England, including acceptance of her doctrine, liturgy, and sacraments, respect for her episcopacy and priesthood; and his devotion to the spread of "scriptural holiness" and the upbuilding of persons in love toward God and man. In case of conflict, the latter concern was paramount. Thus he preached in the open and inspired others to do so, justified extempore prayer, united his converts into little societies for the cultivation of "love and good works," met with his preachers in conferences at least once a year and appointed them to their places of service, and on occasion ordained men to the ministry. Yet all these actions he regarded as fulfilling the true purpose of the church. He refused to separate from the Church of England, believing that would be a sin. Just as emphatically he "varied" from it in the ways named, believing it would be a sin not to do so. To him the church is called of God to be his agent in the salvation of the world. This task takes precedence over all else. Nothing that obstructs it is sacrosanct; everything that advances it is acceptable.

[14] Sermon, "The Ministerial Office" (1789), pars. 3-6, 8; Works, VII, 274-76.

Twentieth-Century Methodist Views

We turn now to an examination of contemporary Methodist conceptions of the church, considering in order its origin, nature, authority, and ministry.

THE ORIGIN OF THE CHURCH

In general, Methodist thinkers agree with R. Newton Flew and Clarence Tucker Craig that the church came into being in consequence of the redemptive activity of God in Jesus Christ. The life, teaching, death, and resurrection of Christ brought forth a new community.

However, the roots of the New Testament community were deeply imbedded in the soil of Israel. In a profound degree its life was continuous with that of the Jewish community out of which it came. The new covenant implied and fulfilled the old. When the New Testament writers refer to the church as the people of God, they are specifically relating it to God's chosen people, the covenant community of the Old Testament. (Cf. I Pet. 2:9-10; Gal. 6:16; Phil. 3:3; I Cor. 10:1; Rom. 2:28; 11:16-24.) The very term *ekklesia*, originally a purely secular word, gained the religious meaning which fitted it to designate the Christian church from its use in the Septuagint to translate the Hebrew *Qahal*, the term used for the people of Israel called out in solemn assembly. This continuity of the new or true Israel with the old lends support to Craig's judgment that Jesus redeemed the church more truly than he founded it.[15]

Yet it remains true that Jesus called together the Twelve, the nucleus of the new Israel. Both the ethical and the eschatological aspects of his teaching suggest that he intended to form a new community of those who responded to the divine call mediated through him. Such a community did in fact emerge, particularly after the outpouring of the

---

[15] *The Universal Church in God's Design* (Amsterdam Assembly Series, Vol. I; New York: Harper & Brothers, 1949), p. 33.

Holy Spirit at Pentecost. Apart from him who incarnated the reconciling love of God, the new community fulfilling the old would not have arisen. In a profound sense, therefore, he was its founder.

We cannot and need not examine here the "faith and order" of the New Testament churches or the various types of ministry which appeared in them. It will suffice to point out four convictions generally held among Methodists: (1) The worship, faith, and order which characterized the apostolic church offer valuable guidance to the church today, and their modern counterparts should be harmonious with them. (2) None of the forms of organization found in the primitive church should be viewed as finally determinative patterns to be slavishly copied in the twentieth century. (3) In view of the functional nature of the ministry in the New Testament period and the variety and change which marked it, none of the forms of ministry prevailing today can claim the exclusive authorization of Christ or the early church, and none should be viewed as binding on the whole church. (4) Any order is valid which is consistent with New Testament faith and practice, and effectively advances the purposes for which God called the church into being.

THE NATURE AND MISSION OF THE CHURCH

In Article XIII of its Articles of Religion, The Methodist Church, like the Church of England, defines the visible church as "a congregation of faithful men in which the pure Word of God is preached, and the Sacraments duly administered according to Christ's ordinance." [16] As we have seen, this statement was regarded as inadequate by Wesley himself, and it is supplemented or modified in important ways by

---

[16] This article, which except for two stylistic changes is identical with Anglican Article XIX, is based on Part I, Article 7 of the Augsburg Confession. In the 1959 poll of Methodist beliefs already cited only 23.7 percent of those replying identified themselves with this classical Protestant conception.

29

current Methodist thought. For example, L. Harold DeWolf lists four requirements for the *esse* or essential being of the church: obedient faith in Christ; preaching and teaching of the gospel, fellowship, prayer, and service; search for unity; and commitment to the teaching of salvation by grace through faith. Also needed for the *bene esse* or well-being of the church are the sacraments, the forms of ministry reported in the New Testament, and the episcopacy or its equivalent. In DeWolf's view these provisions are not indispensable, but they are so desirable that their absence entails movement away from the *optime esse* or maximum well-being of the church.[17]

Methodists affirm both of the main New Testament descriptions of the church—as the body of Christ and the people of God.[18] Craig finds the former metaphor singularly appropriate, since a body is a visible expression of both unity and diversity, an instrument for the expression of spirit, and an organism which develops through inner transformation.[19] Thus the church is a body with many members, constantly renewed from within by the Spirit of Christ, making his life effective in the world. "God created the Church," writes J. Robert Nelson, "to be the continuing vehicle in the world by which His plan and purpose of salvation, testified to in the work of Jesus Christ, may be carried forward." [20] In this sense many Methodists would concur in the view frequently expressed that the church is the extension of the Incarnation.

Others regard the church primarily as the people of God, the new community which fulfills and extends universally the revelatory and redemptive activity begun by God in the covenant community of Israel. The British Methodist

[17] *A Hard Rain and a Cross* (Nashville: Abingdon Press, 1966), pp. 162-69.
[18] I Cor. 12:12-31; Eph. 1:22; 4:4-16; Col. 1:18; 2:19; Hos. 2:23; Acts 15:14; Heb. 4:9; 8:10; 9:15; I Pet. 2:9-10.
[19] *The Universal Church in God's Design*, pp. 39-42.
[20] *The Realm of Redemption* (London: The Epworth Press, 1951), p. 178.

Conference declared in 1937: "God, who has given us the Gospel for the salvation of the world, has appointed his church to witness by life and word to its redeeming power. Through His revelation in Jesus Christ He has called His people to live under His saving rule and to be the instrument of His eternal purpose." [21] Similarly, Albert C. Outler finds characteristic of Methodists in general a functional conception of the church as essentially God's people in action. Having originated as a kind of evangelical order within the Church of England, Methodism today is still marked by "evangelical concern for the Christian mission, witness, nurture—'holiness of heart and life.'" [22] Support for this judgment is found in a seldom recalled assertion in the Historical Statement prepared when three bodies united in 1939 to form The Methodist Church: "The only infallible proof of a true church of Christ is its ability to seek and to save the lost, to disseminate the Pentecostal spirit and life, to spread scriptural holiness, and to transform all peoples and nations through the gospel of Christ." [23]

Clearly there is no conflict between the two biblical images; they point rather to complementary aspects of the church's nature. The church is not a disembodied spirit; it has a definite form and structure and a distinctive kind of corporate life. Yet its central function as the body of Christ is to carry on the work begun by Jesus Christ in his earthly life—that of manifesting or declaring the redemptive love and power of God. This is precisely what the people of God—a real community in time and space, a *koinonia* which knows no barriers—is called to do. The synthesis is happily expressed by Craig when he declares: The church "is the people who have given allegiance to God in response to His

[21] *The Nature of the Christian Church*, p. 38.

[22] "Do Methodists Have a Doctrine of the Church?" in *The Doctrine of the Church*, Kirkpatrick, ed., pp. 24-25.

[23] *Doctrines and Discipline of The Methodist Church, 1964* (Nashville: Methodist Publishing House, 1964), p. 10.

gracious call. It is a body witnessing to His rule by their trust and obedience." [24]

The dominance of these conceptions makes plain that for representative Methodist thought today the church is not a merely human association whose members are loosely joined together by similar interests, but a closely knit community united and empowered by the Spirit of God. The British Methodist Conference affirms that it is primarily "His choice of them and not their choice of Him that is the origin and renewing power" of the church's life.[25] On the human side, says Walter G. Muelder, the church is "a response in faith to the love of God; it is a whole response, not of solitary individuals but of a covenanted fellowship. . . . The historical event which constitutes the Church is always a community." [26]

In summary, it may be said that the church is the worshiping, witnessing, teaching, serving fellowship of those who have responded in faith to the reconciling love of God disclosed in Jesus Christ, and in the power of his Spirit seek to embody that love and realize his kingdom. It exists to manifest the life of God to men and to lift the life of men to God.

THE AUTHORITY OF THE CHURCH

With other Christians, Methodists recognize that in matters of faith the church's ultimate authority lies in God or in Jesus Christ the Word of God, through whom he has acted definitively to make himself known to men. Disagreement arises, however, as to which beliefs and practices can rightly

---

[24] Clarence T. Craig, Report of the American Theological Committee, in *The Nature of the Church*, R. Newton Flew, ed. (London: SCM Press, 1952), p. 253.

[25] *The Nature of the Christian Church*, p. 38; cf. pp. 11-12, 26.

[26] "The Necessity of the Church," *Proceedings of the Ninth World Methodist Conference*, Elmer T. Clark and E. Benson Perkins, eds. (Nashville: The Methodist Publishing House, 1957), p. 144. Cf. Claude Welch, *The Reality of the Church* (New York: Charles Scribner's Sons, 1958), p. 48.

claim divine authority. Since all of man's knowledge of God comes partly through historical and psychological processes in human minds, we still must examine the validity of our human channels of information. Men differ notoriously in their interpretations of divine disclosures.

As R. Newton Flew and Rupert E. Davies have pointed out clearly, for Christians there are three main historical witnesses to the meaning of God's revelation in Christ: (1) the apostles and their immediate followers, and the record of their testimony in the New Testament; (2) the church of Christ through the ages, continuous historically and spiritually with the apostolic church; and (3) the consciences and understandings of Christians illuminated by the Spirit in their search for the truth which is in Christ.[27] Each of the three has been regarded by particular Christian bodies as the decisive source of authority. Significantly, the three norms closely parallel the three main conceptions of the church discussed at the Amsterdam Assembly: the classical Protestant view, which stresses the Word of God contained in the Bible and expressed in confessions of faith; the Catholic conception, which emphasizes the objective, institutional character of the church and its visible continuity, tradition, and liturgy; and the conception of the "gathered" church of the covenant, the community of the Holy Spirit, stressing personal experience, the changed heart, and the Spirit-filled life.

The dominant Methodist view of authority is really a combination of the three sources, with the Scriptures seen as primary. Each norm supplements and balances the others. Flew and Davies express Methodist teaching as well as that of free-church British Protestantism in general when they write:

[27] Flew and Davies, eds., *The Catholicity of Protestantism* (Philadelphia: Muhlenberg Press, [1950]), pp. 116-18.

The protestant doctrine is that to Christ alone belongs supreme authority in matters of faith; that the Scriptures, written under the guidance of the Holy Spirit and embodying the original tradition of the Apostolic Church, possess the greatest authority next to the authority of Christ; that the Church in its interpretation of the Scriptures has also been guided by the Spirit and can rightly claim a large measure of authority; and that the Holy Spirit still bears witness to the truth of the Scriptures in the mind and life of the believer, and brings it home unmistakably to him.[28]

THE MINISTRY OF THE CHURCH

Both British and American Methodists follow Wesley in rejecting the threefold ministry, and in broadly identifying the roles of the presbyters and bishops referred to in Acts 20:17, 28; Phil. 1:1; and Titus 1:5-7. Both are impressed by the rich variety of the ministries carried on in the early church, as indicated by the lists in I Cor. 12:27-31 and Eph. 4:11. In view of this diversity and the evidence of further developments beyond the apostolic age, modern Methodists are less willing than Wesley to acknowledge in "the primitive church" an authoritative basis for clear-cut distinctions in ministerial orders. British Methodists recognize only one order, while their American brothers, more strongly influenced by Wesley through his direct guidance in the formation of the Methodist Episcopal Church, recognize two—elder and deacon. Elders exercise the function of the presbyter-overseers of the New Testament, and deacons are, at least theoretically, their helpers. However, since the only power granted to elders and not to deacons is that of administering the Lord's Supper, and since in practice deacons serving pastorates are usually given this power too, American Methodists are closer to a one-order ministry than appears on the surface. Perhaps the main value in preserving the order of deacon is its probationary function in providing, along with trial membership in an Annual Conference, for a two-

[28] *Ibid.*, p. 126.

year waiting period—and presumably growing period—before
the minister's final ordination.

In spite of the opinion of Bishop John M. Moore that
The Methodist Church "has three offices and no orders," [29]
Methodism takes a serious view of ordination. While recognizing that all the people of God have a *diakonia* (ministry,
service), it believes that some are the recipients of special
gifts for the ministry of the Word and sacraments and pastoral
care. Those who discharge this ministry exercise for the
whole church powers and functions which reside in the
church rather than in a special class within it. For these
responsibilities they are "ordained" by both God and the
church.

According to the Methodist Church of New Zealand,
ordination is: *the sign and seal of the divine commission*
to the ministry of the church universal; *the church's confirmation* of the ordinand's sense of a divine call; and *the
church's authorization* of the ordinand to perform the
characteristic functions of the Christian ministry.[30] Essentially the same view is expressed in the report of an American
Methodist General Conference Commission on the Ministry,
prepared in 1951 by Bishop William C. Martin. Ordination,
says the report, is "an act of the Church by which, after
due examination, it formally and officially accepts, approves,
and commissions the person whom Christ has called into
the ministry." Similarly, Philip C. Watson emphasizes that
the commission is basically that of Christ. The authority it
confers on the minister, though bestowed through his fellow
members, is granted not by them but by Christ himself.
Yet this does not give the ordinand any exclusive rights or
special priestly powers. His authority belongs not to him per-

[29] *Methodism in Belief and Action* (New York and Nashville: Abingdon-
Cokesbury Press, 1946), p. 118.
[30] *Towards the One Church* (Christchurch, New Zealand: National Council of Churches in New Zealand, 1954), p. 25.

sonally but to his office, the purpose of which is the perpetuation of Christ's own ministry.[31]

This conception of ordination provides a clue to the Methodist view of continuity and succession in the ministry. Like John Wesley, modern Methodists reject the doctrine of apostolic succession which regards as valid only ordinations administered by bishops whose authority has been handed down in unbroken line from Christ and the apostles. This view is repugnant for four reasons: (1) It has no clear scriptural warrant. (2) The historical evidence is against it. (3) It assigns to a self-perpetuating hierarchy an authority and responsibility which should belong to the whole church. (4) It puts finite human dignitaries in the place of the Spirit of God. Flew and Davies comment on the High Church tendency of an Anglican symposium on the ministry edited by Kenneth Kirk: "The Holy Spirit is scarcely mentioned in *The Apostolic Ministry*. The bishop takes his place." [32]

In Methodist teaching the basic call of God is not to the ordained ministry or to any other occupation, but to repentance, trust, witness, and service within a fellowship of the transformed. In New Testament times it was therefore not a special segment within the church, but the whole church which was called to minister in Christ's name. The whole church succeeded to the apostolic ministry, and the whole church exercises that ministry today. The ministry of those who preach the Word, administer the sacraments, or perform other special offices within the church is derived from and dependent on the one total ministry to which the whole church is summoned. Genuinely apostolic succession is thus to be found in the ongoing faith and life of the apostolic church, re-created and renewed in each generation by the indwelling Spirit of the living God. However, this

---

[31] "Ordination and Ministry in the Church," in *The Doctrine of the Church*, Kirkpatrick, ed., pp. 133-34.
[32] *The Catholicity of Protestantism*, p. 105, n. 1.

insistence does not deny the unique position of the apostles themselves, derived from their firsthand relation to Christ and their distinctive experience as witnesses of the risen Lord. Thus J. Robert Nelson, seeking a sound criterion for the church and its renewal in our time, finds it in apostolicity, which he defines as *"faithful congruity to the teaching and message of the apostles, in such wise that unbroken continuity is maintained with the earthly life of Jesus Christ."* [33]

In an eloquent passage, the British Methodist Conference finds the church's true continuity with the church of the past in four things: her communication of the Christian experience; her continued loyalty to one Lord; her repeated proclamation of the Christian message; and her continued acceptance of the Christian mission. Christians today are linked by a long line of dedicated men and women with the earliest disciples and our Lord himself. Moving in such a succession, modern disciples may make their own the affirmation of an early apologist: "Christians trace their genealogy from the Lord Jesus Christ."

This is our doctrine of apostolic succession. It is our conviction . . . that the continuity of the Church does not depend on, and is not necessarily secured by, an official succession of ministers, whether bishops or presbyters, from apostolic times, but rather by fidelity to apostolic truth. The office is contingent on the Word, and not the Word on the office. Indeed, the apparent discontinuity of office has sometimes been due to a reassertion of the true and essential continuity of experience, allegiance, message and mission.[34]

All that has been said thus far makes plain that in normative Methodist theory the ministry is not confined to the

---

[33] *Criterion for the Church* (Nashville: Abingdon Press, n. d.), pp. 21, 22-27. Following Acts 2:42, Nelson finds the four main elements of this criterion, hence the primary dimensions of church renewal, in the apostles' teaching, fellowship, breaking of bread (Holy Communion), and prayer.

[34] *The Nature of the Christian Church*, pp. 29-31.

ordained clergy, but is shared by those whom the modern church, like the medieval, has called the laity. In Methodist theory, that is—for frequently our practice has belied our doctrine and our best tradition. The growth and vitality of early Methodism would have been impossible apart from the impassioned labors of its lay preachers and the dynamic witness in daily life of the rank-and-file members of the Methodist societies. In more recent years—in spite of many notable exceptions—too few of our laity have conceived of their lives as a true ministry, and too few of their pastors have helped them to become aware of their real apostleship. The priesthood of all believers still needs to be translated into deed by the multitudes who theoretically assert it.

Fortunately, an exciting new understanding of the ministry of the laity is now rapidly spreading, deepened by the work of various Christian lay centers and encouraged by the World Council of Churches. Methodists are peculiarly equipped by their heritage to contribute constructively to and participate creatively in this movement. This makes it imperative to examine one other aspect of the church's ministry, that of the laity.

As we have seen, the church originated in the experience of those who, confronted with God's forgiving love and transforming power in Jesus Christ, were called out of sin into a new relation to God and their fellows (Eph. 4:1; II Tim. 1:9). God's *klesis* (call) resulted in his *ekkletoi* (those called out), who in turn became the *ekklesia* (called assembly or congregation). Obedience to God's call was thus not merely an individual matter. Christians were summoned to membership in the *laos tou theou*, the people or laity of God. Significantly, the *laos* of God in the New Testament refers not to non-ministers but to the whole church. Within this *laos* each person called had his *diakonia*, whether he was called to be an apostle, a prophet, a teacher, a healer, or something else better fitted to his God-given talents.

38

Thus everyone who responded to the call of God was both a layman, one of the people of God, and a minister, one of those summoned to service. Some were designated bishops, presbyters, or deacons and given special pastoral oversight, teaching responsibility, or leadership in worship and evangelism. Others accepted different responsibilities fitted to their capacities. But all had a ministry, and all were expected to discharge their functions as members of one body, one people of God. In a profound sense all were evangelists, called to witness daily for Christ and to devote themselves wholly to God.

Perhaps no biblical passage expresses this more graphically than I Pet. 2:9: "You are a chosen race, a royal priesthood, a holy nation, God's own people, that you may declare the wonderful deeds of him who called you out of darkness into his marvelous light." This stirring commission is addressed not to ordained clergy but to the whole church, a fellowship of people brought together by a common life and driven forward together by a common mission. The New Testament in general recognizes among Christians different offices and functions, but it knows nothing of a sharp distinction between professional and amateur Christians, between full-time and part-time disciples, between wholly dedicated clergy and laymen who are less active in furthering the gospel.

This false separation can be overcome if we recognize, with the Methodists of New Zealand, that both ministry and laity "are of the *esse* of the Church, and both share its universal ministry." The former is called upon to exercise the ministry of the Word and the sacraments; the latter, a large variety of other gifts and offices. All are called to witness and evangelize. The church is neither a priesthood ministering to the laity nor a lay body appointing a ministry to full-time service in the performance of special functions.[35]

[35] *Towards the One Church*, p. 26.

It is the whole people of God united to do his work.

Yet many Methodists continue to think of the church, if not as a building, as the congregation which assembles in a building and carries on there certain activities, or as the sum total of such congregations. Certainly this is partly what the church is. The worship, education, fellowship, and service which center in our church edifices are the indispensable core of the church's life, and the devoted labors of those who make these activities possible are an incalculably important ministry. But just as certainly the church and its lay ministry extend far beyond this. The church is wherever the people of God live, work, think, play, pray, serve, and struggle for divine ends.

Truly seen, the church is present not only when the worshiping congregation rises in praise on Sunday morning, but equally on Tuesday night when some of its members stand intelligently and courageously for Christian goals in the PTA, the hospital board, the labor union, or the Chamber of Commerce. It is functioning on Thursday afternoon when one of its number, because he is a Christian, advertises his wares honestly or charges a fair price for a careful job of repairing a car. It is active in those who, supported by their sense of belonging to a redemptive fellowship, uphold the rights of racial and other minorities, and work for reconciliation among nations. It is present whenever and wherever its members see in other people children of God for whom Christ died, sense the burdens they bear and the struggles they face, and in spirit, word, and deed mediate the love of God.

In wide circles laymen are still viewed largely as assistant pastors who aid the minister in the performance of activities of particular concern to him. Indeed, in the survey of Methodist beliefs made in 1959, 59.9 percent of the respondents identified themselves with the statement that laymen are "nonordained Christians whose function is to help the clergy do the work of the church." [36] Might it not be sounder to think of the pastor as an assistant layman? As one of the *laos* of God, he has the sacred function of leading people into the presence of God in worship. He is commissioned to help acquaint them with the roots and resources of their faith and relate these to the world in which they live, to deepen their sense of fellowship with each other and with Christ, and to send them out thus prepared for the ministry which they alone can perform. In short, his task is "to equip God's people for work in his service" (Eph. 4:12 NEB). Periodically they return to their physical headquarters for worship, spiritual renewal, mutual strengthening through shared experiences, and deepened understanding of their common task. Then they go out again to be the church in home and school, farm and factory, store and office, court and legislative hall, hospital and hotel, on land and sea and in air—wherever men need to know the power and love of God. So related, pastor and people together make up the laity of God. He and they alike are ministers of Christ.

[36] Schilling, *Methodism and Society in Theological Perspective*, pp. 161, 285.

The Gospel
the Church
and the Mission

L. Harold DeWolf

The church and the mission are not electives of the Christian life. To be in the church and to participate in the Christian mission to the world belong to the very nature of Christian existence. It is proposed to explain why this is so.

The Christian, the Church, and the Churches

To be a Christian implies being in the church, for the church is both the means and an essential aspect of the meaning of being a Christian. If salvation depends upon Christian faith, then it is true that outside the church there is no salvation. The hostility which this affirmation naturally arouses among Protestant Christians is due to its associations with Roman heresy and presumption.

When any man or any organization of men claims to be indispensable to salvation, that claim constitutes a presumptuous usurpation of the prerogatives of God. Since the Roman Catholic Church defines the church without which there is no salvation in such terms as to make absolutely essential the governance of the pope, the claim made by the priests of that church is properly regarded as highly offensive. However, the offensiveness and falsehood are due to the false identification of the Roman Catholic Church with the church of Christ. These matters give cause for much searching thought among Roman Catholic scholars in these days of renewed openness.

On the other hand, when the true church is properly understood as the fellowship of all believers, the followship formed by the Holy Spirit and confined to no organization and to no humanly identifiable groups of men, then it is true that outside the church there is no salvation. It is important to emphasize this in connection with the theology of mission. Otherwise, many people who regard themselves as Christians, but who see no necessary connection between being a Christian and being in the church, would be altogether unaffected by any demonstrated connection between the church and the world mission.

The true church, the *ekklesia* of God, is no theoretical aggregation of believers, an "invisible" church in the sense of being beyond human experience. It is the living fellowship of faith, experienced wherever the Holy Spirit, renewing in human hearts the reconciling work of Christ, overcomes all barriers which estrange men from God and from each other. Where "two or three"—or two or three thousand—"are gathered" in the name of Christ, with him "in the midst of them," there is the church. (See Matt. 18:20.) Such gathering occurs for worship, for work, for home life, for study, and every other purpose for which God calls his people together. The whole company of believers joined in all these mutually supporting "gatherings" of love and faith is the *ekklesia*.

Obviously, the organized churches are intimately related to this true *ekklesia*, as its more or less serviceable instruments. But neither any one of them nor all of them together may be considered identical with it. No human organization has been, from the beginning. Even in the simple organiza-

43

tion of the Twelve there was Judas. Besides, there were loyal disciples of Jesus not counted among the Twelve. When Paul wrote so eloquently to Corinth about the nature of the church, his letter bore abundant evidence that the organized church at Corinth was not a body of such unity and love as he ascribed to the true *ekklesia*. Every organized church is being continually called to be in the *ekklesia*, but none is to be equated with it.

That the church (*ekklesia*), properly understood, is necessary to Christian faith can be seen by reference both to present empirical evidence and to biblical teaching.

The empirical evidence is the simple fact that all who have come to faith in Christ have come to that faith through the agency of other believers linked by direct and indirect ties of witnessing communication with the entire body of Christian believers, past and present. Of course it must be remembered, in this connection, that the Bible has been collected, transmitted, translated, and distributed through this witnessing fellowship, so that even what is learned about Christ and the Way by private reading of the Scriptures has been communicated by the church. It is apparent to present observation that God chooses to make known the way of salvation through Christ by the instrumentality of the frail and unworthy company whom he has previously called.

The scriptural conception of salvation is thoroughly communal. Just as the Old Testament represents Israel as the people of God through whom salvation is mediated to the world; so in the New Testament, although Christ is the mediator and salvation is confined to no race or nation, his work is done in and through the new *ekklesia* gathered to Christ by the Holy Spirit. This is so clearly implied throughout the New Testament, and so emphasized in such books as the Acts and Paul's letters to Rome and Corinth, that we could hardly miss it unless we were blinded by that excessive individualism which so characterizes the past hundred years, especially in the United States. It is not only as instrument or channel that the church is related to salvation. We are called of God not only *through* the church but also *to* the church.

The principal marks of the Christian are faith and love. Faith signifies principally his relationship to God as one of trusting, obedient commitment. Love characterizes both the desire and gratitude with which he lives in this relationship to God and the eagerness with which he seeks to share the mercies of God in fellowship with other human beings. Where this love is released, there is inevitably the church and there is also, likewise inevitably, the Christian mission.

This is not the way in which Christian love is understood in some quarters, so more must be said in explanation and defense of the conception here presented. In any event, this exposition will carry forward the main theme in hand.

Christian Love

It is almost universally acknowledged that love is the supreme virtue of the Christian life, except by those persons who say that it is not only first but is inclusive of all. However, when the attempt is made to define what is meant by Christian love, agape, wide differences appear among Christian thinkers.

Some, following Augustine, have regarded Christian love as primarily Godward aspiration. On this view in its more extreme form, the only proper object of love is the divine. Hence, even when directed toward a wretched sinner its proper object is the image of God in him, however distorted that image may be. Others, following Bishop Joseph Butler or the "New England theology," have defined love as a disinterested benevolence or general goodwill. Yet others have regarded it as a desire for mutuality, a loving in response to being loved or in hope of eliciting reciprocal love. There have, of course, been other views, not here mentioned, and many modifications and combinations of these.

The discussions of love took a new start in the great work of Bishop Anders Nygren, *Agape and Eros,* and all subsequent discussion must take into account what he has had to say. He has rendered an especially important service in showing the inadequacy of most thinking on the subject to reflect the sublime conception of love presented in the New Testament.

Nygren contends that love, in the New Testament sense, is a free giving of self for another in complete disregard of the other's worthiness and with no hope of receiving any good, whether material or spiritual. Let the Christian mingle with his concern for his neighbor the slightest concern for making his own character more kind, generous, or humble, and just so far his love becomes the sub-Christian *eros,* rather than the Christian *agape.* In pure *agape* there is not even a desire to please God by obeying his command to love the neighbor. The center of attention is simply transferred to the neighbor. The Christian has now that kind of spontaneous, direct interest in the *neighbor's* well-being, the *neighbor's* virtue, and the *neighbor's* relation to God which on the sub-Christian level might be devoted to the welfare, character, and relation to God of oneself.

We can hardly fail to find in this teaching of Nygren an authentic Christian note. The transcending of self-concern, the unconditional commitment, the care for human beings regardless of their education, character, or station in life— these are all valid and essential aspects of Christian love.

Yet questions arise. If this be the very essence of that love of which the New Testament speaks, how shall we love God? Can a Christian possibly relate himself to God in such a way that he will be concerned for God and not know or hope that he, the worshiper, will receive from God more than he can hope to give? However spontaneous may be the believer's overflowing of gratitude to God, does he not know from past experience that giving thanks to God purifies and illumines his own soul? Can we possibly so love God that we will pray in order to benefit God without hope of any benefit, even spiritual, to ourselves? It seems quite impossible to find truthful answers to these questions which do not imply the inadequacy of Nygren's position. These are important and relevant questions, for it is made clear in the Johannine writings (especially I John 4:7-21) that God's love toward us, our love to God, and our love for our brothers are all the same love. Of course God's love is original, creative, and infinite, while ours is responsive, creaturely, and finite. Yet in essential quality the love wherewith God loves us and the love wherewith he enables us to love him and our neighbors are the same.

Even as applied to the relations of a man and his neighbor some difficult questions arise. If A and B are both Christians, is each to count the other as proper object of great concern but himself as of no concern—excepting as instrumental to the good of the other? If so, then one or both must be required to suppose what is false. A love requiring such self-deception is not a promising theoretical basis for Christian ethics nor a sound practical basis for the Christian life. Moreover, it is doubtful whether anyone would really want to be loved by such a love as Nygren describes. It makes its recipients too much the objects of "charity," in the aristocratic, condescending sense.

What we really crave and need is a love transcending not only self but also all individual isolation. Neither the "I" nor the "Thou" should be the exclusive object of concern. Rather both should be "lost" in an inclusive "We" in which both are "found," that is, fulfilled.

This is precisely what the New Testament teaches. John represents Jesus as praying for his disciples "that they may

47

be one, even as we are one" (John 17:11), and again "even as thou, Father, art in me, and I in thee, that they also may be in us" (v. 21). In the final sentence of this prayer the word "love" is used with similar connotation: "I made known to them thy name, and I will make it known, that the love with which thou hast loved me may be in them, and I in them" (v. 26).

The book of Acts describes the early blossoming and fruitage of Christian love. Wherever the Holy Spirit was received, love appeared. Wherever love appeared, the separations of race, nationality, language, and individual self-concern were overcome and a very special kind of community (*koinonia*) came into being. In this community there was a glad participation in the blessings of God and a powerful urge to extend this sharing fellowship to include others.

It is significant that Jesus habitually characterized both the relation between the believer and God and the relation between believer and neighbor in terms drawn from family life. God is "our Father" and the neighbor is my "brother." For the family is the social unit in which most universally the isolation of the individual is overcome. The father participates in the life of the son and the son participates in the life of the father. When one member of a loving family experiences some great joy or hears good news, he rushes home to share this treasure with the others.

Such was the love of the primitive church when it was being truly the church. Having received the love of God in Christ, the believers shared this treasure with one another. But like Jesus himself they were eager to extend the circle of participation in this new love. Since this God-given love was the treasure and it was the very nature of this love to be a yearning to share, the possession of it was inevitably expressed in corporate worship and in such evangelism as no boundaries could contain. These expressions are bound to occur whenever God's love is received into human hearts.

The Christian Mission

WHY A MISSION?

If it be asked, then, why there should be a Christian mission, it may be replied that the mission is of the very nature of the Christian faith and so of the church. The church exists as church only in the act of sharing its life—that is, its faith and love—both among its members and with those who are not yet members. Its purpose is not only to exist as the fruit of God's Spirit, but also to be used as his instrument. It is, as Wilhelm Andersen says, the "'bridgehead' of the Kingdom of God, which the Holy Spirit Himself has brought into being in the world." [1] If a church is not eager to share its life beyond itself and beyond all barriers, then it is lacking in the very thing which constitutes a church, namely, the love of Christ. For the love of Christ exists by giving itself boundlessly.

WHAT IS SHARED?

Hendrik Kraemer says truly, "*Heilsgeschichte* [sacred history or history of salvation] has as its purpose the remanifestation of the unbroken [*heil,* whole] relationship of man with God, and of men with each other." [2] Hence Christian love is concerned with the whole of these relationships. Of course the ultimate and supreme objective of our mission must be to share our finest treasure, the reconciling love by which we are sent to our brothers. "In Christ God was reconciling the world to himself" (II Cor. 5:19 marg.). We must testify to this good news. But the testimony is given in many ways. When the love is genuine it includes the sharing of the lesser treasures of life also. Even in the sharing of medical skills, effective agricultural methods, and popular education,

[1] *Towards a Theology of Mission* (London: SCM Press, 1955), p. 49.
[2] *The Communication of the Christian Faith* (Philadelphia: The Westminster Press, 1956), p. 20.

Christian love may be expressed; and such testimony is not to be regarded as in any way inferior.

There are two great perils here against which the missionary needs to keep constant watch. Either the one or the other can be fatal to the effectiveness and even to the genuineness of the Christian mission.

On the one hand, there is the danger of being so pre-occupied with the lesser treasures that "the pearl of great price" is forgotten or neglected. When this happens, the missionary becomes an emissary of Western civilization or of enlightenment, and no longer a missionary of Christ. While sharing many things which are good he will fail to share, by means of them, what is best, without which all else will turn to dust and ashes. When we are true missionaries, "we are ambassadors for Christ, God making his appeal through us," and our appeal is this: "We beseech you on behalf of Christ, be reconciled to God" (II Cor. 5:20). The centrality of this appeal must not be lost, and about this there must be no equivocation.

On the other hand, there is danger of so "spiritualizing" the Christian mission as to cloak a selfish hypocrisy. We may say we are not sent to share Western wealth or techniques but a greater treasure, our Christ. He is, indeed, greater beyond all comparison. But if we keep the advantages of industrial civilization for ourselves, while sharing Christ, there will be a well-founded suspicion that our love is an alloy of religious imperialism and material selfishness. In these days many an African says bitterly, "The white men have given us Bibles and taken our land." Those who say this suspect that the newcomers, despite their professions, cared more for the land than for the Bibles. It is small wonder that they are unconvinced when some of the people who have now most of their countries' wealth under their control talk of separating and so "protecting" the native African culture from foreign "contamination."

If Christian love is truly in our hearts, we are bound to tell the good news of Christ. But we shall do so by giving the "cup of cold water" in his name, as well as by preaching and teaching. The word without the deeds of love will soon be recognized as disclosing a hollow self-deception and not the genuine love of Christ.

BY WHAT MEANS?

Kraemer overstates the case when he says that "communication, which is so essential to human life and also to human nature, seldom succeeds and often fails." [3] However, *adequate* communication of the *Christian* message is, indeed, so difficult as to be altogether beyond our powers. Nevertheless, God has called us—*all* Christians—to this task. Fortunately, as we give our testimony of word and deed we do not labor alone. As Bishop Dibelius said at the Willingen Conference, "*Wir sind Gottes Mitarbeiter*" ("We are God's co-workers"). [4] It is humbling and often discouraging to think that this extremely difficult task of communicating the very Word of Life has been laid upon us. In the mind of the missionary seeking to communicate the gospel to people of a strange culture, it often seems truly impossible to bear. But it is encouraging to know that we are co-workers with God. He will speak through us and beside us, as we give our testimony of faith and love. We are called to plant and to water the precious seed, but it is "only God who gives the growth" (I Cor. 3:7).

In this assurance and with faithful prayer, we must use every means at our disposal. All the talents God has given us must be devoted to this, his work. Some methods are inexpedient, but all the methods which love dictates are appropriate.

[3] *The Communication of the Christian Faith,* p. 17.
[4] Quoted by Ernst Verwiebe, in *Mission zwischen Gestern und Morgen* (Stuttgart: Evang. Missionsverlag, 1952), p. 27.

Among the means employed, the most evident are the church and mission organizations. It is important that the churches be recognized as means and not permitted to become ends or norms. This is a particularly serious hazard in the mission fields where Christians are a very small minority and only a beginning has been made in defining for the larger community the meaning of Christian discipleship. Actually, there are two opposite perils here.

The Christian mission aims to share the love of Christ and so to extend the Christian fellowship, the true *ekklesia*. But how do we define the boundaries of this *ekklesia*?

On the one hand, we may be tempted simply to insert Christian ideas and influences into fundamentally non-Christian institutions. Similarly, we may consider our mission to individuals accomplished when Christian sentiments permeate to a greater or lesser degree lives basically committed to other gods. But this road leads to a formless eclecticism in which Christian faith and love become ever more thinly dissipated among contrary elements. Such a danger is especially obvious in a country like India today.

The problem is seen in better perspective when we observe that it is also a grave peril in a land like the United States of America. Here, too, many worshipers add Christ to their pantheon of deities, with a minimum of disturbance to their basically non-Christian loyalties. The deities placed alongside Christ in the American and Indian eclecticisms go by different names and have different meanings. But they are equally idolatrous.

There is also an opposite danger. In seeking to escape the perils of eclecticism, we may identify the *ekklesia* of Christ with the formal membership of a particular church organization. But to identify the body of Christ with any membership roll or with all the membership rolls, or even with all the people whom men have baptized, is itself a usurpation of God's own place and so, again, a kind of idolatry.

Most of us would refuse to exclude from acknowledged Christian fellowship members of the Society of Friends who have never been baptized but who show all the evidences that the Holy Spirit blesses and empowers them in his service. What, then, shall we say of an unbaptized Indian scholar who, by deed and explicit word, testifies to his faith that "in Jesus Christ God came uniquely into our common historical humanity," and who seeks with an earnestness which would shame most members and even ministers of our churches to rid his professedly christocentric life of all contrary loyalties and discordant elements? He has not accepted baptism because his Christian associations have been principally with the Friends and because he believes it a part of his own Christian vocation to "help hold open the door" between the Christian community and other religious communities. He believes that keeping relations between these communities fluid is at this time of great importance to the communication of the Christian message, hence to the effectiveness of the Christian mission in India.

At the same time, he regularly takes his place among others to worship, study, and serve in the name of Christ, and he testifies gratefully to the sustaining power of the Christian fellowship. Such membership in the living *ekklesia*, without formal membership in an organized church, could hardly be the normal relationship. He regards it as belonging to his special Christian calling. Yet such an exceptional instance brings into sharp focus certain important issues, especially concerning the distinction between the *ekklesia* of Christ and the organized churches which testify to that *ekklesia*, cultivate it, and seek to extend it.

He has not formally severed ties with other religious communities. The freedom with which he gains acceptance in these communities gives him many opportunities to testify to the unique power and the unique authority of Christ. Some Christians would condemn him for this. They call him and others like him "non-Christians," often despite

53

earnest protests. Would they also condemn Jesus because he did not sever his ties with Judaism?

Like Paul, some modern disciples selectively renounce those ancestral religious requirements which conflict with the new freedom and the new responsibilities given them by Christ. Yet they seek to retain, rather than violently sever, their ancestral associations, for the love of Christ. Even so, Paul wrote, "To those under the law I became as one under the law—though not being myself under the law— that I might win those under the law. . . . I have become all things to all men, that I might by all means save some" (I Cor. 9:20-22). Have we lost the flexibility and freedom which Paul enjoyed and used? Would our Christian legalists now call Paul a non-Christian because he never disavowed his Judaism? Has a new legalism replaced the old? Was the letter to the Galatians written in vain?

We may as well recognize that God alone knows who are truly members of the *ekklesia* at any given moment. This does not keep us from knowing the extremely important role of our church organizations in the world. But it should remind us to give thanks for every sign of Christian consecration we observe, and leave final judgments to God.

Church organizations and membership rolls are means to be used in the Christian mission. They are instruments of the Holy Spirit and servants of the true *ekklesia*. As such they are to be generously supported and carefully cultivated. But they are not the only instruments of God nor do they include in their membership all Christ's faithful witnesses. Much less are they entitled to be the norms of the Christian mission. There is one norm and one only, namely Jesus Christ himself.

WITH WHAT ATTITUDE?

Our mission is to be carried on with courage and hope. There is a current tendency in some circles to recommend that the Christian church take a defensive stance in its relations with rival ideologies and religions. In such circles there is a shrinking from real communication of heart and mind with non-Christian movements. Some Christians seem to fear dilution or perversion of the Christian message by non-Christian elements more than they hope for persuasion and winning of non-Christians to Christian faith. Such defensive rigidity is a counsel of despair. It can lead only to stalemate or defeat. Salvation is by faith, not by fear. The Christian gospel has everything to gain by seeking all possible communication. True faith is not afraid of the risks inherent in real communication, but seeks maximum involvement, that by all means the testimony may be introduced in all possible circles in all possible ways. Faith has nothing to fear from such involvement save our own fear, which is lack of faith.

From What Beginning?

The Christian mission, the task of communicating the creative, life-giving Word to a world estranged and stifled by sin, began when God spoke to the world by the Word made flesh, even Jesus Christ. We should not be surprised to find that communication is difficult and costly for us. It was costly to God himself, as Calvary bears witness. Today, too, the way of communication may lead to a cross. But that is the way of Christ.

The Christian mission begins again whenever the Word comes to a man or woman and is received with repentance and thanksgiving. For the Word is love, and love lives by going forth to be freely given.

History of Salvation
and World History

John D. Godsey

Beneath the facade of its prosperity there is a growing
sense of frustration in American Christendom, a dis-ease that
is sapping its vitality. In part, this is an ecclesiastical reflection
of our national frustration over the loss of our traditional
American messianism, which perforce dissolved the unholy
alliance between the Christian way and the American way.
But more significant, it is an expression of a deep-seated
anxiety concerning the truth of the Christian message and
its meaning for human life and history.

Undoubtedly many factors are involved in the ques-
tionings that accompany the current "crisis of faith," but
none seems so dramatic as the shrinking of Christianity
within the population of the world. Wendell Willkie's dream
of "one world" is suddenly a reality, and with it has come
for the Christian community the shocking consciousness of
its minority position within the world. The informed have
always known this, of course, but even they had sometimes
set this fact within a comfortable picture of an ever-
expanding, triumphant religion.

It took the technological revolution, with its rapid worldwide communications and transportation, to etch indelibly on the Christian mind a new picture of the world we face: a world of competing ideologies and resurgent religions, of nationalism and racism, of population explosion and nuclear threat, of secularism and nihilism. In the foreseeable future there is no other possibility than that the Christian church, long identified with the white man and Western colonialism, will diminish in size and probably in influence. Is it any wonder that even Christian laymen are beginning to ask the question: What is the meaning of Jesus Christ for the teeming millions on this earth who either have not heard of him or, having heard, reject him? Or, to put the question another way: Can the Christian claim that a particular holy history has universal and decisive significance for world history be validated?

The urgency of answering these questions in an age which is largely controlled by functional thinking, and in which belief in God is considered by many to be irrelevant, cannot be overestimated. It is not simply that the present situation forces the church to face the questions, but rather that the gospel itself demands that we be responsible to our missionary obligation. In this light, it is not too surprising that the most sensitive indicator of ecclesiastical disquiet is precisely the denominational boards of missions, for here both the questions and the feeling of responsibility are encountered in concentrated form. Here it is recognized that church and mission are identical, so that either the mission is clear or the church falters. Today our beclouded vision and faltering steps cause us to return together to the wellsprings of our faith in the quiet conviction that, if we drink deeply, the Spirit will lead us into all truth.

Some Current Views

Before we attempt to answer questions regarding the relation between "history of salvation" and "world history," it will be helpful to examine some of the issues that are being debated in contemporary theology with reference to these concepts. Perhaps the easiest way to grasp the issues is to explicate the views of certain key theologians.

OSCAR CULLMANN AND HEILSGESCHICHTE

Cullmann has championed a view of *Heilsgeschichte* (variously translated as "history of salvation," "redemptive history," and "holy history"), which conceives of salvation as bound to a continuous linear time-line embracing past, present, and future, the mid-point of which is the ministry, death, and resurrection of Jesus of Nazareth. This is fundamentally opposed to the Greek cyclical view of time, which takes its analogies from the recurrences of nature, but it also conflicts with any metaphysical idea of salvation in the "beyond," as well as any notion of "contemporacity" that overleaps history either backward (Kierkegaard) or forward (Roman Catholicism). The only symbol of time true to the Bible, declares Cullmann, is the continuous "upward sloping line." [1]

Primitive Christian thought, he continues, did not proceed on the basis of a spatial contrast between "here" and "beyond," but on that of the temporal distinction between "formerly," "now," and "then." It worked with two conceptions of time: *kairos*, which designated a point in time with a fixed content, and *aiōn* or age, which referred to a defined or undefined duration of time. The history of salvation is constituted by divinely chosen *kairoi*, which join together to form a meaningful time-line. The New Testament also knows three ages: an age before creation, which corresponds to the divine predestining of the revelatory process; the present age, which stretches from creation to the *parousia*, the return of Christ that begins the eschatological end-time; and the coming age, the consummated kingdom of God

[1] *Christ and Time: The Primitive Christian Conception of Time and History* (Philadelphia: The Westminster Press, 1950), p. 51.

that will continue eternally, i.e., for an endless duration of time. Cullmann argues that primitive Christianity differs from Judaism, not in the conception of time, but in the division of time. For Judaism the mid-point of the history of salvation is expected in the future, whereas for Christianity it has become past, namely, in the historical life and work of Jesus Christ. For Judaism the mid-point coincides with the parousia, whereas for Christians the mid-point has fallen in the midst of the time prior to the parousia. From this mid-point, in which God reveals his lordship over time, the Christian gains a completely new understanding of his situation. The age prior to creation and the history of Israel are now interpreted "prophetically" as preparatory to the redemption accomplished by Jesus Christ, whose crucifixion and resurrection mark the decisive battle (D day) and guarantee the ultimate victory (V day) of God over sin and the evil powers that characterize the present age. The Christian, therefore, knows by faith that he lives in the peculiar intermediate period between D day and V day, having been already redeemed and given the gift of the Holy Spirit, which is characteristic of the new age, and yet having still to contend with the sin and evil powers of the old age until the final consummation inaugurated by the parousia.

From the perspective of Christ as mid-point, primitive Christianity proceeded to refer the entire line of the history of salvation to him as Mediator. This is illustrated by the New Testament titles bestowed on the same Christ with reference to his functions in the successive stages of redemptive history: the Mediator of creation, the Suffering Servant who fulfills the election of Israel, the Lord ruling in the present, the returning Son of man who consummates the entire process and is the Mediator of the new creation. Moreover, the theological principle that determines the movement of this development in time is declared to be

59

that of election and representation. In order to save all men, the Old Covenant proceeds from the many to the One through a progressive reduction, in which are chosen representatively, first, the people of Israel, then the "remnant," and finally Jesus Christ; the New Covenant, on the other hand, progresses from the One to the many: from Christ to the apostles, then to the church, and finally to all men in the kingdom of God.

Thus through the principle of representation Cullmann sees an intimate connection between the history of salvation and the general history of the world. World history takes its start from the same line and finally passes over into the same line. All dualism between creation and redemption is excluded. Even now the world process has begun to touch the redemptive process, although only at the consummation will the two fully coincide. The broadest universalism, then, is the paradoxical result of extreme concentration on the history of salvation.

As we have seen, the church lives during the interim between Christ's ascension and his coming in glory, between mid-point and end, between present and future. Christ already rules as hidden King and Lord and Head of all, although only in the church, his body, does his lordship become visible on earth; only here does the Spirit work as the first fruits or "earnest" of the coming eschatological period. The church has one great task during this intermediate period, namely, to proclaim the gospel to all the world. The church proclaims the salvation that has already happened in the death and resurrection of Christ, the present lordship of Christ over the world, and the coming kingdom of God. Through this activity the church becomes an instrument in the eschatological plan, for the end will come only when the gospel shall have been preached to all peoples. Lest this sound as if the coming of the kingdom of God depends not upon the success but upon the fact of preaching, and because it is God who initiates the consummation, there can be no reckoning of dates, and the church must proclaim the gospel anew in every generation.

Finally, the Christian attitude toward the world, according to Cullmann, can be neither one of simple affirmation nor one of simple denial. Insofar as the world is the framework of the present stage of the history of salvation, it must be affirmed; but insofar as it is destined to pass away, it is to be denied. The entire life of the individual Christian is determined by his knowledge of his place in the history of salvation. Faith is the conviction that the past act of salvation is for him; love is the "principle of application" that is based upon the indicative of the history of salvation and applied in the ethical decisions of the present; hope is directed toward the consummation of redemptive history, when the entire creation will be released from the power of death and the resurrection of the individual will take place.

RUDOLF BULTMANN AND HEILSGESCHEHEN

In Bultmann's instructive review of Cullmann's book *Christ and Time*, he indicates his virtually complete disagreement with Cullmann's interpretation of the New Testament from the standpoint of the history of salvation. His basic criticism is that Cullmann turns the theology of the New Testament into a Christian philosophy of history, and he elaborates this charge in four "critical comments." [2] First of all, in attempting to present a unified theology of the history of salvation Cullmann has practiced an illicit harmonizing of New Testament writings, which in fact exhibit very different patterns of thought. Second, Cullmann has not faced the many problems posed by the history of religions, and as a result he has underestimated the influence of Jewish apocalypticism on the New Testament understanding of the history of salvation. What he presents as

[2] *Existence and Faith* (New York: Meridian Books, 1960), pp. 234 ff.

the Christian philosophy of history, asserts Bultmann, is really "Jewish apocalyptic speculation, modified only by the 'mid-point's' having been pushed back on the time-line." Third, Cullmann's designation of Christ as the mid-point of history or of the history of salvation is not in accordance with primitive Christian thought, which rather considered Christ to be the end of history and of the history of salvation. Christ is the eschatological event that puts an end to the old age, and everywhere, apart from John, the final events of the eschatological drama (*parousia*, resurrection of the dead, and the judgment) are expected to take place in the immediate future. The subsequent delay of the *parousia* created a problem for early Christianity, the seriousness of which Cullmann trivializes by an unconvincing D/day-V/day scheme. Fourth, Cullmann's elimination of the problem of the delay of the *parousia* has the effect of obscuring for him a problem which Bultmann considers far more important, namely, the problem of the temporality of Christian existence. If Christians are a new creation, set free from the world and translated into the eschatological mode of existence, how can their eschatological existence still be understood as temporal existence? Bultmann does not think Cullmann's interpretation of the eternity of the new age as a time-line, which would make eschatological existence a mere existence in time, is an adequate answer at all.

Anyone familiar with Bultmann's own theology will not be surprised by this critique. According to Bultmann's interpretation of the New Testament, in the primitive Christian community history is swallowed up in eschatology. Taking over Jesus' own eschatological preaching and embellishing it with themes from Jewish apocalypticism, the community understood itself not as historical but as an eschatological phenomenon, expecting the imminent end of the world. With the delay of the *parousia*, however, the church was forced to recognize its existence as a world-historical phenomenon and to take up a new position toward eschatology. On the one hand, eschatology is historicized (made applicable to man as an historical being), first by Paul, who nevertheless does not abandon altogether the apocalyptic picture of the future, and later by John, who radically carries through an interpretation of the eschatological event occurring in the present. On the other hand, eschatology is neutralized through the sacramentalism and the hope of immortality that emerge in the later writings of the New Testament and eventuate in Catholicism. Here eschatology was not abandoned, but the expectation of the end of the world was removed to an indefinite future.

It is Bultmann's conviction that the historicizing of eschatology by Paul and John—that is, the demythologizing of the cosmic-naturalistic-futuristic conceptuality by interpreting its existential meaning for man's existence in the present—is the only legitimate interpretation for Christian faith. Jesus Christ is now understood as God's eschatological act of salvation through which God sets an end to the old world—namely, the world of the "old man" who is determined by the past (his own sinful self) and devoid of the freedom requisite for historical decisions—and creates the "new man," who, being freed by the grace of God from himself, his sin, and his bondage to the world, is now able to make responsible decisions born of love. God's revelatory act may not be divided into successive events in various periods of history (a history of salvation), but is a *Heilsgeschehen*, an occurrence of salvation that happens again and again in the hearing of the Word of Christ preached by the church. The Word addresses man, calls him to respond in the decision of faith, and imparts to him the grace of God that makes him free from himself and free for responsible living in the present. Inauthentic existence becomes authentic existence. The man of faith lives continually from the future; his God is the "coming" God; and every moment contains the possibility of being an eschatological moment. To find meaning in history, concludes Bultmann, one does not look to universal history, for one cannot stand outside history and see it in its totality and thus judge its meaning. One rather finds meaning by looking to his own history, that is, to the present where he is involved in making responsible decisions.

KARL BARTH AND URGESCHICHTE

To understand Karl Barth we must understand what he means when he declares that God's election of grace is the sum of the gospel, the best news man can ever hear. This election, according to Barth, refers to an eternal decision, choice, and decree of the triune God to become one with sinful man in the person of Jesus Christ. That is, from all eternity God wills to be gracious to a reality separate from himself, bestowing on man not only the gift of being but also the gift of salvation, the fulfillment of being. The event of this election is the eternal preexistence of Jesus Christ, the Son of God as man. Jesus Christ, in whose person the electing God and the elected man meet and unite in an eternal covenant of grace, is the content of *Urgeschichte*, the primal history that forms the basis and hidden meaning of all other history, be it the temporal history of salvation or world history in general.

We might assume that Barth is attempting to think God's thoughts after him in some speculative, supralapsarian fashion, but this is not the case. His thinking does not move from an abstract plan in eternity to its execution in time, but vice versa. Barth looks to Jesus Christ, the God-man, as the point where eternity and time are united, but where God's eternity retains its priority. Primal or eternal history has as its content nothing other than the life, death, and resurrection of Jesus of Nazareth. This earthly history is the temporal realization and revelation of God's eternal decision and choice.

When Barth speaks of God's eternity, he does not mean that God is timeless or, for that matter, that eternity is infinitely continuous time (Cullmann). God is a living God whose being is an event, namely, the event of his own decision to be who he is, the One who loves in freedom. He has his own time of eternal vitality, a time in which past, present, and future are possessed in an enduring "now," a time that encompasses and forms the basis and model for our created time, a time that is at once pre-temporal, supra-temporal, and post-temporal. We know of God's time because in Jesus Christ he reveals that he has time *for us* and that he is Lord of our time.

This dynamic interpretation of the eternity of God prepares us for the fact that when Barth defines history, he makes it clear that God rather than man is the eminently historical being. "The history of a being," he declares, "begins, continues, and is completed when something other than itself and transcending its own nature encounters it, approaches it and determines its being in the nature proper to it, so that it is compelled and enabled to transcend itself in response and in relation to this new factor." [3] In the man Jesus, historical being is revealed: the self-transcendence of the Creator in his movement to the creature, the confrontation and communion of persons in time.

The eternal reconciliation of God and sinful man in Jesus Christ is revealed as reality in the midst of human history. The history of Jesus is the history of salvation, and it involves two simultaneous movements: God's self-condescension in entering human history as a servant in order to take upon himself the burden of man's plight, and man's elevation into fellowship with God as his child. In this history in which God accepts man by becoming a man himself, God's covenant of grace with all men is fulfilled once for all. The divine judgment and mercy revealed here is attested by the prophets and apostles, and it is to be

[3] Barth, *Church Dogmatics,* III/2 (Edinburgh: T. & T. Clark, 1960), 158.

Christian Mission in Theological Perspective

proclaimed by the church as the one order of reality for all mankind. The being of all other men depends on their togetherness with Jesus, their participation in his history. The hidden foundation, content, and goal of human history is none other than the history of the covenant of grace fulfilled in Christ.

The task of the church is given in the fact that the eternal accomplishment of salvation is not yet perfectly known. God's eternal election of grace is meant for all humanity, but it follows in temporal realization the "unhurried biblical order" of the election of Jesus Christ, of the community, and of the individual. What for God is an ever-present event takes the form in created time of a succession of events. God wills that what has happened apart from us (extra nos) and for us (pro nobis) be an event in us (in nobis). That is to say, salvation is not a general truth, but an event that occurred eternally in Jesus Christ and occurs in us, secondarily but really, in our knowledge of it. This knowledge comes to the individual through the proclamation of the community and calls man to faith and obedience. When man responds to this call, acknowledging the truth of the gospel and living in dependence on God's grace, he exercises his true being.

This presupposes, of course, that it is possible for man to live as if God had not been gracious to him in Jesus Christ, to think of himself as self-sufficient and in no need of a savior. But this, says Barth, is to live a lie, to exist in the unfreedom of an "impossible possibility," to live in abstraction from reality. Thus the urgency of the witness of the church becomes evident: that men may know the truth and become free covenant partners in the community of faith and love and hope that represents and reproduces and reflects on earth the very life of Christ himself. Between the first and the second advent God patiently gives Christians time and space to perform their task.

REINHOLD NIEBUHR AND THE INTERIM

Reinhold Niebuhr's prophetic ministry has been based upon a profound understanding of the meaning of history that is disclosed in the event of the cross of Christ. His reflection upon this occurrence, seen against the background of prophetic messianism in the history of Israel, has produced a theology of history which illuminates its mystery as well as its meaning, its ambiguities as well as its divinely given unity. On the cross, where innocent suffering Love judges and forgives sinful mankind by taking the burden of guilt upon himself, there is revealed both the wisdom of God that orders history and the power of God that bears history. What is disclosed there is the justice and the mercy of God, his unceasing conflict with evil and his power to overcome it.

No theologian has been more perceptive than Niebuhr in pointing out the ambiguities of history, that complex human realm of commingled freedom and necessity, good and evil. History, he declares, does not yield its own meaning. Indeed, it cannot, for the observer of history is himself caught up in its moral ambiguities and tragic antinomies. Niebuhr has been unremitting in his effort to unmask the falsehood and pretension involved in those modern utopian views of history which claim that the solution of the problem of history lies within history through man's moral or scientific progress. On the other hand, he is just as opposed to the pessimistic view that no human progress is possible and that history has no meaning at all. The truth lies between the two, which must be held in dialectical tension. Meaningful progress is possible in history, but it is limited by the fact that every achievement of good is tainted with evil. Only the end of history will bring the complete fulfillment of God's victory over evil on the cross.

The Christian church exists in the "interim" between the disclosure of the meaning of history and the fulfillment of history, between Christ's first coming and his coming again. It is called to proclaim to all men the amazing mercy of God which is greater than his judgment, and to live a life of responsible action that will reflect the love and justice of God within the personal and social structures of human history. It should affirm the sovereignty of God that gives history its unity, but because of the complexity of history manifested in the cross, it should never attempt to reduce the meaning of history to a Christian philosophy of history. Because the meaning of history is set in the context of mystery, it cannot be reduced to complete rational intelligibility, although Niebuhr firmly believes that the truth of the Christian revelation can be validated in experience.

Since the church lives in the interim, it must be conscious of not only its responsibility to manifest the reality of reconciliation in the present, but also of its character as an eschatological community. It must not divinize itself or introduce "false eternals" into history, for absolutely nothing in this world can escape the ongoing moral ambiguities. Christians remain sinners even though saints, and the Christian life must ever be based on justification by faith alone. It is just this faith that provides the resources of spirit that are necessary for effective engagement in our common social tasks.

In conjunction with his consciousness of the eschatological dimension of faith, Niebuhr takes seriously, though not literally, the biblical symbols of the "end" of history. No finite mind can hope to comprehend what will take place beyond history, but this does not negate the meaningfulness of the symbols. For instance, the symbol of the Antichrist precludes any utopian illusions about the gradual attainment of perfection, and that of the second coming distinguishes the Christian hope from any rationalistic or mystical otherworldliness. Resurrection implies that the problem of history will not be solved in history, and yet that eternity will not annul but will fulfill what is begun in time; and the last judgment means that the distinction between good and evil abides to the end and that history is not its own redeemer, although its ultimate judge is One who has lived in history.

An Assessment

These brief sketches neither do justice to the thought of these influential theologians nor adequately represent the variety of contemporary positions with respect to this subject, but it is hoped that they will contribute to an understanding of the major alternatives.

The deepest cleavage exists between Cullmann and Bultmann. Cullmann bases his entire theology on the idea of a divinely revealed plan of salvation that unfolds chronologically in analogy with world history. All of history—and, for that matter, eternity too—is bound to one ongoing time-line. Christ is the mid-point of the history of salvation, but the victory that he achieves on the cross, although real, will not be consummated until the eschatological drama unfolds at some unknown date in the future. In the meantime, the church enters the continuing struggle between good and evil with the knowledge that the risen Christ is already the hidden Lord of all earthly powers. With a firm faith in the past victory and a hope for the speedy return of the Lord, the church undertakes the task of preaching Christ in word and deed to all peoples in the belief that this preaching plays a definite role in bringing on the events of the end-time.

This short recapitulation is meant to highlight the main features of the history-of-salvation type of thinking that Bultmann considers a grotesque misinterpretation of the New Testament faith. It is not that Bultmann does not acknowledge that this type of thinking exists, in a certain sense, in the Old Testament and to a limited degree in the New. Wherever one finds the concept of the "people of

God," there will also be found the idea of a history of salvation. What he denies is that this type of thinking is characteristic of, or relevant to, Christian faith, for which Jesus Christ is God's eschatological act of salvation, an occurrence that sums up and brings to an end the history of salvation. For Bultmann, consequently, the Old Testament history of salvation has no revelatory character and thus no vital significance for the Christian. Bultmann believes that the dominant influence in shaping the consciousness of the early Christian community was Jewish apocalypticism, with its fantastic picture of the Son of man coming on the clouds to inaugurate the events of the "last days," an occurrence that was considered imminent. It was the genius of Paul and especially of John to demythologize the apocalyptic imagery by interpreting it anthropologically, that is, as the self-understanding of faith. Bultmann considers his own theological program of existentialist interpretation to be nothing more than the logical consequence of the Pauline-Johannine logic of faith for our day. What is involved is not salvation-history, but salvation-historicity. The concept of time congruent with faith is not that of chronology, but that of personal decisions which make life meaningful.

Bultmann's own achievement and his trenchant criticism of Cullmann's position is impressive. Cullmann's concept of time, particularly his idea of eternity as endless time, does not seem to do justice to the Christian assertion of God's free lordship over time. The latter makes possible the conceptions of "eternity entering time" and of "contemporaneity," which for me are not only legitimate but necessary expressions of Christian understanding, Cullmann's objections notwithstanding. Furthermore, to include in the content of faith a whole series of events in a history of salvation appears to be an objectification that contradicts the essence of faith, which is to be a direct encounter with the *Eschaton*, God himself. Would not such belief require a *sacrificium intellectus*, and does it not presuppose a false understanding of revelation, namely, knowledge about God rather than knowledge of God? And is it legitimate to turn primitive Christianity's eschatological expectation of an imminent end into a history-of-theology expectation of a distant end?

When all this is said, however, I still question whether Bultmann's total elimination of the history of salvation provides a viable option for Christian theology. Is there not an intrinsic connection between God's saving act in Jesus Christ and the revelatory action of this same God with Israel as the people of God of the Old Testament? Does not the New Testament witness to Christ understand the saving deed attested by it as the fulfillment of Old Testament prophecies and thereby point to a planned sequence of divine promise and fulfillment? And does not New Testament faith look forward to an eschatological goal of "beholding," of seeing face to face? Does it not look to a consummation of history that will bring an end to the problem of evil in history? I think these questions must be answered affirmatively. It seems to me that Bultmann's thinking is too individualistic. It simply will not do to emphasize faith as direct encounter between the individual and God and neglect the attachment to the church and the solidarity with the people of God. Bultmann's seeming abhorrence of the *historisch* ("objective") makes him a target for the charge of docetism, despite his demur; and what is ultimately at stake is the meaning of the incarnation itself. Does Bultmann understand John 1:14 to mean that God became *man*? Or merely *Word*, one through whom God spoke and still speaks?

For me, Karl Barth and Reinhold Niebuhr offer more adequate interpretations of our subject matter than either Cullmann or Bultmann, because in their theologies they

71

hold together a view of the history of salvation and the idea of contemporaneity. Thus they overcome Cullmann's monotonous view of time and Bultmann's volatilization of history into eschatology. I believe their superiority rests ultimately upon their more profound interpretation of Christology, wherein they preserve the intention of the Council of Chalcedon with its subtle dialectic, without continuing its substantial categories. For Barth and Niebuhr, God really enters human history in the form of man, yet without ceasing to be God. Therefore, God in Jesus Christ becomes worldly-historical reality, but precisely therein he shows himself to be truly God, the Lord of history, who is not bound to our time but steps opposite us as our "eternal contemporary." Furthermore, these two theologians maintain a dialectical view of eschatology: the kingdom of God is present and yet is still to be consummated. This view makes for a healthy attitude toward world history and forms the basis for a discriminating ethic. Both can take the world with great seriousness, but they have prophetic noses that can smell idolatrous claims of false absolutes from miles away! Because of the cross, they are serious; because of the resurrection, their seriousness is not deadly (thus the "laughing Barth" and Niebuhr's "nonchalance of faith"). With respect to the task of proclaiming the Christian message to the world, perhaps Barth has erred on the side of giving undue attention to the analysis of the message, Niebuhr to the analysis of the world. The result is that they go well together!

Conclusion

THE RELATION OF HISTORY OF SALVATION AND WORLD HISTORY

It is my belief that there are certain basic affirmations that ought not to be omitted in the elaboration of a Christian view of the relation of the history of salvation and world history. These are as follows:

1. God is the sovereign but hidden Lord and providential ruler of all history.

2. From an empirical viewpoint, there is no difference between the history of salvation and world history.

3. The election of God differentiates salvation history from world history.

4. This differentiation has only noetic significance: In the history of salvation the secret meaning of all history is made known.

5. The revealed meaning is the divine will to serve and to save fallen man.

6. The history of salvation which manifests the divine will is a history of suffering, begun in God's election of Israel and completed in Israel's Suffering Servant, the Incarnate One who representatively bears the judgment of all and brings God's grace to all.

7. The relation of the history of salvation and world history consists in the contemporaneity of all history with the one representative suffering and resurrection of Jesus Christ. Here all human history (every man of every age) is pronounced guilty and receives pardon.

8. The cross and resurrection mean that world history is ultimately the history of man with God and that its fulfillment is not from the world but from God, in new creation. The Christian, therefore, will not expect salvation from world history and will indulge in neither a pessimistic nor optimistic view of the world. He will not believe in an immanent striving of history toward a goal, but he will believe that each time and each individual is placed before God and called to responsibility. He will therefore join in the life of the world and witness to the victory and lordship of Christ by concrete service to the neighbor,

free in the confidence that the consummation of history is God's affair.

THE MISSION OF THE CHURCH TODAY

This chapter began with some observations about the situation of the church in the perplexing, often frightening, ever-changing, secular world in which we live. We asked what Jesus Christ can mean for the teeming millions who have worldly concerns and do not look to God for their answers, and whether the church can validly claim universal significance for the "history of salvation." Everything comes to focus on the question of how the church is to understand its mission today.

When I reflect on our responsibility as Christ's missionaries, several words from the past come to mind. When I think of the ground of our responsibility, I am reminded of Christ's great commission. When I think of the place of responsibility, there rings in my ear the audacious declaration of John Wesley that the world was his parish. When I think of the scope of responsibility, I remember these words of Dietrich Bonhoeffer: "The more exclusively we acknowledge and confess Christ as our Lord, the more fully the wide range of His dominion will be disclosed to us." [4] When I meditate on how our responsibility is to be fulfilled, I keep coming back to Paul's remark about "being all things to all men" and John's admonition that we are to "do the truth." I think we ought not fret about the "scandal" of our universal claims for Jesus Christ, but simply affirm and presuppose in all we do that Christ is Lord of all and the center of history. Reinhold Niebuhr has spoken significantly about this matter:

The scandal that the idea of universal history should be the fruit of a particular revelation of the divine, to a particular

[4] *Ethics*, Eberhard Bethge, ed. (New York: The Macmillan Company 1955), p. 180.

people, and finally in a particular drama and person, ceases to be scandalous when it is recognized that the divine Majesty, apprehended in these particular revelations, is less bound to the pride of civilizations and the hopes and ambitions of nations, than the supposedly more universal concepts of life and history by which cultures seek to extricate themselves from the historical contingencies and to establish universally valid "values." [5]

Precisely from our claim should follow those resources of love that Niebuhr stresses so strongly: humility, tolerance, and the nonchalance of faith.

The greatest threat and obstacle to the mission of the church is not the world it faces but the church itself. In what we do we are to become like him, to grow into his likeness. Jesus lived his life entirely for others. Have we learned to do this, so that our time is radically filled with God's glory? Jesus prayed. Have we learned to pray, so that what we do and say has spiritual depth and power? Jesus lived a worldly existence, at least in comparison to John the Baptist. Have we learned to be "worldly" in the best sense of the word, or does our religiousness separate us from many types of peoples and levels of society? Jesus risked suffering. Dare we venture with radical trust into areas of life where the cost may be great?

I do not think anyone can give a simple answer to the question of how the church is to accomplish its mission. However, I want to close by quoting part of an outline of a book that Bonhoeffer had hoped to write on this subject:

The Church is her true self only when she exists for humanity. As a fresh start she should give away all her endowments to the poor and needy. The clergy should live solely on the free-will offerings of their congregations, or possibly engage in some secular calling. She must take her part in the social life of the world, not lording it over men, but helping and serving them. She must tell men, whatever their calling, what it means to live

---

[5] *Faith and History* (New York: Scribners, 1949), pp. 113-14.

in Christ, to exist for others. And in particular, our own Church will have to take a strong line with the blasphemies of *hybris*, power-worship, envy and humbug, for these are the roots of evil. She will have to speak of moderation, purity, confidence, loyalty, steadfastness, patience, discipline, humility, content and modesty. She must not underestimate the importance of human example, which has its origin in the humanity of Jesus, and which is so important in the teaching of St. Paul. It is not abstract argument, but concrete example which gives her word emphasis and power.[6]

[6] *Prisoner for God: Letters and Papers from Prison*, Eberhard Bethge, ed. (New York: The Macmillan Company, 1954), pp. 180-81.

The Issue:
Ultimate Meaning in History

Carl Michalson

I

The Christian gospel is a proclamation which strikes the ear of the world with the force of a hint. Some "get it"; some do not. To those who do, it is "the power of God unto salvation." To those who do not, it can seem a scandal and an offense. The scandal and offense of Christianity is that a bare hint in history should become the occasion for something the whole course of history taken together cannot provide. That is the sense of ultimacy which a Christian experiences when he hears about Jesus of Nazareth as the Word of God. If the gospel scandalizes and offends when it is preached, however, the ministers of God can know they have failed in their proclamation. For the purpose of the gospel is reconciliation with God and not offense. The purpose of the hint is the illumination of human experience with ultimate significance. When the act of proclamation gives way to acts of examination into its truth value, it is a clear sign that the proclamation has failed. Not that such an examination is ruled out, or even unprofitable; but only that examination does not fulfill the intention in the proclamation.

Christianity can never be more than a hint in history. Its subject is the eternal God, but its mode of communication is history, and in history nothing is evidently eternal. Christianity need never be more than a hint, because where its proclamation is heard, it creates the possibility of an ultimately meaningful life. That meaning reorganizes man's whole experience at a new level of significance. The New Testament calls it the new age—the body of Christ, eternal life. In this respect the hint has the revelatory power of a clue. It does not say everything there is to say. It simply supplies what is lacking to make the story of our life complete. Christianity *ought* never be more than a hint, because anything stronger conveys a falsely expanded, hence misleading impression of the eternal's verifiability under conditions of history.

The first Christians who caught and communicated the faith could scarcely have anticipated its consequences for the very structure of history as we experience it today. "History as we know it now began with Christ," Uncle Kolia says in *Doctor Zhivago,* "and . . . Christ's Gospel is its foundation." What that means is not so favorable to the Christian cause as it may sound. The hint about the availability of ultimate meaning to history has made mankind restless with an existence which pursues its ends without such hints. It has given rise not only to obedience to God, which was its purpose. It has also set off such protean human efforts to achieve ultimacy within history as states like Soviet Russia project. In that sense it is true to say that Communism is a Christian heresy and that the Marxian philosophy of history is a secularized Christian eschatology.

On the other hand, since it has suggested the historical reality of ultimate gratifications, the Christian proclamation has sponsored a deep-seated historical despair, the fear arising from the fact that such gratifications have not seemed forthcoming. Although the American historian Herbert J. Muller deplores it, he is correct when he observes that "the absolutist tradition of Christendom leads men to assume that if we don't have absolute standards we can't have any standards, and that if we are not standing on the Rock of Ages we are standing on nothing." [1] Existential nihilism is the result. To say as it does that nothing significant is ultimately possible in history identifies existentialism as a secular offspring of the Christian line.

Where history has been given the sense of absoluteness in life, the very structure of historical existence is changed. It is the intention of the Christian proclamation that mankind should receive its life from beyond itself, which is a life by grace. That would be to have a history in an ultimately meaningful sense. The failure of the world to get that hint from the Christian faith expresses itself in either revolt or resignation. The man in revolt denies there are such gratifications as Christians speak of and sets up rival absolutes. The resigned man settles for life at some less than absolute level, taking minor gratifications from the perishing moments of a history that is ultimately destined to die.

Like Archibald MacLeish's J. B., who fails to catch the hint in God's silence, the nihilist resolves to rebuild his life upon a perishing humanity.

> Blow on the coal of the heart.
> The candles in churches are out.
> The lights have gone out in the sky.
> Blow on the coal of the heart
> And we'll see by and by . . .[2]

[1] H. J. Muller, *The Uses of the Past* (Mentor Books; New York: New American Library, 1952), p. 47.
[2] MacLeish, *J. B.*, Scene II (Boston: Houghton-Mifflin Company, 1958). Used by permission of the publisher.

Like Albert Camus' restless, biblical-type heroes, he satisfies his taste for ultimacy in a form of "mysticism with the world." Some fevered prisoners of the world have been known to see the face of the Holy Mother of God on the walls of their cell. Camus' nihilist sees only the face of Marie, his mistress. In history one can learn to settle for minor gratifications. But in a time that has heard there are ultimate gratifications, such a settlement turns every intercourse with the world into what Camus seems willing to call an experience of being "taken in adultery." Nihilistic forgiveness for inadequate adjustments to life inheres in the heroism with which one goes about them. The hero knows that simply the fact that life is ultimately meaningless does not mean one may not salvage meanings.

II

Revolt and resignation are kindred efforts to cope with the history to which Christian proclamation has given rise, the history in which it has been revealed that there is an absolute meaning in life. The significant thing about the new religious situation in the world today, then, is not that Christendom is now becoming a mission field for non-Christian religions. That fact is a mere accident of history. The world is now small enough and the economic strength of non-Western religions large enough to facilitate such reciprocal missions. Nor is the significant thing that the religions with which Christendom is now being confronted are themselves "post-Christian," meeting Christianity with positions already accommodated to Christianity. The really significant thing about the mission to America today is that for the first time in its history Christianity is encountering the non-Christian religions in the framework of a history which Christianity itself has formed. It is a history in which the thirst for ultimate meaning has been induced and in which the failure to drink expresses itself as revolt and resignation. The effect of the encounter between the religions within that framework should, therefore, be markedly different from the effect the encounter has had upon the soil of non-Christian cultures. It is no longer simply the paramountcy of Christianity as a religion which is being placed in question. The very desirability of any ultimacy within history is now being challenged.

The eagerness with which non-Christian missions have come to America is rooted in the very characteristic which has made it so difficult for Christianity to succeed on non-Christian soil. Christianity in the past has been blocked in its mission because of the apparent satisfaction of non-Christian cultures with less than ultimacy in history. Now Christians are being made the object of a mission by these very religions which have made their peace with historical meaninglessness. Their chief success will, therefore, be among the rebellious and resigned who experience the structure of Christendom without having appropriated its substance.

Islam, for instance, affirms the existence of the absolute God but denies he is really present in history. For that reason the Christian doctrine of the incarnation of God in Christ is the chief target of its apologists. Christians can make Jesus Christ the source and the form of their existence, the beginning of their new age, because God is believed to be present in him. Jesus Christ then becomes the focus for both the understanding of God and the understanding of man. On the other hand, Mohammed for Islam is the final prophet, the miraculous author of the final book, in the light of whose finality Jesus is only a penultimate figure. It is understandable by that canon that the transcendent reality of God is needed by Islam to account for both Jesus and Mohammed, but that nothing in history—neither Jesus nor Mohammed—can be said to account for the reality of God. [3]

The only historical finality known to Islam is the chrono-

[3] See the account of Islam by Edmund Perry, *The Gospel in Dispute* (Garden City: Doubleday & Company, 1958), chap. 6.

logical finality by which the prophet is believed to say the last word for God. The finality which Christianity sees in history is an attribute of the presence of the fullness of the Godhead bodily in Jesus of Nazareth. Islam is said to combine the absolute monotheism of Judaism with the universalism of Christianity. That is a misleading part-truth. For that combination overlooks the real genius of the New Testament faith, which is its particularism. In the New Testament a single event is endowed with finality by virtue of the presence of God in history. The possibility of an ultimately meaningful history is formed by that event. The absence from Islam of this sort of particularism could well account for the fact that so syncretistic and universalistic a "religion" as Bahai had its source in Islam.

Vedanta affirms the reality of ultimate truth but denies that it can be embodied anywhere in history. Its chief missionary target, therefore, is the exclusiveness found in self-conscious Christianity. The quasi-religious metapsychology of C. G. Jung has much in common with the Vedanta mission to the Western world. As Jung has said, "To the psychologist there is nothing more stupid than the standpoint of the missionary who pronounces the gods of the 'poor heathen' to be illusions." [4] The statement by itself would be applauded by current Christian mission circles. What it intends to convey, however, ought not be classified as missionary etiquette but as theology. For Vedanta the statement would imply that the ultimate is too deep and still to enter the concrete and transitory life of history. That witness should leave a dearth in history from which man would wish to flee as from a desert.

For psychology, according to Jung, the statement means that "anything that acts for us is real, irrespective of the name we give it." When Sigmund Freud, therefore, wrote

[4] Jung, *Modern Man in Seach of a Soul* (Harvest Book; New York: Harcourt Brace, 1955), p. 72.

The Future of an Illusion, he could not have meant the same by "religion" as Jung did. Freud anticipated a day when religious ideas would wither away because their usefulness as emotional props had been superseded by psychological stability. Jung, on the other hand, anticipates a day when the universality of historico-religious symbols will be achieved by a movement toward trans-historical archetypal symbols. Vedanta's mission shares that goal. When it comes about it will be seen that the contest between Christianity and "heathenism," between enlightenment and superstition, was avoidable. All religious symbols are believed to participate in some nonhistorical realm of common human validities. Individual histories are therefore translatable beyond individuality into that collective humanity through a participation mystique.[5]

Christians find, on the other hand, that the naming of God is not a matter of indifference. "The God and Father of our Lord Jesus Christ" is a God who makes himself known. That is the ultimacy in which Christians are involved. Furthermore, the God whom Jesus names makes himself known not beyond or beneath our individual histories, but within them. That indicates the historical ultimacy of the Christian's archetype. Historical meditation is of the essence of a faith in which it is believed that God is present in history. All history is thought to derive its hope from the event in which God is named. That is why Christians hold so stubbornly to their vocation to witness that the ultimate hope of history is tied up with "the name that is above every name." The indissolubility of the Christian witness, however, ought not be looked upon as an axis of exclusion. It is really only the access to the possibility of a finally meaningful history.

Ramakrishna, the modern Hindu saint and foremost inspiration of the Vedanta mission, took as a motto for his

[5] *Ibid.*, p. 172.

movement *Siva-Seva*, God and service. There are also expressions of responsibility toward the world among Hindus in India today, such as the "Land Gift" movement of the venerable Vinoba Bhave. But the Vedanta position does not support this practical concern for history in principle. Contrariwise, while Christians default in their responsibility toward the world in practice, their faith does support historical responsibility in principle.

III

Zen Buddhism, like modern existentialism, abandons all hope in a historical absolute. Unlike existentialism, however, it can do so without agony. All the methods by which Zen justifies its life in history are characterized by abstraction and esthetic detachment. In this sense, the "beat Zen" of the Americans Allen Ginsberg and Jack Kerouac is closer to existentialism (and Christianity) than the rather "square Zen" of the former Episcopal priest Alan Watts. Ginsberg must

> live
> in the physical world
> moment to moment
> I must write down
> every recurring thought—
> stop every beating second.

Watts himself leans toward the more orthodox Zen. He prefers *Haiku*, the seventeen-syllable Japanese poetic form originated by the seventeenth-century Zen poet, Basho. To cite one instance he selects,

> The sea darkens,
> The voices of the wild ducks
> Are faintly white.[6]

[6] Alan W. Watts, "Beat Zen, Square Zen, and Zen," in *Chicago Review*, Summer, 1958, p. 8.

According to the Japanese theologian Kazoh Kitamori, the aesthetic observer attitude preeminently heralded in Japanese culture by Basho is the chief hindrance to the Christian mission in Japan. Because it has become the spiritual element in which the Japanese people live, it is the greatest enemy of Japan's evangelization. *Haiku* and *Zen* are filled with "the pathos of *things*" (in Japanese, *monono aware*). In an existence in which ultimate meaning is anticipated, aesthetic pathos is an anesthetic which kills the pathos of the person, the pathos which appears when the ultimate possibility in history seems unrealized. In Japan the aesthetic, detached way of life is called *iki*. Christians who live an involved life are felt to be rude and uncouth by comparison. That rudeness is known as *yabo*. As Kitamori says, *iki* people will have nothing to do with Christianity because of its *yabo*-ness.[7]

There are some structural respects in which Zen and Christianity seem a good deal alike. These are usually the respects in which Christianity has a kinship to existentialism. Martin Heidegger is said to have commented after reading a piece by the Zen philosopher D. T. Suzuki, "This is what I have been trying to say in all my writings." The point of similarity referred to is the Zen, Christian, and existential way of grasping the truth inwardly. Each of these emphases knows that the truth can only be communicated in hints, indirectly. Zen actually has a discipline, the *koan*, contrived to make the grasping of truth in objective categories impossible. According to an American novelist who has flirted with the eastern faiths, J. D. Salinger, "Logic" was in the apple Adam ate. "What you have to do is vomit it up if you want to see things as they are."[8] In his more

---

[7] See *Ajiya ni okeru Kirisutokyo* (Christianity in Asia), ed. H. R. Fox and Kano Yamamoto (Tokyo, 1955), pp. 117 ff. James Bissett Pratt in *The Pilgrimage of Buddhism* may have had in mind the *iki-yabo* contradiction when he likened the conversion of a Buddhist to Christianity to making Thomas Aquinas a Methodist.

[8] See his short story "Teddy" in *The New Yorker*, January, 1953.

sedate way Joachim Wach has observed that this passion for inwardness is found nowhere in Western culture except in some modern philosophy "and in Methodism!"

A Methodist or an existentialist could say as the twelfth-century Zen monk Doken did, "When you are hungry or thirsty, my eating of food or drinking does not fill your stomach. You must drink and eat yourself." Or, "borrowed plumage never grows." But it is not true for Christianity as it is for Zen that existence in the truth is an attribute of one's realization of oneself. Zen believes that man must find his salvation within himself or nowhere, therefore the hints in all its communication are contrived to block alliances beyond oneself. Zen's aesthetic detachment from the world serves as an opiate which quiets the surmise that on such a basis nothing will have the last word. It is no accident that many of Salinger's heroes confront the perils of their historical existence by dozing off. The device borders closely on what Vedanta knows as *nirvana*, Zen as *satori*, and psychotherapy as neurotic sleep. The Christian gospel, on the other hand, speaks to the world in such a way as to evoke a nexus of faith with Jesus Christ, who is the Eternal God's way of being present in history. That presence provides a basis for responsible awareness in history.

IV

In its proclamation of God's presence in Christ the Christian gospel has disturbed the world with a restlessness which has often been written off as Western *yabo*-ness. The motivation of the non-Christian mission to America, therefore, is quite unlike the motivation of Christian missions to non-Christian lands. Christians go to non-Christians to proclaim that history can be ultimately meaningful because of Christ. When non-Christians fail to take the hint, possibly it is because it has not occurred to them to require history to be ultimately meaningful. The non-Christian history never remains quite the same, however, for having been exposed to the suggestion.

That fact is evidenced precisely in the non-Christian missions to America. These missions come with the avowed purpose of persuading Christians to abandon the disquieting expectation of ultimacy in history. Salinger's "Teddy" exposes their concern. Teddy is an American boy who believes that in a previous incarnation he was a holy man of India. Due to some misdemeanor in his previous life he was punished, as he believes, by being reincarnated in an American body. For, as he says, "It's very hard to meditate and live a spiritual life in America." A mission to a "Christian" land is a non-Christian culture's alternative to and first line of defense against the Christian mission and against its psychologically perilous by-products, infiltrating the world in the form of Americanism and Western rudeness.

The non-Christian mission will be stubbornly resisted within a Christianly structured history because of the penchant for the absolute which Christianity has developed here. It will be as stubbornly resisted here as Christianity is in the more relativistic and detached non-Christian cultures. But it may also be more enthusiastically received than Christians would care to concede. The grounds of that enthusiasm cannot be found in any detailed delineation of the comparative similarities and differences between the doctrinal systems of Christianity and the non-Christian religions. It may be found, however, in the fact that the difference is expressible in one name, Jesus Christ. That difference reduces the significance of the similarities to a merely academic level. Jesus Christ has a twofold meaning for the religious experience of mankind. He is God's call to the world to take history with absolute seriousness and he is God's sign in history that the invocation has his eternal benediction. Those who hear the invocation without the benediction are either fatigued by the prospect of realizing anything ultimate in history or inflamed by the desire to do so on their own terms.

The whole gospel is not at hand, however, until it is known that in Christ God gives what he commands. That knowledge is the ground of repentance for the rebellious and the resigned alike. That is why there is a thirst on Western soil for what these non-Christian faiths can offer. The thirst can be attributed to the reactions of revolt and resignation which the Christian proclamation has produced among us in the West. The non-Christian religions, which come appealing to the West to surrender the Christian claim to ultimacy, at the same time offer these dissident elements in Christendom an attractive alternative to Christian repentance. They offer it in the form of new possibilities for revolt and resignation, and with the blessing of organized religion. That sweet seduction will not be easy to resist.

The Work
of the Holy Spirit
in the World

D. T. Niles

"Did you receive the Holy Spirit when you believed?"
And they said, "No" (Acts 19:2).

"Come"—"Come and see": that was the Lord's first invita-
tion to his disciples (John 1:39). "Go"—"Go and preach":
that was his last command to them (Mark 16:15). This
reversal of direction is a constitutive part of the Christian
life.

The story, which the Gospels tell, begins with Bethlehem
when God in Jesus came to dwell with men. But that story
comes to a definite end where the Gospel writer says, "He
parted from them" (Luke 24:51). He himself had said to
them a few hours before his death, "It is to your advantage
that I go away, for if I do not go away, the Counselor will
not come to you; but if I go, I will send him to you"
(John 16:7). Mary of Magdala, when she met her risen
Lord, clung to his feet. He said to her, "Mary, do not hold
me, for I have not yet ascended to the Father" (John 20:17).
Of course, the story continues; but with the coming of the
Holy Spirit, it moves out of the villages of Galilee and

towns of Judea into the highways of life. It is with this movement that we are concerned in this chapter.

When Paul came to Ephesus, he found some disciples there. They had been baptized into the baptism of John, but they had not even heard of the Holy Spirit. Paul baptized them again into the name of the Lord Jesus, "and when [he] had laid his hands upon them, the Holy Spirit came on them; and they spoke with tongues and prophesied" (Acts 19:1-6).

Peter and John came to Samaria. There were some disciples there who had already been baptized into the name of the Lord Jesus. But they had not received the Holy Spirit. Peter and John laid their hands upon them and prayed for them that they might receive the Holy Spirit, and they received him (Acts 8:14-18).

Nicodemus came to Jesus to talk with him about the signs he did (John 3:1 ff.), and the way in which God was with him. Jesus said to Nicodemus, "You cannot see the signs of the Kingdom, you cannot see them as signs, unless you are born anew. This birth is by water and the Spirit. John baptizes with water, I baptize with the Spirit."

Jesus said to his disciples (Acts 1:4, 8), "Depart not from Jerusalem but wait for the promise of the Father. Before many days you shall be baptized with the Holy Spirit. And when the Spirit has come upon you, you shall be my witnesses in Jerusalem and in all Judea and Samaria and to the end of the earth."

The Experience of the Spirit

What do these incidents add up to? Is it not clear that they show the absolute importance of the coming of the Holy Spirit into the lives of Christ's disciples, and that it is by the Spirit alone that men see and understand the signs of the kingdom of God in the life and ministry of Jesus, as well as find power and authority to proclaim these signs to the world? On the day of Pentecost, the disciples spoke with tongues (Acts 2:4). The gospel became a gospel for all the nations. Whenever the Holy Spirit comes into the life of a person now, nothing less takes place. He is swept into that movement which would take the gospel to the uttermost parts of the earth. It is said that when the apostles laid their hands on those who believed, with prayer for the Holy Spirit, the Spirit came: so he comes even now when the mission of the church claims a person, lays hands upon him, and he surrenders to that claim.

The Christian faith is more than a "Jesus religion." It is concerned with the consequence to men of who Jesus is.

Jesus is ascended on high. He sits at the right hand of the Father. His kingdom is exercised upon earth. He must rule till all God's enemies are subdued.

Jesus is risen from the dead. He is alive on earth. He is constantly seeking the lost, upholding the fainthearted, strengthening the weak, spreading his love abroad in the hearts and lives of men.

The Holy Spirit is come to lead those who believe to participation in power in this ongoing ministry of Christ. He is come also to prepare a believing response to Christ among those who have not as yet accepted him.

It is said that, when God made the heavens and the earth, the Spirit of God was moving over the face of the waters (Gen. 1:2). Because of that movement of the Spirit, chaos responded to the creating Word of God. When the angel brought his announcement to Mary (Luke 1:35), it is said that the Holy Spirit came upon her and the power of the Most High overshadowed her. That was how Mary brought forth Jesus.

That is how it always is. It is the Spirit in our hearts that teaches us to say "Abba! Father!" (Rom. 8:15). It is when the Holy Spirit comes that we even learn to pray as we ought (Rom. 8:26). "Do not grieve the Holy Spirit" (Eph. 4:30), is Paul's warning. The Holy Spirit has come. He is preparing a response to the gospel here, there, and everywhere; and he is seeking to lead the church in its mission into those places and to those persons whom he has so prepared. The Holy Spirit guided the first Council of Jerusalem (Acts 15:6 ff.) to fashion a policy that would meet the kind of preparation among the Gentiles which he had already effected. The Holy Spirit would not allow Paul and Silas to go to Bithynia (Acts 16:6, 7) but took them instead to Troas where Paul received the call to take the gospel to Europe. Paul went, on his last visit to Jerusalem, bound in the Spirit, not knowing what should befall him there (Acts 20:22). What happened to him there took him ultimately to Rome, the center of the empire.

The fact is that the possibility of Christian obedience is bound up with the experience of the Holy Spirit. He directs the campaign in which the Christian is a participant, so that without him the Christian life simply becomes a religious exercise. The issue is never only, "Do you believe in Jesus Christ?"; it is also, "Have you received the Holy Spirit?"

To avoid serious misunderstanding, let it be insisted that the way in which the distinction is here made between Jesus Christ and the Holy Spirit should not lead anyone to theorize about distinctions within the Godhead, as if man can understand or explain what the life of God is like. The distinction is drawn only because it is an important distinction when we are considering God's work of salvation. When God dealt with human history, that was how he dealt with it, so that it becomes determinative for us and our obedience. However, it affords no basis on which altars can be set up to three gods. There is only one God about whom, when men approach him, they find that their obedience has three decisive moments in it. I accept Jesus Christ. I receive the Holy Spirit. I am a son of the Father. But, when Jesus Christ is accepted, we find that he and the Father are one (John 10:30). When the Spirit is received, we know that the Lord is the Spirit (II Cor. 3:17). When we seek to live as children of the Father, we see that it is only Jesus who is able to establish us in this relation (John 14:6), and that it is only the Spirit who is able to maintain us therein (Rom. 8:27). There is one God in three persons, not an identity of the three but a unity of them, a unity which reflects itself in the Christian experience.

Jesus said to Nicodemus, "The wind blows where it wills, and you hear the sound of it, but you don't know whence it comes or whither it goes; so it is with everyone who is born of the Spirit" (John 3:8). An electric fan can circulate the warm air in a room. Many church activities and even some evangelistic missions achieve little more. It is a different matter when one is able to go out where the breezes blow and feel the breeze on one's face. To receive the Holy Spirit, one must stand where the Spirit blows. There, where God is so obviously at work, is the place to be caught by the Spirit of God. To come into close association with a person alive in the Spirit is to come where one may catch contagion. The symbol of the Spirit is not only wind but fire. Some men are so aflame with the Spirit that to draw near to them is to be where the sparks fall. A Christian congregation is a failure if, in its midst, the Spirit does not break out into flame and fire; if, there, those who do not have the Spirit do not receive him. Jesus said, "If you, who are evil, know how to give good gifts to your children, how much more will the heavenly Father give the Holy Spirit to those who ask him?" (Luke 11:13). To any other prayer God's answer may be "no"; but to the prayer for the Holy Spirit, God's answer is always "yes."

When our Lord said to his disciples, "Wait for the Spirit," this was what he asked them to wait for. They needed the Holy Spirit in order that in their own lives they may be filled with the presence of Jesus Christ. They needed the Holy Spirit in order that they may be led to follow their Master in his continuing ministry in the world. And they needed the Holy Spirit so that each may find the locus of his own obedience. "When the Spirit comes," said Jesus (John 14:26), "He will bring to your remembrance the things I have taught, he will take what is mine and declare it to you, he will make me glorious in you" (John 16:14).

The Launching of the Mission

But when our Lord said, "Wait for the Spirit," he meant also, "Wait until the mission of God is launched in the world." In their different ways, Christmas and Pentecost both celebrate the coming of God to become part of human history, to be involved in it. The coming of God in Jesus Christ determined what man's history shall be. The coming of God in the Holy Spirit regulates the tides of this history.

I was discussing this point with a friend of mine when I was preparing this paper. He was a person greatly influenced in his thinking by the writing of the mystics of all religions. He said to me, "It is generally thought that the postulate of a personal God is a concession to the religious instinct. In your thinking you seem to make God even time-bound." My answer was "Yes: but probably not in the sense in which you mean it. God is time-bound until time itself will be redeemed and set free. He entered into time, and that entrance is the basis of our hope in cosmic redemption." "But the incarnation," my friend countered, "was only for the purpose of revealing God." I said, "No. Certainly, by the incarnation God is revealed, but the incarnation is not just a revelation. It is what it means—the entrance of God into human life in order to be part of it. The avatars of Hinduism are not incarnations in this sense. They are revelations. They are interventions in human affairs and in human lives. Jesus is God incarnate. That is why the Christian faith announces not only an incarnation but a resurrection—a continuous participation of God incarnate in the movement of human history. That is also why the Christian faith announces an end-event when this action of God entering into time will have reached fulfillment, and time itself is no more because death is swallowed up in victory" (I Cor. 15:54). "All this is dogma," my friend said. "What is the experiential proof?" "The experiential proof," I replied, "lies in receiving the Holy Spirit. God's entrance into history is a double entrance. He becomes part of it in Jesus Christ. He makes this part embrace the whole through the Holy Spirit. Jesus Christ is the content of the gospel—the good news of what God has done. The Holy Spirit is the missionary of the gospel. It is he who makes the gospel explosive in men's lives and in human affairs."

"Until Jesus was glorified," says John (7:39), "the mission of the Holy Spirit could not be launched." But when Jesus was glorified, the Spirit came. He came to lead men to see the glory of God in the face of Jesus Christ (II Cor. 4:6). Acceptance of the Christian witness must be prepared for by the Holy Spirit in the lives of men. Apart from that preparation, they will neither understand nor believe. Ask any convert and he will tell you that he is unable to explain how he came to believe. C. S. Lewis gives to the story of his conversion the title *Surprised by Joy*. It is always a surprise when one suddenly sees life according to a new pattern, when, within the soul, one's knowledge of Jesus catches fire and becomes a living awareness, when the will accepts the mastery of Christ and is satisfied.

What of Unbelief?

But what of unbelief? No consideration of the work of the Holy Spirit can avoid this question. In the teaching of Jesus there are two emphases which determine the perspective in which this question must be viewed. He spoke of those who were known as believers but whom the Lord would not acknowledge (Matt. 7:23). He also spoke of those who were known as having said "no," but who turned out to be those who had done "yes" (Matt. 21:28-30). The elder son who stayed with his father finally stayed outside the home, while the younger son who left his father finally found his place within the home (Luke 15:11-32). "The men of Nineveh will arise at the judgment with this generation and condemn it" (Luke 11:32). "Many that are first will be last, and the last first" (Mark 10:31).

The second emphasis in the teaching of Jesus on this question is that on the Holy Spirit as the author of true discipleship. The scribes and the Pharisees persistently rejected Jesus and opposed his work, but his judgment upon them is pronounced precisely at the point where they attributed his work to the devil (Matt. 12:24; Mark 3:30). "A word against the Son of man," he says, "will be forgiven; but whoever speaks against the Holy Spirit will not be forgiven" (Matt. 12:32). Unbelief is a refusal to say "yes" to Jesus Christ, but such refusal may be based on a rejection of Jesus Christ because of who he is. It is this rejection which is the sin against the Holy Spirit, for by the Holy Spirit Jesus has been made known and yet rejected.

Any reflection, then, on unbelief as one meets it in the course of one's Christian ministry of witness must be a reflection in the shadow of the last judgment which will be an event of many surprises. It will also be a reflection on the work of the Holy Spirit as he witnesses to Jesus Christ and draws men to him. In his last discourse in the upper room, Jesus spoke of the work of the Holy Spirit as that of convincing the world of sin because they do not believe in him, of righteousness because of his death, and of judgment because by his triumph the ruler of this world is judged (John 16:8-11). Here becomes evident the inextricable link between the person and work of the Holy Spirit and the person and work of Jesus Christ. The Holy Spirit works, as it were, by applying Jesus Christ to the souls and consciences of men. Who can say where and in whom this work is being performed?

How does he work? He works through the ministry of the church, which ministry he surrounds with his previousness and impregnates with his presence.

The life and mission of the church is the result of the coming of the Holy Spirit into the world. Because of him, the church is engaged in the proclamation that Jesus is Lord. By the Holy Spirit alone is the announcement born that Jesus Christ has come in the flesh (I John 4:2). He thrusts the church out to make this proclamation, he empowers the church to make it under all circumstances, he effects in the church a demonstration of it, he gives to men the gifts of repentance and faith by which they accept the Lord who is proclaimed and confess him.

But here precisely is the problem that not all who hear demonstrably believe, so that the question is raised: What of unbelief? An answer, to be true to the New Testament, must say two things, the one said under the shadow of the last judgment and the other said in the light of the warning about sin against the Holy Spirit.

Can we put into words what needs to be said in the shadow of the last judgment? At least one instance can be given, that which it is necessary to say when the question of belief and unbelief is discussed with respect to the uniqueness and particularity of the Christian gospel and its relation to other faiths. This discussion always runs into difficulty precisely because the relationship being discussed is never a static one. The Holy Spirit is at work. He is eliciting response in the hearts and minds of men to the working of God upon their lives. Their lives are lived within their faiths, sometimes as those who accept them and sometimes as those who do not. Into this situation, the Holy Spirit brings the witness of the church to the lordship and saviorhood of Christ. This witness evokes the response of faith. It sometimes meets with rejection. It oftentimes results in raising questions in the minds of the hearers and leaving those questions there. The Holy Spirit takes all these ways in which people respond to the gospel, and uses them in his own ministry of leading them to confess Jesus as Lord; or even where that confession is absent, of making

Christ's lordship a felt pressure upon their lives. The whole business is too complex for neat answers. We cannot meet a dynamic situation with rigid orthodoxies; we can only recognize it through lives of sensitive obedience. It cannot be otherwise since the mission of the church is a mission within the mission of the Holy Spirit.

But just because this is so, the other word is of equal importance: that it is the gospel proclaimed which causes the double movement of faith and unbelief. Mark sets forward the story of Jesus in this very form, a story culminating in the cross. In John this double movement centers in the figure of Judas. "So, after receiving the morsel, he immediately went out; and it was night" (John 13:30). In the light of the gospel, unbelief is the terrible tragedy of sin.

Is there, then, nothing more to say? There is, because the world's hatred, which the gospel precipitates, itself creates the suffering church, which is for the world's redemption; and the coming of the Holy Spirit will bring to bear his own witness to Christ on the church's witness to him (John 15:18-27). Also there is more to say because the world's hatred is not a surprise to God (John 15:19); it was known in his great wisdom always.

The classic discussion in the New Testament of the problem of unbelief is that by Paul in his Letter to the Romans concerning the unbelief of Israel (Rom. 9:11). At the very outset of his argument Paul moves away from the unbeliever as his starting point. Not all Israel were faithless, there were those who believed (Rom. 9:27). Besides, this faith was possible to all because all heard the good tidings (Rom. 10:18). Why, then, did they not believe? The answer has to be in terms of the actual consequences which their unbelief produced. Because of the unbelief of Israel the gospel went to the Gentiles and, by their acceptance of it, became manifest as God's offer of free salvation to all men (Rom. 11:32). So it became clear that Israel' unbelief itself was held within the wisdom and design of God (Rom. 9:18), while the promise implicit in the faith of those in Israel who believed has also been fulfilled (Rom. 11:31-33).

The inner significance of this argument of Paul becomes luminous when we read what he has to say in the previous chapter. "The hope is," he writes (Rom. 8:11, 14, 19, 21), "that in the end the whole of created life will be rescued from the tyranny of change and decay, and have its share in that magnificent liberty which can only belong to the children of God. They are God's sons who follow the leading of God's Spirit. Within them lives the Spirit that raised Jesus from the dead, bringing to their whole being new strength and vitality. The whole creation is on tiptoe to see the wonderful sight of the sons of God coming into their own." A direct connection is here made between the liberty of the sons of God—those who are in Christ—and the liberation of the whole cosmos. Faith and hope jump from the redeemed community to the redemption of all things, a jump which is possible only because the in-between situation of belief and unbelief is comprehended within the mystery of God's plan of salvation.

The Holy Spirit is the agent of the new creation, the new heavens and the new earth, which he creates in Christ. And, because this is so, the church comes to see its own meaning as the community of the Holy Spirit, becomes aware of the encompassing ministry of the Holy Spirit by which its own ministry is sustained, and understands the task of its own upbuilding in relation to the great work of salvation.

In speaking about salvation, the thrust of the Christian hope is to include "all": it is in speaking about the church that the selective principle applies. A direct consequence of the church's mission, when men find faith in Christ, is that the mission itself is strengthened. The mission is intended to produce missionaries, the evangel must produce evangelists. Bishop Azariah introduced the practice in his diocese of people confirmed placing their hands on their heads and saying, "Woe to me if I do not preach the gospel" (I Cor. 9:16). That is what the confirmation service is about: prayer for the Holy Spirit that one may live the witnessing life. But it is just here that the selective principle applies (John 15:2). The army of Gideon had to be reduced, the vine needs to be pruned, the confessed and confessing people of God in the world will necessarily be a remnant. It is of the church that it is true that "many are called but few are chosen" (Matt. 22:14).

In the work of the Holy Spirit, then, there is the quality not only of comprehension but also of selection, not only of wideness but also of narrowness—a contradictoriness which ought to be no surprise for anyone whose faith is grounded in the Bible. For, as the Bible makes plain, the work of God is always characterized by universality of intention as well as particularity of method. Israel is for the nations, the church is for the world. When the gospel is proclaimed there are the few who are led by the Spirit to faith, who become members of the community whose task it is to proclaim the gospel. When the gospel is proclaimed it becomes also, within the ministry of the Holy Spirit, the power of God for the salvation of the world.

There is only one Savior, Jesus Christ (I Tim. 2:5), and all who are saved will be saved by him. There is only one end-event toward which all things move, their re-creation in Jesus Christ (Eph. 1:10). There is only one finale to the story of man and that will be its fulfillment in the eternal city where God and his Christ are the light by which men will walk and into which the treasures of the nations will be gathered (Rev. 21:23-26). The ministry of the Holy Spirit in the world is to recall the world to its moorings, to reestablish it on its true foundation, to make actual the once-for-allness-for-all-men of what God has done for man in Jesus Christ. "The Holy Spirit is my witness," said Jesus (John 15:26). "He will claim on my behalf all truth that belongs to me" (John 16:13-15). "He will own on my behalf the light wheresoever the light may be. I am the truth, I am the light—the light that enlightens every man" (John 14:6; 8:12; 1:9).

This argument must now be concluded, and yet no way of concluding it seems to be wholly satisfactory. Paul concludes his argument with a shout of praise: "O the depth of the riches and wisdom and knowledge of God!" (Rom. 11:33). God has unlimited resources of grace and mercy. He also remains wholly free so that no one has rights over him. His people have no claims on him above those of others. But this is only one half of the conclusion of the argument. The other half lies in the fact that this shout of praise is the shout of the people of God, those who have found their sonship in Jesus Christ. They witness to the fact that for all men God has provided a place of reconciliation, a mercy seat, a visible Savior, and a visible company which is the saved and saving community.

Let our Lord's own parable concerning the last judgment say the last word. The sheep and the goats are separated (Matt. 25:31-46). So, at the last, will God's judgment separate men. And the judgment turns on the question, Had they accepted him? But, as the parable makes clear, the form in which he had presented himself to them for their acceptance was the form of one despised and rejected of men. There is no salvation except in Jesus Christ, but who shall decide how and in what guise Jesus comes to men and claims their acceptance!

The Nature of the Church's Mission

There we must leave it, and turn to a search for an understanding of the nature of our own obedience, of the meaning and significance of the mission of the church. First of all, the church's mission is to be the people of God. Redeemed by Christ and raised from death in him by the Holy Spirit, the Christian community exists as the result and the demonstration of the facts of the gospel. "You are the light of the world," Jesus said (Matt. 5:14). The Christian community cannot escape this responsibility. In the night, it has to be the moon reflecting the light of the sun. In the day, it has to be the mirror in which men can see themselves. Its task is to make plain the way of life, to reveal life, and to direct it. The proclamation of the Christian gospel must arise from a demonstration of what it means. The Christian must be a witness of what he proclaims, he must be an evidence of it. "We are," says James, "the first specimens of his new creation" (Jas. 1:18). It is true that the treasure will always remain in earthen vessels (II Cor. 4:7), but the treasure will be there. There will be proof that the door of heaven has been opened and that God has come among men. "If a man loves me," said Jesus, "he will keep my word, and my Father will love him, and we will come to him and make our home with him." Emmanuel is the promise "God with us" (John 14:23). To us who believe in Jesus Christ, it is the promise of God's presence and companionship; to those who do not yet believe in Jesus Christ, it is the promise that the presence of God will be mediated to them. God has made us priests (Rev. 1:6); we are no priests unless we mediate God to the world.

"Men are not so foolish," said Jesus (Matt. 5:15), "as to light a lamp and put it under a bushel. Neither is God less wise. When he lights a lamp he puts it where it will give light to the whole house." The sanctuary is the place where the lamp is lit, where it is filled with oil, where its wicks are trimmed. It should never become the place where the lamp is left. The lamp is meant for the world outside. It is not a sanctuary lamp but a street light that the church represents. An ecumenical conference, called by the World Council Youth Department and held in Berlin in May, 1960, was reported on in the Ecumenical Press Service.[1]

[1] E.P.S. No. 19, May 20, 1960.

The report says that there was a session at the conference when the participants were asked to write press articles on peace arising out of Paul's Letter to the Ephesians. One conference member is said to have remarked, "I should prefer to write a book on systematic theology. It is easier." Of course it is. Systematic theology is an exercise within the precincts of the temple. Press articles demand converse with wayfarers on the road.

The church, it is commonly said, is a divine society. It is. But its divine nature lies in the actuality of its mission as the herald and carrier of the divine. The divine nature of the church is in its dynamics. It is, and remains wherever it is, the place where men find God; whether they find him as One who is troublesome or satisfying, as effecting their obedience or causing their rebellion.

Secondly, the church's mission is to be the people of God everywhere—in every situation, in every land and nation, in all areas of life. The church anywhere represents the gathering of the firstfruits (Rev. 14:4, 15), which is the promise of the final harvest. That there be firstfruits everywhere, that in every city of earth there be a colony of heaven (Phil. 3:20): that is the task of the Holy Spirit through the mission of the church. The unfinished task of evangelism is the task of bringing the gospel to those who have not heard it, of building the Christian community within a people among whom such a community does not exist, of maintaining the Christian witness amidst current problems and tensions in all areas of human relationships, of exerting the pressure of the Christian way of life on those who do not yet accept it.

There is a sense in which, until all men are confessing Christians and all life is lived in the Christian obedience, the task of evangelism is not over. But the task to which the church is committed is not so much the finishing of it as the beginning of it. It is the beginning that is yet unfinished. When the leaven is hid in the meal (Luke 13:21), the beginning of the task is over. But there are so many situations in which the leaven is not yet so hid. Where the seed is sown (Mark 4:26), the beginning of the task is over. But there are hundreds of thousands of villages in Africa and Asia alone where the seed has not yet been sown. Where the city is built (Matt. 5:14), the beginning of the task is over. But there are many places in which the Christian city has not yet been built. "This gospel of the kingdom will be preached throughout the whole world, as a testimony to all the nations; and then the end will come" (Matt. 24:14). The end cannot come where the beginning is not over. To be the people of God everywhere, that is the mission. To go to the ends of the earth, that is the task. As we think of it cannot we hear the word of the Lord that came to Israel long ago, "You have compassed this mountain long enough. Go north"?

For a whole generation they had lived on the slopes of that mountain. (See Deut. 1.) It was their home. They had left Egypt, a crowd; here on this mountain they had been welded into a nation. Why could they not continue to live here? They could not, because they were a pilgrim people. The promised land lay north of where they were. They had to strike their tents and set off again on the march.

This mission of the church is to be the people of God. It is to be the people of God everywhere. It is also to be the people of God on a journey. A church at rest is no church. I was present one day at a discussion conducted by Dr. Nolde on some aspect of international affairs. During question time he was asked, "And for what solution are you prepared to settle?" His answer was, "For none." The Christian community," he said, "cannot settle for any answer. We shall press for the best possible compromise in the present situation, but we shall also press for a complete change in the situation itself." This is a good illustration of what it means for the church to be a pilgrim people.

A pilgrim people is bound to have a set of values which

are different from those held by people who have settled down. It will tend to accumulate less luggage, it will not be overconcerned with creature comforts, it will enjoy its food provided for the journey.

When I was studying in the Theological College at Bangalore, I was to go one day with three of my friends to visit the waterfalls at Shimoga. We had planned to leave early in the morning. Sandwiches for the trip were prepared, and we had our thermos flasks filled with coffee. Unfortunately for us, at the very last moment, the picnic had to be called off. We decided to eat the sandwiches and have the coffee for breakfast. I can still recall how flat those sandwiches tasted and how insipid the coffee. On the picnic they would have been wonderful, on the breakfast table they were awful.

The sacraments of the church, the worship of the congregation, the study of God's Word, the practices of religion in the home and in one's personal life—all these are food for the journey. So many neglect them because they do not need them. Theirs is a sedentary life, and all this food is unnecessary. And even what food they take they do not relish. A beautiful cloth and flowers on the breakfast table will not make much difference. Even "music while we eat" is quite irrelevant. The sandwiches are for the road. Get up and get out. Go north.

This challenge to the church to take to the road implies also another consequence. It means that the church can never be satisfied with its forms of obedience. What the church is today in our several countries is the result of the obedience of our fathers in the faith. But their obedience cannot necessarily be ours. In one of the discussions in the Negotiating Committee for Church Union in Ceylon, a suggestion was made by one of the Anglican representatives that a paragraph be included in the Scheme of Union expressing repentance for the past sin of division. "I shall never repent," said a Congregationalist, "for the action of the pilgrim fathers." We don't have to. It is not necessary for the past to have been wrong in order to make repentance now necessary. Repentance is our essential response to new tasks and new commands. There is no entail on the church's past. A great deal has to be left behind. That is what it means to be a pilgrim people, that is what is involved in being called to take to the road.

In the Gospel narrative the challenge of Jesus, that those who would follow him must take up the cross and follow him (Mark 8:34), appears before there is any mention of the cross on which he himself must die. What meaning then could it have conveyed to those who heard him? It would have only suggested to them that they must be prepared to die at the hands of the Romans, a likelihood contingent on Jesus' leading an insurrection. Explaining this difficulty, Dr. Findlay quotes a traveler familiar with Bedouin life as saying that in the Aramaic the word "cross" simply meant "something sticking up from the ground" and that it was used generally to describe a tent peg. Even now, this traveler remarked, the Bedouin sheikh when he orders a move, says to the women of his harem "take up the cross and follow me." [2]

Peter has confessed Jesus as the Christ, Christ has said that he must suffer and die and rise again. Peter has protested that this cannot be and been rebuked by the Master. Then Jesus says to them all, disciples and multitude: "You cannot follow me by staying where you are. You must break camp. You think that your security lies in the well-trodden paths of yesterday. I tell you that it lies only in following me along the unknown paths of tomorrow and sharing there both my passion and my victory. If you seek to save your life you will lose it. And what will it profit you if by staying behind you gain the whole world and lose your own soul?"

[2] J. A. Findlay, *A Portrait of Peter* (New York: The Abingdon Press, 1935), p. 88.

It is said of Abraham that he obeyed, not knowing whither he went (Heb. 11:8). The unknown is the pilgrim's goal and obedience, it is also his hope and his heritage. And what a magnificent thing the unknown will be when finally the pilgrim arrives! A city with foundations, whose builder and maker is God! And, all along the way, what an exhilarating experience to find that, while one leaves behind that which one has made his home—whether spiritually or materially— and takes to the road with fear; God provides safety for the journey, sustenance for the road, and a foretaste of one's inheritance. "In his hands," sang the psalmist (Ps. 16:11), whatever those hands will dispense, "are joys for evermore."

"It is not enough," I heard Dr. Hoekendijk say at a conference, "to speak of the church as engaged in a mission. It is essential to realize that the church is a mission." To use a phrase of Bishop Newbigin, "The church is an expedition." And, because it is an expedition it creates consequences for other people, for those in whose midst this expedition has been launched. These consequences, too, are part of the church's task in the world.

The consequence for others of having a pilgrim people in their midst is that such a people will exert a peculiar pressure on the forms of common life. Theirs will be a worldliness that is holy. They will live the common life as those who are soon to leave it behind. Also, they will cause even those who are not on the pilgrimage to serve it. The church loses one of its greatest opportunities of fulfilling its mission when the Christian community seeks to be self-contained. This is an insistent temptation for the small Christian groups that are scattered throughout the large lands of Asia and Africa. A pilgrim people must maintain their differentia as pilgrims, but they must belong to the society among whom their journey is set. This common association is of the heart of the business.

By far the greater part of the church's mission is to bring to bear on people the pressure of the Christ. So will their living be influenced by him even when they are not Christians by commitment. In the Western world, there is a Christian national past in the lives of the nations on which such pressure can depend; in the lands of the younger churches such pressure must depend on the normality of the relationship between Christians and their fellow citizens in all walks of life. The Christian community has always to be a witnessing community but its intention to convert to Jesus Christ is never a conditioning factor in its relationships. It qualifies but does not condition, and because it qualifies, the church becomes in human affairs the instrument of the inescapability of the Christ.

So be sure you do not refuse to hear the voice of God! . . . Now he promises:

> Yet once more will I make to tremble
> Not the earth only, but also the heaven.

This means that in this final "shaking" all that is impermanent will be removed, . . . and only the unshakable things will remain. Since then we have been given a kingdom that is "unshakable," let us serve God with thankfulness in the ways which please him, but always with reverence and holy fear. . . . Our God is a burning fire. (Heb. 12:25-29; tr. J. B. Phillips.)

Christian Theology
and the Living
Faiths of Men

J. Robert Nelson

Great difficulties are inherent in every attempt to deal with
the relation of the gospel of Jesus Christ, the church, and
Christian theology to the faith on the one hand and to the
practice of various world religions on the other. A purely
disinterested, objective inquiry is impossible; the Christian
thinker cannot detach himself from the claims of his faith.
Neither can he understand with perfect empathy the nature
of other faiths. Moreover, the Christian inevitably identifies
himself with the particular understanding of the Christian
faith which his own church tradition and theological discipline have bequeathed to him. If the Lutheran, the Baptist,
and the Russian Orthodox stand in such fundamental
disagreement with regard to essential matters of the faith,
how can there be conceived the Christian attitude toward
non-Christian faiths? Yet these difficulties need not paralyze
our efforts to understand the component faiths of mankind
and make judgments about them. Such attempts, constantly
being made, are indispensable to Christians in the church
in their need to strive after integrity of thought and faith.

The Church in the Mission of God

Two factors determine the Christian's attitude toward other living faiths. First, he is a member of the church. Second, the church is the instrument of God's mission to all his creatures.

1. In virtue of his personal faith in Jesus Christ as Son of God and Savior, the Christian is a member of the living, historical community called the church. Membership in church is not incidental to his confession of faith, but integral to it. It is through the historic life of the community that the message of God's action in Jesus Christ and the broad implications of the gospel have been conserved, thus enabling the man in each generation to become a Christian disciple. Through the ongoing activity of the church in teaching and interpreting the faith, and in the recurring acts of corporate worship and sacramental communion, the person is nourished in the faith and also given a clearer apprehension of what it means to be a Christian and a member of the church. He is not merely set on the way to personal salvation and self-fulfillment; not merely guided in the worship of God; not merely permitted to enjoy the satisfaction of living within the community where divine love is expected to be the rule; not merely enlightened in mind by wise teachers of the Bible and instructors in the ways of God with man. These are important, indeed indispensable concomitants of the Christian's life in the church. In addition to these, however, is the equally essential perception that the church is a distinct historic people, called together by God, without respect to natural and national differences, for the double purpose of embodying the regenerate human life in Christ and of extending to all mankind the faith and community which make this life possible.

The church is more than an association for the pursuit of certain religious ends, more than an organization for promotion of a desirable way of living. It is a uniquely universal people set in the midst of mankind in its historical existence. There is a clear distinction, therefore, between the church and all the rest of the human race which is "not-church." The fact that the line of demarcation between the church and the rest of the race cannot easily be determined does not invalidate the claim of a distinct difference. Neither can one tell exactly the moment when night ends and day begins, though the difference between the two cannot be denied.

Between the beliefs, practices, and attitudes which characterize the church and those which constitute the totality of life under other religions, there are innumerable differences. It is the task of the science of comparative religions to note and describe these; and the person of tolerant mind may conclude that they represent nothing more than variations on certain basic religious themes. Such comparison seldom takes seriously the self-consciousness of the Christian, which is exceedingly serious to him and his brethren in the church; namely, that the community of which he is a member is sent by God with the message of Christ, and the adherents of all other faiths, or of no faith at all, are those to whom the church is sent to bear witness to this message. What appears to be religious imperialism in the eyes of the Hindu or the contemporary liberal humanist is nothing other than the inherent sense of mission which the church has held since its beginning and has implemented with varying degrees of intensity and success. When the Christian today both defends and advocates his faith in witness to non-Christians, he remains faithful to the distinction expressed many times in the New Testament between the Israel of God (*ekklesia*, church, people of God) and the "nations of the world" (*panta ta ethne*, Gentiles, heathen, pagans). [1] Without equiv-

---

[1] Georg Bertram, "Ethnos," *Theological Dictionary of the New Testament*, ed. Gerhard Kittel (Grand Rapids: Wm. B. Eerdmans Publishing Co., 1964), II, 367-69.

ocation the apostle addresses the Christians of Ephesus, center of the living religion of Artemis, as former Gentiles (*ethne*) who were once atheists (*atheoi;* Eph. 2:12). But now, as members of the church, being "in Christ Jesus," they have become "members of the household of God" and consequently missioners to the people whence they came. It is difficult to see how any subsequent experiences of the human race or of the church have altered this difference between those who are sent and those to whom they are sent.

2. "As the Father has sent me, even so send I you" (John 20:21). The Christian, as disciple of Jesus Christ and member of the church, is a participant in the mission of God himself, who takes initiative to come to men and restore them to obedient fellowship with himself. Even those Christians who feel most responsive to the missionary command must guard against the false notion that the Christian faith is a religious system or body of belief which they must somehow persuade non-Christians to accept. Their zeal is misdirected, and they may even prevent the gospel from having its intended effect, if they regard the faith as just the best and truest competitor on the religious market of the world. The gospel and the church, on the contrary, are God's means of breaking through the stubborn resistance of men and attracting them to himself in faith, which works through love and engenders hope. Whether this resistance be based upon ignorance or pride or attachment to another center of religious devotion, it must still be attacked by the witnessing Christian who is thereby extending the saving work of God in Jesus Christ.

In his penetrating book, *The Mission of God*, Georg F. Vicedom makes the point that the church, in its movement toward the world, does not possess a mission of its own or a mandate to carry on a religious crusade. Rather, the mission is of God, through Jesus Christ the incarnate Word, *to* the church and *through* the church to all persons. "We must do mission work not because we possess the Gospel, but rather, we have the Gospel only because it is intended for the heathen." [2] Bearing, but not possessing for itself, the treasure of the gospel in its common earthen vessels, the church is constrained to meet every person in his peculiar situation and share with him the saving revelation of God in Christ.

The present condition of most persons alive today who are not Christians is that of being adherents of Judaism, Islam, Buddhism, Hinduism, Shintoism, or some form of animistic religion (not to mention those who, quite literally, are without any religion at all). Therefore the explicit and legitimate posture and purpose of Christians, according to Edmund Perry, is to "undertake the study of religions in order to convert their adherents to faith in the Gospel of Jesus Christ." [3]

It is a fact that much of the pioneering work in the systematic study of the great religions of the East has been done by Christian missionaries, who were enabled to pursue it by critical methods developed in the Christian West, and motivated by the desire to win the adherents of these religions. The Muslim or Hindu rightly feels that such study is therefore subversive of his own religious convictions. He thinks, further, that it expresses the kind of arrogance which he has long held to be the property of Christianity. It would perhaps be as difficult to persuade the non-Christian that this study and missionary effort are undertaken out of love and concern for him, as to make the medieval heretic, bound to the stake, believe that the Inquisition was burning him for the good of his soul. Yet it is love, not arrogance, which motivates the Christian witness—love both for God and for the person who does not yet know him in the reconciling work of Jesus Christ.

What the Christian has to offer the non-Christian is not

---

[2] (Saint Louis, Missouri: Concordia Publishing House, 1965), p. 82.
[3] *The Gospel in Dispute*, p. 83.

simply a "better way of life" or a "better way of salvation."
The Christian believes and makes the bold claim that the
gospel is the way of both life and salvation. Such has been
the claim from apostolic times to the present. As Vicedom
asserts it, "Since Jesus died and rose for the salvation of
men, any redemption apart from him is impossible, even
though men ever and again strive to classify Christ among
many figures who try to indicate a way of salvation." [4]
Here arises again, as it must, the bluntly intransigent declaration of the church's conviction that the one, holy God has
acted decisively and unrepeatably in Jesus Christ for the
salvation of all men. Its corollary is that religious systems or
doctrines which deny the absoluteness and particularity of
God's act in Jesus Christ are not partners with Christianity
in man's search for God, but are obstacles and hindrances to
be overcome.

Religious Values and Saving Truth

Having declared his unbending conviction that whatever
man may expect of a saving knowledge of God is to be
found only as a result of the act of revelation in Jesus Christ,
the Christian is by no means obliged to conclude that no
value or truth is to be found in the teaching and practice
of other religions. The erroneous deduction from the Christian affirmation of exclusive claim to saving revelation, that
other religious systems are wholly and damnably false and
corrupt, has caused much confusion and bitterness. Such
an attitude of total rejection would indeed be arrogance
and as indefensible as its opposite attitude of unrestrained
syncretism. The "Declaration on Non-Christian Religions" of
the Second Vatican Council asserts the proper appreciation
of many elements of Islam, Buddhism, and Hinduism.

Fortunately the Christian claim to unique truth is not
proved valid or invalid by the moral fruits of faith. Un-

---

[4] *The Mission of God*, p. 53.

fortunately the majority of people who compare Christian faith with the other religions are more interested in discovering signs of moral superiority and supremacy in piety and devotion than they are in dealing with the differences theologically. It must be acknowledged that the sages and holy men of Eastern religions are often superior to leading Christians in both charity and piety. Jean Daniélou freely admits that "Buddha and Mohammed are greater religious geniuses than St. Peter or the Curé d'Ars." [5] The faithful regularity of the Muslim in his daily pattern of prayer and his disciplined observance of the rules of Ramadan fill the Christian with admiration and shame. The serenity of the devout Buddhist, in contrast to the anxiety and frenetic activity of the average Christian, make it seem that the Buddhist has learned more than the Christian of the "peace which passes all understanding." And the gentleness and sensitivity of the Hindu or the Jain in his practice of non-violent *ahimsa* actually seem to approximate the pattern of Jesus Christ more closely than the behavior of Christians does. Clearly there are such values in non-Christian religions which may well be emulated by Christians. And insofar as the Christian can explain the overt goodness of man only in terms of the working of God's Spirit in all men, as bearers of the *imago Dei*, which is not totally defaced, he may conclude that certain aspects of the other religions testify to the undelineated, universal work of the Holy Spirit.

Having said "*sic*" to certain qualities of non-Christian religions, the Christian must declare a resounding "*non*" to the notion that it is legitimate to evaluate the truth and integrity of religions according to the norms of piety and morality. The so-called "Christlike" character of Mohandas K. Gandhi does not invalidate the ancient conviction that "there is no other name under heaven among men by which

[5] *God and the Ways of Knowing* (New York: Meridian Books, 1957), p. 14.

we must be saved" than that of Jesus Christ (Acts 4:12).
Nor do the non-Christian virtues, however praiseworthy,
compel the Christian to accept the thesis of Professor Arnold
Toynbee that the church should "purge our Christianity
of the traditional Christian belief that Christianity is
unique." [6]
In the last analysis the comparison of religions with the
Christian faith does not yield a syncretizing solvent which
promises to dissolve the great barriers between the religions
and produce eventually either a universal amalgam of religions or an agreement on the part of all to surrender
their claims to saving truth in order to support a universal
tolerance of religions. There is a widespread notion in both
East and West today that the great religions are divided
only by matters of marginal importance but united by
essentials of faith and revelation. Nothing could be more
fallacious. Even Rudolf Otto, with all his disposition to
relativize the central claims of the religions by painstaking
comparison of them, could not honestly expect the emergence of a universal religion.[7] Still less was Gerardus van
der Leeuw, after years of the most intensive study of the
phenomenology of religion in the history of mankind, constrained to regard the Christian gospel as anything less
than the distinctive fulfillment of man's religious aspirations
and the final answer to them.[8]

More accurate than the popular notion cited above would
be the assertion that the common elements of the religions,
especially their moral and devotional manifestations, are

[6] *Christianity Among the Religions of the World* (New York: Charles
Scribner's Sons, 1957), p. 95. The idea that Christians have no legitimate
cause to seek the conversion of a non-Christian to Christianity is likewise
held by the New Testament scholar Rudolf Bultmann (in private conversation, 1964) and by the late Paul Tillich in *Christianity and the Encounter
of World Religions* (New York: Columbia University Press, 1963).

[7] Cf. his essay "A Universal Religion?" in *Religious Essays* (London: Oxford University Press, 1931).

[8] *Religion in Essence and Manifestation* (2nd ed.; London: Allen & Unwin,
1964), p. 646.

of a marginal character while their points of division on matters of ultimate truth and the way of salvation are central and essential. Prof. Walter Freytag of Hamburg, also a respected scholar of the great religions, finally concluded: "It is the simple fact that the religions do not stand closer together the higher they are, but are, on the contrary, more distinctly divided from one another." [9]

The points of irreconcilable contrast between the gospel and the chief religions (excepting Judaism) were presented definitively in the Beecher Lectures given by D. T. Niles in 1957. He asked friends who were adherents of three religions to write him a concise explanation of why they could not regard conversion to Christianity as a possibility. In each case the christological *skandalon* was at stake.

For the Hindu, the barrier was the historical incarnation, the decisive revelation in a particular person. The friend quotes the *Bhagavad Gita*: "Howsoever men approach Me, even so do I accept them, for on all sides whatever path they choose is Mine." Niles's comment on this is: "The Hindu needs no doctrine of redemption within history. The Christian is lost without it. That is why the Christian faith insists that the Incarnation, the Cross, and the Resurrection are not only acts of revelation but also of redemption." [10]

The Muslim is also offended by the idea of incarnation, and repulsed at the Christian belief in Jesus' crucifixion. He holds these to be fabrications of the church rather than descriptions of reality. "To speak of Jesus as an incarnation of God is to sin against God's majesty as well as His unity. . . . It is too materialistic a conception and derogates from God's awful majesty. Also, the Christian teaching is contrary to the unity of God. There is only one God and no other." [11]

[9] *The Gospel and the Religions* (London: SCM Press, 1957), p. 20.

[10] *The Preacher's Task and the Stone of Stumbling* (New York: Harper & Brothers, 1958), p. 32. See also Niles's *Upon the Earth*, pp. 227-46.

[11] Quoted in *The Preacher's Task*, p. 41.

The Christian understanding of sin and the reality of redemptive value in the crucifixion and death of Christ are thus unacceptable. As the infallible Qu'ran itself declares, in Niles's quotation: "The Jews did not kill him, nor did they crucify him; but he was made to appear to them like one crucified." [12]

The Buddhist correspondent is even more extensive in his detail of the essence of the gospel. Buddhists are "unable to accept the theory of an omnipotent and merciful Creator"; they see no reason for "the Christian concept of having to appease a God by prayers to obtain one's salvation." Even without engaging the gospel's claim concerning Jesus Christ, but limiting himself to negations of the idea of a good, almighty, and personal God, he concludes that "the doctrines of Christianity and of Buddhism are divided by a vast chasm." [13]

These contrasts are familiar enough, and for many they are so patently irreconcilable that efforts in this direction are considered futile. In each relationship between the Christian gospel and another religion something of vital necessity to the gospel is at stake. This does not mean that Christians are prevented from recognizing "good" in other religions or even from borrowing certain ideas from them, even as Christianity did so significantly in its encounter with Hellenic and Roman civilization. Nevertheless, the heart of the faith, the faith in the person and work of Jesus Christ, can scarcely be sacrificed or changed for the sake of a "higher religion" beyond any we know. Professor William Ernest Hocking's criticism of the Christian fear of syncretism as being a "timorous attitude to alien religions" and a "smallness of faith" may be partly justified. [14] The church

[12] *Ibid.*, p. 51.
[13] *Ibid.*, pp. 72-73.
[14] *Living Religions and a World Faith* (New York: The Macmillan Company, 1940), p. 186. A most trenchant exposure and repudiation of religious syncretism is presented by W. A. Visser 't Hooft in *No Other Name* (Philadelphia: The Westminster Press, 1964).

ought to have sufficient confidence in the reality of the mission of God to risk its teachings in dialogue and encounter with other religions. But it is exceedingly questionable whether Hocking respects the truth and integrity of the Christian message when he advocates a calculated process of religious synthesis culminating in the "reconception" of all religions to become a "world faith." While most Christians are constrained by faith to proclaim a gospel based upon "the scandal of particularity" of God's work in Jesus Christ and his calling of the church to extend this work, Hocking finds the multiplicity of religions in the world to be "a scandal of plurality." So the lines of disagreement remain sharply drawn.

Is the Christian Faith Incomparable?

Thus far we have been dealing with the Christian faith and Christianity and the church as though they constituted one religion among many in the world. Most persons would not take exception to this usage. Christianity has specific beliefs, rites, institutions, and traditions which can be compared empirically with those of other religions. In this act of comparing, most Christians are confident that the essential truth of the gospel is vindicated. But certain theologians are dissatisfied with the very notion that the truth of the gospel as divine revelation can be in any sense designated "a religion." They do not deny that Christianity has the marks of a religion and can be called such. But they hold that Christianity itself, as a religion among others, is subject to the judgment of the decisive revelation of God in Jesus Christ. The gospel thus stands above the historic and institutional forms in which it has been cast.

The most radical expression of this distinction, as may be expected, has been given by Karl Barth. The plumb line of judgment falls upon all religions, Christianity not excepted. The revelation of God in Christ spells the annulment of all religions.[15] Indeed, he concludes, "Religion is unbelief. It is a concern, indeed, we must say that it is the one great concern, of godless man." [16] Religion is the gravest temptation of all, in the judgment of the gospel, because it tempts man to self-justification and self-righteousness by believing and doing "religious things." The irreconcilability of non-Christian religions and the gospel is, in this view, far more radical than the disagreements exposed through comparison would indicate.

The same kind of criticism, though somewhat milder, was made earlier by Emil Brunner.[17] Brunner recognizes the fact that the exponents of most religions base their faith on some form of divine revelation. Since Christianity is also a religion of revelation, it is commonly assumed that the Christian claim to revelation is comparable to similar claims, and one must decide for himself which of these to believe and which to reject. But the astonishing thing, he observes, is that there are very few claims outside Christianity to a divine revelation possessing universal validity. Indeed, the Christian gospel is here quite incomparable.

The claim of the Christian faith, in its radicalism, is as solitary as its content: the message of atonement. It is this: Only at one place, only in one event, has God revealed Himself truly and completely—there, namely, where He became man. . . . No "other religion" can assert revelation in the radical, unconditional sense in which the Christian faith does this, because no "other religion" knows the God who is Himself the Revealer.[18]

That the two Swiss theologians should recoil from liberal dilutions of the gospel and consequent inclinations on the part of some Christians to yield to relativism and syncretism

---

[15] *Church Dogmatics*, I/2, 280.
[16] *Ibid.*, pp. 299-300.
[17] Cf. *Die Christusbotschaft im Kampf mit den Religionen* (Stuttgart: Evang. Missionsverlag, 1931), and *Revelation and Reason* (Philadelphia: The Westminster Press, 1946).
[18] *Revelation and Reason*, pp. 235-36.

among the religions is both understandable and right. They have done much throughout the Protestant churches to call Christians back to a serious evaluation and proclamation of the gospel. The most telling influence of their type of theology upon the Protestant missionary venture has been effected by the writings of the late Dr. Hendrik Kraemer. In his last large book, *Religion and the Christian Faith*, he conceded that in his earlier work of 1938, *The Christian Message in a Non-Christian World*, he "far too one-sidedly characterized the religions as human performances and achievements, good or bad, and dealt with them too unilaterally as purely human products." [19] Even so, he had to assert in the new book: "The world of religion and religions (of culture as a whole) belongs to the realm of the 'old man,' the unredeemed man, not yet re-created into the Image of God in whose likeness man was originally created, and therefore, with all its marvellous achievements and Satanic deviations, under divine judgment, dimly or unwittingly awaiting its redemption." [20] Comparison between the gospel and the religions is still, in the view of Kraemer, a precarious and suspect undertaking.

Despite the sanative effect this strong medicine has had upon the churches and their missionary movement, there is growing resistance to so stark and radical delineation as Brunner, Barth, and Kraemer have made. J. Russell Chandran questions whether the idea of absolute discontinuity between the gospel and religions, or even between Christianity and the other religions, is an inevitable consequence of the biblical revelation. [21] Though he is fun-

---

[19] (Philadelphia: The Westminster Press, 1957), p. 316. A briefer statement of Kraemer's conviction and understanding of the issue is given in his book *Why Christianity of All Religions?* (Philadelphia: The Westminster Press, 1962).

[20] *Religion and the Christian Faith*, p. 257.

[21] "The Christian Approach to Non-Christian Religions," *Christianity and the Asian Revolution*, R. B. Manikam, ed. (New York: Distributed by Friendship Press, 1954), pp. 185 ff.

damentally in sympathy with a rigorous theology of uniqueness, Walter Freytag opposed the idea of the utter annulment of religion. He admitted the complicity of Christians in general with the ranks of non-Christians in "man's attempt to master the Eternal." But he asked rhetorically whether we must really abandon the attempt to affirm the superiority of Christianity, as well as to find good in others.

Is everything in the religions really only Godforsakenness and rebellion? Has God really forgotten the works of His hands? Is there no humanity in the religions, in the rectitude and truthfulness we can encounter, in the tenderness of conscience, the genuine coming together in human community, the heart-felt sympathy for the suffering, in the honest quest for God, in the resolute obedience to that which a man has perceived as being right, in genuine modesty, in humble self-moderation? [22]

Moreover, one has to question whether the church as God's people, the body of Christ and bearer of God's mission, is not unduly minimized by the theology of radical discontinuity. Even when it is admitted that Christianity as a religion and the church as a people are not adjuncts of particular cultures or the results of human striving after salvation-by-works, it must be further declared that it is only the church, as Christianity made manifest, which continues to proclaim and explicate the saving revelation in Christ. As Edmund Perry rightly says: "Christianity in this sense is not a *cursed* religion but so inevitably derivative from the Gospel as to be intrinsic to the Gospel itself." [23]

So far as the Christian mission is concerned, then, the affirmation of the gospel need not carry with it the unconditional negation of Christianity as a religion among religions, nor even of all elements of the religions.

[22] *The Gospel and the Religions*, p. 29.
[23] *The Gospel in Dispute*, p. 220.

Christianity as Different in Degree and Kind

The perennial debate on the continuity or discontinuity of the gospel and the religions of the world has been marked by an antiphony of "yes" and "no" choruses. Perhaps this has been so for no more reason than that theologians usually disagree; for the "yes" and the "no" are inherent in the nature of the gospel itself.

In his essay on "Christianity and Other Living Faiths," Walter M. Horton[24] implies that a new and promising stage of the debate has been attained by H. H. Farmer in his Gifford Lectures of 1950. Farmer finds the theologically and philosophically satisfying middle way between syncretism and absolutism by holding that the Christian revelation and faith are at once different in degree and different in kind from other religions. Referring to R. G. Collingwood's theory of the "overlap of classes," Farmer writes: "Difference of degree, when it reaches a certain point, may become a difference in kind without ceasing to be a difference in degree."[25] In other words, while Christianity remains in the category of religion, it is also the given *normative* concept of religion itself. He does not seek to demonstrate how the Christian norm is applicable to the range of components which make up religion, but concentrates on the act of *worship*. He finds in worship, rather than in preaching, teaching, or theology, the focal point of the continuing apprehension of the gospel. In seven distinguishable, but inseparable, elements of Christian trinitarian worship, Farmer discerns the meaning of the revelation of God in Christ which constitutes the norm of other kinds of worship and hence of all other religions.[26] This normative worship is based upon the apprehension of God as "ontologically and

---

[24] *Christian Theology: An Ecumenical Approach* (rev. ed.; New York: Harper and Brothers, 1958), pp. 303-304.
[25] *Revelation and Religion* (New York: Harper & Brothers, 1954), p. 33.
[26] *Ibid.*, pp. 78-79.

axiologically other," as "personal," as "asking all" of men and yet "giving all" for their salvation, as "intimately present and active within the worshipper's own being" and as giving the "feeling-tone" of the living encounter with himself. In all these respects the content of the revelation in Jesus Christ is brought to bear upon the Christian at the most significant time in his life, that is, at worship. And it is precisely at this time and in this experience that the distinctive truth of Christianity is seen to be set over against the competing claims of other faiths. Farmer's insight, and the thesis based upon it, cannot be considered the definitive answer to the problem. But he points a new direction toward a more profound examination of the life of faith as distinct from propositions about faith.[27]

Conclusion

However wide or narrow, however open or closed the attitude of Christian theologians may be, as exemplified in the whole discussion described above, it is still to be contended that the basis for the church's exercise of the mission of the gospel is essential and indispensable. Not that mission by itself is an unalterable concept; but mission is the inevitable consequence of the Christian apprehension of the love and purpose of God in Jesus Christ. Neglect of mission or hesitancy about it are equivalent to a betrayal of the essential Christian faith. Refusal to carry on the mission, out of deference for truths inherent in other religions, is really rejection of this faith. It remains the theologians' task, probably an unending task, to attempt to describe the terms under which the Christian can approach the non-Christian and witness to the uniqueness, the saving efficacy, and the truth of the message of Jesus Christ.

[27] I have attempted to present still another mode of understanding the critical distinction between Christian faith and other religions in terms of attitude toward suffering, in the article "Tolerance, Bigotry, and the Christian Faith," *Religion in Life*, XXXIII (Autumn, 1964), 540-58.

Toward a Theology
for the
Christian-Jewish Encounter

A. Roy Eckardt

I

The past twenty-five years have witnessed the hope that Christendom was going to change its ways and its thinking concerning the Jewish people and Judaism. Adolf Hitler's so-called final solution (*Entlösung*), the program for the total annihilation of European Jewry and ultimately of all the world's Jews, constituted no more than an extreme application of the centuries-long *Mahnung* (warning-exhortation) by the Christian world: Beware of the menace of "the Jews"![1] The history of the West discloses as impossibly abstract any attempt to separate antisemitism from anti-Judaism. Indeed, the Hitler program could succeed to the extent it did only because the Western world had been exposed for so long to the teachings of the Christian church concerning "the Jews." Yet at last, when the Nazis in effect told the church how to bring to fulfillment one prevailing dimension of its doctrinal logic, the dimension of oppression and persecution, and then put their own words into action,

[1] The definite article here says much about non-Jews who use it, nothing about "the Jews" themselves.

it was too much even for Christians. Some in the churches recoiled before Nazism and before their own conscious and below-conscious drives, if only by turning inward upon themselves in funereal silence. This shock, the waves of which still reverberate throughout Europe and across the oceans, seemed for a time to be capable of converting the Christian world away from its traditional stance respecting the Jewish community. The new Christian attempt to make amends was born.

II

Although considerable progress has been made in the direction of Christian friendship for Jews and of the understanding of Judaism,[2] regrettably it cannot be claimed that any fundamental change of mind or heart has occurred in the church. There remain many grave obstacles to the achievement of righteousness, humanity, and justice for the Jewish people. No theology for the Christian-Jewish encounter can ignore these obstacles. By taking them into account, we shall be helped to speak more positively to our subject.

For one thing, we will have to stop hedging when it comes to the historical culpability of the churches and of ourselves for antisemitism. We cannot avoid a telling indictment by James Parkes: "The fact that the action of Hitler and his henchmen was not really motivated by Christian sentiments, . . . the fact that churches protested and that Christians risked their lives to save Jews—[such] facts come into the picture, but unhappily they do not invalidate the basic statement that antisemitism from the first century to the twentieth is a Christian creation and a Christian responsibility, whatever secondary causes may come into

[2] See, e.g., Eckardt, "The Jewish-Christian Gegenüber: Some recent Christian Efforts in Europe," *The Journal of Bible and Religion*, XXXIII (1965), 149-55. Helpful articles on developing trends may be found in these periodicals, among others: *Common Ground, Encounter Today, Foi et Vie*, and *Freiburger Rundbrief*.

the picture." [3] And yet, in 1965 a Christian clergyman could publish a book entitled *The Anguish of the Jews*, which, while honestly revelatory of the crimes of Christians and the church, nevertheless dares to maintain the "coresponsibility" of Jew along with non-Jew for antisemitism.[4] In a day after Auschwitz, probably the only moral course open to us before so unspeakable an allegation and such incredible self-justification is that of emesis. We could be given no more fateful reminder of where the real "anguish" lies: our anguish as Christians.

Second, we will have to give up our casuistry, our doubletalk, concerning the New Testament and antisemitism. Many Christian scholars and spokesmen have, of course, recognized and lamented the antisemitic proclivities within the church's Scripture. But the opposite view still persists. Thus, one recent and rather influential study, *The Jews and the Gospel*, states flatly that "there is no foundation for the accusation that a seed of contempt and hatred for the Jews can be found in the New Testament." [5] Alas, numerous passages give the lie to such special pleading (cf., as examples, John 5:18; 7:13; Acts 3:14-15; 14:2; I Thess. 2:14-16); the prevailing moral-logical defect is to fabricate discriminate judgments out of New Testament statements about "the Jews" which are mostly indiscriminate in character.

What is the cause of such linguistic gymnastics? While many of us have emancipated ourselves from fundamentalism-of-the-letter (every unalterable word of the Bible is the Word of God) we remain captives of fundamentalism-of-the-spirit—a condition that induces us to follow a double standard of morality. Accordingly, we are quite ready to

[3] "The History of Jewish-Christian Relations" (unpublished address to the London Society of Jews and Christians), p. 3. See also Eckardt, "The Theology of Antisemitism," *Religion in Life*, XXXI, (1962), 552-62.

[4] Edward H. Flannery, *The Anguish of the Jews* (New York: The Macmillan Company, 1965).

[5] Gregory Baum, *The Jews and the Gospel* (Westminster, Md.: The Newman Press, 1961), p. 5.

denounce for their anti-Judaism and antisemitism John of Chrysostom and other postbiblical fathers of the church. But when it comes to John the Evangelist and Peter and Paul—the New Testament—we pull up short. Somehow or other we must try to prove to ourselves or to somebody that the New Testament is morally unassailable. We do not seem to know—perhaps we do not wish to know—that until the Christian church admits unqualifiedly the antisemitic dispositions within parts of its basic canon, hostility to Jews will not be finally rooted out anywhere in Christian teaching.

Third, we Christians will have to overcome our obsession with so-called Jewish responsibility for the death of Jesus of Nazareth. The word "obsession" is introduced for its psychiatric import, for we are faced here with a matter of social pathology.

Consider these words: "The question of the responsibility of the Jewish people for the crucifixion of Christ may well become one of the major theological issues of the day." This recent statement was made, not by a knave or a fool, but by a clergyman and official in the Church of England. [6] There was of late some sentiment to grant unapprehended murderers of Jews the protection of a twenty-year statute of limitations (an indefensible view, I believe). But nineteen hundred years are evidently not long enough when alleged collective "guilt" is at stake as a dogma. Could the interpreter cited somehow not comprehend that it is entirely impossible to speak as he does without insinuating a link with the Jewish people today? Or perhaps he does not care to deny this link. [7] The question of "the Jews" and the crucifixion must be raised again and again, no matter

[6] George H. Stevens, "The Jews and the Crucifixion," *Christianity Today*, December 18, 1964, p. 18.

[7] Stevens identifies the phrase "suffered under Pontius Pilate" as "a timely reminder that the Gentile as well as the Jewish world must take its share of the blame" (*ibid.*, p. 10). His use of the present tense, rather than the past tense, is most revealing.

how many centuries have passed, because it has become an obsession within the Christian soul.[8]

To apply to today the guilt, real or imagined, of men who lived so long ago is either laughable or insane. The application cannot be dismissed as laughable because those who make such allegations are deadly serious and are able to exert considerable social influence and power. Any allusion at all to the participation or collaboration of some first-century Jews in the events of Jesus' death serves to distort the real problem. Even the *denial* of Jewish responsibility for the crucifixion plays into the hands and minds of the obsessed ones—by keeping the subject alive. Should a man be convinced that a dragon with twenty heads is constantly lying in wait to seize him, we do not overcome his delusion by repeating that no such dragon is about. We have to comprehend the nature of the victim's obsession. Thus, when the present pontiff says, on the occasion of a Lenten mass in April, 1965, that when Christ came, the Jewish people "not only did not recognize Him, but fought Him, slandered and injured Him; and, in the end, killed Him," [9] we do not face up to the problem by calling attention to the prevailing falsity of the charge as history. We meet the problem responsibly only by exposing and comprehending the nature of the papal obsession, an obsession made infinitely grievous by the truth that the pope is *der Stellvertreter*, the representative of Christendom before the world.

What perpetuates the obsession? The answer is that when Christians speak of the *historical* culpability of "the Jews," they are actually insinuating, and even directly charging, *continuing* and *current* sin. Here they are aided and abetted by their own dogma, since the crucifixion is for them not a mere past event; it is reenacted every year of the Christian

[8] Eckardt, "Can There Be a Jewish-Christian Relationship?" *The Journal of Bible and Religion*, XXXIII (1965), 125-26.
[9] As cited in *The New York Times*, April 5, 1965.

calendar. This brings us to a fourth necessity—the most decisive of all.

We Christians must somehow be delivered from our monstrous assumption, a contemporary and pervasive charge, that the Jewish people in any age have been unfaithful to their calling, for having (allegedly) rejected Jesus as the Christ, and that, correspondingly, their only ultimate hope lies in conversion to the Christian faith.

Here at once are the crux and the stumbling block of the entire Christian-Jewish relationship (from the Christian side), a condition that lies at the root of every other facet of the problem. This condition is brought home to us through various contemporary ecclesiastical pronouncements—Orthodox, Protestant, and Roman Catholic. The Greek Orthodox community of Damascus recently issued a statement condemning any decision "to declare the Jews innocent of the blood of Christ," while a certain Syrian Christian patriarch has stated categorically that it "is a dogma of the Church that the guilt of the crucifixion of Christ must fall upon the Jewish people to the end of the world." [10] A world gathering of Lutheran theologians meeting in 1964 declared, despite its admission of Christian guilt for antisemitism, that the "division" within the "old" and the "new" Israel will be healed only when "all Israel," the people of God, "recognizes Jesus of Nazareth as its Messiah." [11] And The Second Vatican Council, despite that body's protestation of solidarity with the people of Abraham and its deploring of antisemitism, insisted that "Jerusalem did not recognize the time of her visitation . . . , nor did the Jews, in large number accept the gospel; indeed, not a few opposed the spreading of it. . . . Authorities of the Jews and those who followed their lead pressed for the death of Christ." (There is the obsession again; why not

[10] "The Anger of the Arabs," *Herder Correspondence*, II (1965), 81.
[11] *The Lutheran World*, XI (1964), 265-66.

say "*religious* authorities"?) And then, as the final and climactic words of the entire section dealing specifically with Judaism and "the Jews," the cross of Christ is identified as "the fountain from which every grace flows." [12] No divine grace at all apart from the cross! As David Polish has pointed out, the Vatican declaration, devoid as it is of any hint of Christian contrition or reconciliation, does not in any tangible way surmount the age-old, dreary charge that the Jews are rejected of God until and unless they see the Christian light; accordingly, the statement offers an evangelistic thrust as its culminating theme.[13]

That this woeful, condescending assertion of the Vatican Council should constitute in important respects the very consummation of twenty-five years of Christian effort offers a sobering commentary. The Catholic document has a Protestant counterpart in the preamble to the "Principles of Church Union" put forth by an eight-denomination Consultation on Church Union, meeting in May, 1966: "The people of God exist as one people, and *only one*, of every nationality and race and tongue. They have been made so in Christ; and He wills that they make this unity evident." [14] We should have to go far to find a greater insult to the original Israel of God. Such effrontery comprises further support for justifiable Jewish fears of the whole movement of Christian ecumenism. The one consolation is that the grand alliances of millions of Christians are coming only in the age after Christendom, an age of massive desacralization. The great armies will probably be soldiered mostly by ghosts.

[12] "Declaration on the Relationship of the Church to Non-Christian Religions," *The Documents of Vatican II*, W. M. Abbott, ed. (New York: Guild Press–America Press–Association Press, 1966), pp. 663-67.
[13] David Polish, "The Statement on the Jews: An Inadequate Document," *The Christian Century*, December 1, 1965, pp. 1475-77; see also Eckardt, "End to the Christian-Jewish Dialogue," *The Christian Century*, March 23, 1966, pp. 360-63; March 30, 1966, pp. 393-95.
[14] "The Text on Preamble on Church Union," *The New York Times*, May 6, 1966 (italics mine).

We have never overcome the Nazi logic, however great our revulsion with Nazism and however different our moral presuppositions from those of Hitler and his cohorts. The Jewish people can still attest: "The Nazis sought to destroy us in the gas ovens; you Christians seek to annihilate us by baptism and conversion." Our ambivalence remains. For years on end we in the churches have oscillated between pagan, antisemitic diabolism and the imperialistic compulsion to turn Jews into Christians. Yet even today we have hardly begun to face up to our own history; it afflicts us as a past that is as yet unmastered (*eine unbewältigte Vergangenheit*).

The task of trying to transform the prevailing, if false, dogmas of almost two thousand years is perhaps foolhardy. But the attempt must be made, since there is no other way out of the prison in which we have held ourselves. In this day, amidst the tensions and the guilt, signs appear of a new confession: that it is we who have played the prodigal within the house of Israel. Here, on the foundations of history, repentance, and hope, a new theology for the Christian-Jewish encounter may begin.

III

The relation between the church and Israel is among the most serious and enigmatic questions in all Christian theology. One conceptual instrument for grappling with this matter is the spectrum of discontinuity and continuity.

Christian advocates of discontinuity declare the brokenness of original Israel's election. Christianity has taken the place of Judaism in the divine plan of redemption. When Rudolf Bultmann insists that the events that meant so much to Israel "mean nothing more" to us as Christians,[15]

[15] Bultmann, "The Significance of the Old Testament for the Christian Faith," in B. W. Anderson, ed., *The Old Testament and Christian Faith* (New York: Harper & Row, 1963), p. 31.

he may seem to typify this point of view. In truth, Bultmann's argumentation has no relevance to the Christian-Jewish encounter. The recognized principle that faith cannot be finally authenticated by history is driven by Bultmann to absurd limits: History comes to have no decisive significance for faith. But, of course, this must mean the history of Jesus of Nazareth as well as any other history.

As we would expect, Bultmann has nothing to say on the Pauline theology of history.[16] In recent years the apostle Paul's exposition in Romans 9-11 has received much attention and has even been hailed as wonderful New Testament support for Christian-Jewish solidarity. For example, to Rudolf Pfisterer, Paul's testimony that God has not rejected Israel is unambiguous and clear; "only a stepping aside [*Beiseitetreten*] of Israel" is asserted by Paul "and not any collective and final exclusion from the Covenant with God."[17] A fatal difficulty is seen here when we keep in mind that three, rather than only two, possibilities obtain: (1) Original Israel has been cast off forever. (2) Israel continues as the elect people of God without essential qualification. (3) Though Israel is not ultimately rejected of God, its place *in the present dispensation* has been taken by the church. The first two alternatives are explicitly disallowed by Paul. But the third is just as explicitly avowed by him. Although one may attest that the church has not now taken original Israel's place—such is the point of view of the present essay—he cannot use Romans 9-11 (or Paul's writings as a whole) to vindicate this claim. To Paul, original Israel gives birth to the Messiah, rejects him, and then enters a state of spiritual occultation which will be transformed only at the end of time.

The position of Karl Barth is sometimes interpreted as

---

[16] Eric Voegelin, "History and Gnosis," *ibid.*, pp. 76-77.
[17] Pfisterer, "Das Judentum in der Verkündigung und im Unterricht der Kirche," an address before the Lutheran Consultation on the Church and the Jewish People, Lögumkloster, Denmark, April 29, 1964.

having broken out of the Pauline type of discontinuity. This is not the case. True, Barth speaks much of the faithfulness of God toward his original chosen people.[18] Yet here as elsewhere Barth weighs everything upon the scale of christomonism. Together with Bultmann,[19] he insists that the history of original Israel has come to an end. Israel has refused "to confirm its own election by uniting with the Church—by abandoning, that is, its self-assertion with respect to it, and breaking out into the confession of Jesus as its own and promised Messiah." The true Israel is the New Testament community, the New Israel.[20]

J. Coert Rylaarsdam expresses well the grave moral consequences of the theory of discontinuity. "We must raise the question whether the relation of our two communities of faith . . . can be most profoundly understood in terms of such a chronological framework. If we are dealing with a temporal sequence in which the vocation of one ends when that of the other begins, there is no place for colloquium between us. Confrontation between the dead and the living does not occur."[21] Accordingly, it is not strange if some Christian interpreters should seek to avoid the dead end of discontinuity and to advocate instead varying forms of continuity. These advocates celebrate a simple fact: Judaism today, as in any time, can and does offer a living, vital faith in the only real God as King and Redeemer. The celebration leads to an equally simple but far-reaching conclusion: Original Israel must occupy a positive place along with the church in the divine economy.

Such an advocate is the noted English historian, James Parkes. Insisting that Judaism and Christianity are different

---

[18] *Church Dogmatics*, III/3, 217; *Against the Stream* (New York: Philosophical Library, 1954), pp. 196-97.

[19] Bultmann, "The Significance of the Old Testament for the Christian Faith," p. 31.

[20] *Church Dogmatics*, II/2, 204, 214; III/3, 181.

[21] Rylaarsdam, "Common Ground and Difference," *The Journal of Religion*, XLIII (1963), 266.

kinds of religions, Parkes nevertheless avoids any conclusion of incommensurateness by emphasizing, first, that humanity manifests differing religious needs and, second, that the channels of divine revelation correspond to these human differences. Judaism is directed to man as social being, Christianity to man as personal being. The "Power that flows from Sinai" and the "Power that flows . . . from the life and death of Jesus of Nazareth" are equally divine. We must speak at once of the *elect nation* and the *elect from every nation*.[22]

Although Parkes is quite correct that the dimensions of social existence and personal existence have a certain significance with respect to the history and psychology of faith, must we not say that they lack ultimate significance for the life of faith? In Judaism and Christianity alike, both the group and the individual are caught up in the blessed community of the divine kingdom. The only genuine center of value is God.

While Parkes construes the relation of the two faiths as broadly ecumenical—Jews "are there already as foundation members" of the ecumenical movement [23]—he recognizes the divine and human tensions implicit in "Sinai" and "Calvary." Aside from the issue of the propriety of applying the concepts of ecumenism to the Jewish-Christian relation, must we not insist that the real tension is between "Sinai" and the "empty tomb"? Parkes himself reminds us that at the trials of both Paul and Peter "the issue turned on the resurrection and not on the Law." [24] Yet the resurrection

[22] Maurice Eisendrath and James Parkes, *Jewry and Jesus of Nazareth* (Barley: Parkes Library Pamphlets, 1964), pp. 15, 20. See also, among Parkes's many writings on this subject, *The Bible, the World and the Trinity* (Barley: Parkes Library Pamphlets, 1964); *The Foundations of Judaism and Christianity* (London: Vallentine, Mitchell, 1960); *Judaism and Christianity* (Chicago: University of Chicago Press, 1948); and "A Reappraisal of the Christian Attitude to Judaism," *The Journal of Bible and Religion*, XXIX (1961), 299-307.

[23] Eisendrath and Parkes, *Jewry and Jesus of Nazareth*, p. 16.

[24] Parkes, *Judaism and Christianity*, p. 82.

of Jesus Christ, which stands at the center of the Jewish-Christian *Auseinandersetzung*, receives no more than passing reference in Parkes' constructive expositions.

In a widely discussed essay, "The Relations of Christians and Jews in Western Civilization," Reinhold Niebuhr presents an avowedly liberal ethic for Christian-Jewish relations, without wishing to abandon the more apologetic emphases of his Gifford Lectures.[25] He agrees with Martin Buber that the heart of the messianic issue between the two faiths lies in the Christian claim that in an unredeemed world, redemption has somehow already taken place. With respect to the conflict of particularity and universality within Judaism, "the tension of having a potentially universal religion standing on the historic base of a particular nation," Niebuhr emphasizes that the Christian, whose faith ideally resolves this dilemma, is tempted to self-righteousness until he realizes "that history is full of realities which violate solutions in principle" and remembers as well that the issue is a human, rather than a peculiarly Jewish, one.[26]

The conclusion of Niebuhr that has received most attention is his opposition to Christian missionary efforts among Jews:

These activities are wrong not only because they are futile and have little fruit to boast for their exertions. They are wrong because the two faiths despite differences are sufficiently alike for the Jew to find God more easily in terms of his own religious heritage than by subjecting himself to the hazards of guilt feeling involved in a conversion to a faith, which whatever its excellencies, must appear to him as a symbol of an oppressive majority culture. Both Jews and Christians will have to accept the hazards of their historic symbols. These symbols may be

[25] Niebuhr, *Pious and Secular America* (New York: Charles Scribner's Sons, 1958), chap. 7; cf. *The Nature and Destiny of Man* (Charles Scribner's Sons, 1941, 1943), especially Vol. I, chap. 5, and Vol. II, chaps. 1-4.
[26] Niebuhr, *Pious and Secular America*, pp. 100, 107, 111.

the bearers of an unconditioned message to the faithful. But to those outside the faith they are defaced by historic taints. Practically nothing can purify the symbol of Christ as the image of God in the imagination of the Jew from the taint with which ages of Christian oppression in the name of Christ tainted it. [27]

Niebuhr is right in his denial of a conversionist position but his reasons are wrong. There is nothing in Christian faith to support the notion that hoped-for success is a precondition for proclaiming the gospel. Further, because antichristian forces within or without the church act to debase Christian symbols, it hardly follows that the evangelical obligation of the church is thereby negated. If we are to vindicate the denial of the Christian attempt to convert Jews, we must move beyond Niebuhr's pragmatic, prudential reasoning. From a human concentration upon "finding God," we must turn to Christian theological affirmation. James Parkes and Reinhold Niebuhr offer valuable correctives to the theory of discontinuity, but neither of them takes us into the full depths of the dialectic between the church and Israel.

IV

A primary reason why the theory of discontinuity leads to a dead end is the impossibility of numbering Jesus of Nazareth among its friends. Jesus was a Jew; it is more than a little difficult to make him out as a Christian. The persuasion, "It is from the Jews that salvation comes" (John 4:22 NEB), is paid provisional tribute by exponents of discontinuity; they at least recognize its place and necessity within an earlier dispensation. But what becomes of the confession that redemption is brought through *this Jewish man*—not the mere "spirit" of such a man but Jewish "flesh and blood"? Is nothing at all to be said of or for this Jew

[27] *Ibid.*, p. 108.

who once toiled as a woodworker in the ancient village of Nazareth? The claim of discontinuity scarcely knows what to do with the history of Jesus, just as the position of sharp continuity finds it hard to know what to do with the trans-human dimension of the incarnation.

The true dialectic of Israel and the church rests upon the sovereignty of God. God's sovereignty is disclosed in his faithfulness. In the thinking of Karl Barth, the Lord's faithfulness finally becomes contingent upon human responses. This can only mean the denial of God's sovereignty. At best, the theory of discontinuity seeks to maintain God's faithfulness "despite" the decisive rupture of the covenant caused by original Israel's (alleged) rejection of the Messiah. This explains why Barth, for all his dislike of the word "missions," ends up with a call to "missionize" "the Jews." [28] Against all this, we must testify to the Lord's faithfulness *as such*, as it is presented in Jesus: his merciful willingness to stay with his human children amidst all their disobedience-obedience. As Christians we can never say that the validity of the election of original Israel turns upon the reality of the Christian revelation.

How can it be that original Israel has endured until the present time? Admittedly, theology cannot rely upon the mere fortunes of history for an authentication of faith. But Christian theology is not permitted to turn its back upon history. The simple truth is that the everlasting covenant—there are *not* "two" covenants[29]—antedates Christianity. History and theology are brought together in the affirmation that original Israel's persistence is a mystery made possible and sustained by the strange providence of God. Israel is the people of God in independence of subsequent divine measures to open the covenant to the world.

For the Christian as younger brother to insinuate that

[28] *Church Dogmatics*, IV/3, 877-78.
[29] *Israel und die Kirche* (Zürich: Evz-Verlag, 1961), pp. 25-26.

the Jew as elder brother does not already live within the household of God is the height of presumptuousness. It means a reversal of the course of salvation-history. For the church to endeavor to "convert" the Jewish people to Christianity is forbidden; it is a theological impossibility. There is no exit from the following logic: "If God's covenant with Israel is indeed an enduring one, all attempts to put it out of business by missions, however well intentioned, contradict God's purpose." [30] The true Christian witness can only be one of gratitude for Israel's responding faithfulness to God and a humble exhortation to Israel to be steadfast in faith, to sanctify the name of the Lord, to adore the God beyond all the false gods of men, to rejoice in Torah, and to await the coming of God's messianic kingdom.

The disallowance of a conversionist stance toward original Israel does not in any way call into question the missionary task of the church in the world; the very opposite is the case. Such disallowance is the other side of the truth constituting the soul of missionary obligation. The Christian church is called to proclaim to the world the blessings of the covenant in the Jew, Jesus Christ.

The relevance of Rudolf Bultmann's experiential witness is to be acknowledged at one point: We have to make our own moral choices from within a congeries of conflicting and baffling testimonies. It is possible, of course, to seek to equate the "Saviour of the world" and the "Saviour of Israel" (cf. Acts 13:23). But there are two grave, closely linked difficulties: (1) The relationship among Israel, the nations, and the world (*kosmos*) is not finally worked out in the New Testament. We simply cannot take refuge in some allegedly unanimous, dogmatic testimony of Scripture for a complete resolution of the Christian-Jewish dialectic. (2) Much more seriously, the place of the so-called Old Testa-

---

[30] Rylaarsdam, "Common Ground and Difference," p. 266.

ment in Christian faith remains as "the fundamental problem of biblical interpretation and theology." [31] The obligation to make choices is grounded, however, in faith in an objective event: We Gentiles, who were "strangers to the community of Israel, outside God's covenants and the promise that goes with them," devoid of hope and without God, have been brought into the covenant by Jesus Christ, who "has broken down the enmity which stood like a dividing wall" between Jew and Gentile, and has made us "fellow-citizens with God's people, members of God's household" (Eph. 2:12-14, 19 NEB). [32]

If God's faithfulness to his people Israel is the nemesis upon discontinuity, the latter persuasion cannot be wholly gainsaid. Exodus-Sinai is for original Israel what the life, death, and resurrection of Jesus Christ are for the church. [33] And Exodus-Sinai has the utmost significance not only for Judaism but also for Christianity. But no parallel affirmation can be made from the Jewish side: Jesus Christ does not belong in any crucial or normative way to the history of original Israel. The Christian faith testifies that in Jesus Christ the problem of universality and particularity is resolved in principle. The faithfulness of God extends to humanity: the Lord has acted decisively to open the covenant to the nations.

V

If, as already implied, the New Testament materials remain problematic to any theology for the Christian-Jewish en-

[31] John L. McKenzie, "The Significance of the Old Testament for Christian Faith in Roman Catholicism." in Anderson, ed., *The Old Testament and Christian Faith*, p. 102. McKenzie is making the point that Catholic scholars of recent years have more and more seen this fact.

[32] Of course, the author of the probably pseudo-Pauline Epistle to the Ephesians maintains that the way this unity of Gentile and Jew is implemented is through common life in the church, the body of the Christ who has "annulled the law" (2:15).

[33] James Muilenberg, *The Way of Israel* (New York: Harper & Brothers, 1961), p. 49.

counter, the nature of the witness of the so-called Old Testament is the fatal stumbling block to the theory of discontinuity. We have stressed the faithfulness of God amidst human disobedience-obedience. In point of fact, the prevailing Jewish nonacceptance of the messianic character of Jesus Christ falls within the category not of disobedience but of obedience.

The traditional Christian consensus has at once fallen into moral travesty and taught us intellectual foolishness.[34] The attempt has been made to establish three principles simultaneously: (1) The Old Testament (so-called) contains the Word of God. (2) Without any substantive qualification, Jesus of Nazareth is the Messiah "prophesied" in the "Old Testament," and he was spurned by Israel. (3) Human culpability is proportionate to human responsibility.

The first and second propositions cannot be reconciled. There is no debate respecting the third. It enters the discussion simply because the church has taken the indefensible position of affirming Jewish culpability where there has been, in actuality, an absence of moral responsibility. The first and second affirmations could be made noncontradictory only if a very heavy price were paid: the assigning of perverseness to God and the withdrawal of the third affirmation.

How are those who adhere to God's providential guidance of history to live theologically with the truth that the crucified Prophet of Nazareth was essentially not the Christ whom Israel had come to expect (insofar as Israel was expecting anyone)? True, H. J. Schoeps goes too far when he alleges that the faith of the Tanak is not "in any sense a preparation" for Christ Jesus.[35] Remove Jesus of Nazareth

---

[34] This and the ensuing four paragraphs are adapted from Eckardt, "Can There Be a Jewish-Christian Relationship?" pp. 127-29.

[35] Schoeps, *The Jewish-Christian Argument*, trans. D. E. Green (New York: Holt, Rinehart & Winston, 1963), p. 50.

completely from the spectrum of messianic expectation, and the story of salvation is broken. But make Jesus of Nazareth the sole fulfillment of the expectations, and the story of salvation is tortured. The idea of a God-man is, of course, sacrilege to Israel. How could the Christian conscience ever justifiably summon human beings to such a sin as sacrilege? To object that the sacrilege would not be real begs the entire question; the presence of sacrilege is tied to a certain state of the human conscience. Even if Jesus himself made no claim to divineness—and as a faithful Israelite, how could he?—the way in which he finally interpreted, or at least lived out, the messianic role was to stand in conflict with the dominant view grounded in the Tanak: When Messiah comes he will vindicate the people of God by throwing off the yoke of the oppressors. But Jesus suffered death at the hands of the oppressors. The world to this day remains unredeemed. The resurrection only begs the question further; testimony to that event presupposes adherence to Christian faith.

Had the Christian community not been led to attribute dogmatic status to the Hebrew Bible, there would obviously be no problem. The discrepancies between the Jewish messianic promises and hopes on the one hand and the acceptance of the Prophet of Nazareth as Messiah on the other hand could have been put down as proof of the great disparity between the two faiths. But the church has testified differently: a denial of the so-called Old Testament is heretical. Yet the church is committed to the faith that its Messiah is a genuine consummation of the covenant of election. Thus has the almost unbearable problem confronted the church across the centuries of trying to reconcile the divine authenticity of one constituent part of its canon with the fact that the acclaimed guarantor of its own election cannot be ultimately fitted into the canonical promises. This predicament helps to account for the persistent appeal both of Marcionite impulses which sunder the two Testaments (how enticing was the "Faith Movement of German Christians"!) and of latitudinarian impulses which join the Testaments in happy marriage and reduce Christianity to a version of Judaism (are we not tempted every day by unitarian simplicities?). A Marcionite affirmation of the Christian irrelevance of the so-called Old Testament is much more consistent than other nondialectical views of law and gospel which try nevertheless to retain, or at least rescue, the Tanak as canonical literature. If one mark of heresy is contradiction, the Marcionite conclusion is, in this one respect, less heretical than that prevailing Christian view which seeks to have things both ways: to abandon, and yet hold on to, the Hebrew Bible.

The Israel of Jesus' day, and the Israel that lives upon Torah in any day, not only bears no real moral liability for the alleged nonacceptance of Jesus but is to be praised for undeviating fealty to its recognition of the divine promises. Yet at least two serious issues remain: the truth that the New Testament church was constituted primarily of Jews; and the question of the divine integrity.

1. Is it not true that the call of Jesus was originally addressed to Jews? This straightforward question deserves no less straightforward a response: To whom else could the call have been addressed?

Apart from the occurrence of certain historical events, how could the two rooms of the covenantal household have been built? Are we to believe that God is some kind of magician? The critic is challenged to provide an alternative response that will avoid pure speculation and be faithful to first-century history. If history cannot demonstrate faith, the testimonies of faith can never subvert history. That the Christian church soon lost its Jewish constitution and moved into the Gentile world is not in itself a proof that the nonacknowledgment of Jesus as the Christ by (many of)

the Jewish people was providential. But had this development not transpired, we could not maintain theologically
the providential nature of such nonacceptance. Here is our
basic theological proposition: History becomes definitive
and demonstrative for faith if and when it is a constitutive
part of salvation-history, i.e., if and when it is tied to the
universal thrust of divine election.

The primitive church's acknowledgment of Jesus as Messiah was linked to, and made possible by, the strange jointure
of Messiah and resurrection along the edge of human history.
Following upon their bitter distress because of their Master's
death, the disciples were enabled to proclaim as risen Lord
the same Jesus who had been killed (cf. Acts 2:32-36).
These Jewish Christians ranged themselves against the very
tradition of faith in which they had been reared. Are we to
assert, in consequence, that they betrayed their ancestral
faith? There is no human defense against an affirmative
answer. But there is a divine defense for a negative answer,
the simple testimony of Paul: "No one can say 'Jesus is
Lord!' except under the influence of the Holy Spirit" (I Cor.
12:3 NEB). Defensible claims of conscience have their
foundation in the Spirit of God—a quite different legitima-
tion from a purely humanistic avowal of an ultimate "right"
of conscience. A Christian defense of conscience implies, at
the opposite end, that the absence of a manifestation of
that divine Spirit which is intertwined with the spirit of
Christ can only mean the absence of a confession that Jesus
is the Christ. In this respect, in the first-century nonacceptance of Jesus Christ by many and in the acceptance of
him by others, there is unassailable unity of conscience.
Theological emptiness and theological arrogance are alike
avoided—as they must also be in any consideration of the
place of Jewish Christians within the church today. Of
course, no human resolution of the enigma of the one and
the many is ever possible. By the power of the Spirit alone,
the first-century Christians constituted a unique bridge-

community. "O depth of wealth, wisdom, and knowledge in God! How unsearchable his judgements, how untraceable his ways!" (Rom. 11:33 NEB.)

2. The challenge confronting us would not be so formidable if mere human attitudes to a given body of literature were involved, or even if a Spirit-supported conscience were at stake. The infinitely more painful question cannot be escaped of how the Lord of truth could possibly nurture the messianic consciousness of his people in several directions, only to count Israel blameworthy for not pursuing one of these rather than another. Hence, at stake as well is the question of the divine integrity: *Is God true to his word?* [36]

Could it be that God misled original Israel? The question has nothing to do with his ways not being our ways; it is whether he is trustworthy. We are God's little children; therefore, we have to contend honestly with him. But we are also men, and we must make responsible decisions. If we answer "yes" to the question of whether God misled original Israel, the consequences for our relation to God are enormous and shattering. If we answer "no," there appear to be only two other choices: We may deny the objective veracity of the reputedly divine elements of the biblical witness that have taught Israel to hope for a messianic consummation so different from the church's persuasion. Or we may attest—it is a very bold saying—that it was not God's revealed will or purpose that the great majority of original Israel should come to acclaim Jesus as the Christ. The present exposition presupposes the oneness and integrity of Scripture in a theologically normative sense. And I just cannot believe that God misleads his human creatures. Therefore, I must advocate the second choice.

Acknowledgment of the abiding fidelity of God to Israel

---

[36] This and the next paragraph are adapted from Eckardt, "Can There Be a Jewish-Christian Relationship?" pp. 129-30.

together with the confession that through the Jew Jesus, his life, death, and resurrection, we Gentiles are given a place within the everlasting covenant, means the end of theological antisemitism in the church. There is no other end to this horrendous phenomenon, no other atonement for the dreadful crimes of Christendom against the people of God. But neither is there any other way to celebrate the integrity and uniqueness of the Christian faith.

Christian Responsibility
with Respect
to Revolution

Walter G. Muelder

I

The church has a positive responsibility with respect to the social order. Its involvement is direct since salvation is an integral whole of persons-in-community. Social action is not a peripheral by-product of the church pursuing other goals. In itself social action is not the gospel, but the gospel to be whole includes political, along with other, concerns of man. To speak of social action "in itself" is an abstraction with little meaning. This essay differs frankly from the position taken by the late Gustave Weigel, a leading Roman Catholic who said: "Religion can contribute to the welfare of the general community; it can help society. My only worry is whether it should. It certainly cannot be the prime purpose of religion to make . . . the secular enterprise more satisfactory. That can indeed be the consequent of religion. But consequents are not the goals of deliberation; they are casual accretions to the proper goals of a planned effort." [1] Human salvation and social salvation are interpenetrating processes. The one cannot be complete without the other.

[1] "The Present Embarrassment of the Church," in *Religion in America*, John Cogley, ed. (New York: Meridian Books, 1958), p. 224.

The notion that Christian responsibility is only indirect has defenders among Protestants as well as among Roman Catholics. Waldo Beach argues for an "indirect" relationship as follows: "The church does not exist in order to produce racial justice, or to achieve racial inclusiveness in its own life. The Church [sic] exists to honor its Lord and Head, through a corporate life of worship and service. Its racial inclusiveness within, and its witnesses for racial justice without, are the inevitable by-products, not the intention, of this corporate life in Christ." [2] Such a division of mission and unity would seem to violate the nature of the church. Where racial inclusiveness is violated worship is not truly corporate, and where racial injustice without is condoned Christ is dishonored.

Christian responsibility to be political must also be pre-political, for the state rests on a firmament of law which has deep social foundations. The present essay will emphasize the inclusive context of political change and revolution, and in this it follows the position developed at the Oxford Conference in 1937.

Whatever limitations there may be on the action of the church as an organized society, Christians must give expression to their faith not only in what one may call the pre-political sphere of the aims, standards and values that determine political action, but also in the field of concrete political decision and political struggle. To doubt this would be to deny the sovereignty of God over the whole of life and to surrender larger areas of life to the unfettered control of the forces of evil. [3]

The life of worship and the call to radical social action must not be divorced. Harry F. Ward once quipped that

[2] Beach, "Ecclesiology and Race," *Union Seminary Quarterly Review*, XIV (1959), 22-23.

[3] W. A. Visser 't Hooft and J. H. Oldham, *The Church and Its Function in Society* (Chicago: Willett, Clark & Company, 1937), pp. 199-200.

"mysticism is the refuge of the tired radical." Edgar S. Brightman has replied, "If you are going to be a mystic you must pay attention to God, and if you pay attention to God you must be radical." The ax of God is at the root of all institutions.

In a remarkable essay prepared for the Amsterdam Assembly Jacques Ellul deals with the failure of the church in the context of the situation in Europe. The failure of the church he noted in three areas: (1) "The Church has left the care and protection of man to others." (2) "The Church has left to others the responsibility for revolution." (3) "The Church has left to others the responsibility for the spiritual life of the peoples." [4] Of these three the second thesis bears directly on the present essay. Professor Ellul writes as follows:

The Church exists in order to insist on constant change in society and civilisation, in order to bring them more into conformity with the order of God. This is a mission of "permanent revolution." But the Church has completely lost sight of the fact that an order of God exists, and it has accepted the established order of things. Hence instead of representing values of transformation and judgment (justice, freedom, etc.) founded on Jesus Christ, the Church has merely stood for conservative values, and has left the revolutionary function in the hands of political parties.[5]

There is a certain Trotskyist flavor to the term "permanent revolution," but as employed by Ellul it presents an image which discloses the heart of the Christian social ethic. It involves such concepts as judgment, crisis, mission, conversion, fundamental change, and transformation. There is in it an eschatological element of hope for men and society. Hope involves the prospect of release from captivity. Mission

---

[4] Ellul, "The Situation in Europe," *The Church and the Disorder of Society,* in *Man's Disorder and God's Design* (The Amsterdam Assembly Series; New York: Harper & Brothers, 1948), III, 59-60.
[5] *Ibid.*

is hope in action. A permanent revolution in Christ is an ongoing eschatological event in which God guarantees the instability of every order of injustice, since it mocks the creation; Christ effects redemption for those who accept God's new order in faith; and the Holy Spirit creates a new community in Christ. This ongoing revolution takes place concretely in history, therefore in earthen vessels, and for this reason it involves the constant reformation and renewal of the church as well as of society, for Christ is the meaning of man, society, and history.

The doctrine of "permanent revolution" is not universally acknowledged in the church. Some parts of the church lack a sense of political responsibility entirely. Some parts of the church wrongly translate the idea of political responsibility into church political parties. In no part of the church do we find an unambiguous awareness of the relation of political revolution to the mission of the church. Where the responsibility of the church for revolution is unacknowledged, the mission of the church is not fully accepted. Since mission is hope in action, the church has a permanent vocation to take steps to release men from whatever bondage holds them. Political revolution derives its meaning from the nature and destiny of man.

From what we have just said, we must place political responsibility within the context of a view—well described by H. Richard Niebuhr—of Christ as the transformer of culture. One of the great names in this tradition of Christian social ethics is Augustine. Niebuhr says of Augustine: "Christ is the transformer of culture for Augustine in the sense that he redirects, reinvigorates, and regenerates that life of man, expressed in all human works, which in present actuality is the perverted and corrupted exercise of a fundamentally good nature; which, moreover, in its depravity lies under the curse of transiency and death, not because an external punishment has been visited upon it, but because it is intrinsically self-contradictory." [6] Augustine could see clearly as a Christian that it was not Christianity that was causing the decline and collapse of Rome but the self-contradiction of its total culture. The false will and the false loves were the root sources of the decay. But within the womb of the old society, as Marx would put it, a new order was in the making. The source of that new order was not where Marx would have looked for it. In the womb of the Roman Empire a new love and a new will had been conceived. This new love was creating a church which would one day shape a new civilization.

Along with Augustine, Wesley belongs in the tradition of Christ's transformation of culture. In Wesley this motif is part of his idea of perfection. Niebuhr says,

He shares with Paul, John, Luther, Augustine, and Calvin the understanding that Christ is no new lawgiver who separates a new people from the old by giving them the constitution for a new kind of culture. Christ is for Wesley the transformer of life; he justifies men by giving them faith; he deals with the sources of human action; he makes no distinctions between the moral and the immoral citizens of human commonwealths, in convicting all of self-love and in opening to all the life of freedom in response to God's forgiving love. But Wesley insists on the possibility—again as God's possibility, not man's—of a present fulfilment of that promise of freedom. By the power of Christ believers may be cleansed from all sin, may be like their Master, may be delivered "in this world." [7]

S. Paul Schilling develops the Wesleyan theology of salvation into a completer theology of society. He says:

A conception of Christian social responsibility which centers in the gospel of redemption has a built-in point of contact with

---

[6] Niebuhr, *Christ and Culture* (New York: Harper & Brothers, 1951), p. 209.
[7] *Ibid.*, pp. 218-19.

Wesleyan thought. It may also provide a perfect medium for working out the social implications which were clearly present in Wesley's teachings but which Wesley himself never fully developed. There are thus three good reasons for believing that in the concept of redemption we have found the key principle for a sound theology of society. (1) A social theology centering in salvation broadly interpreted will be true to the deepest meaning of the Christian gospel, which calls on men to respond in trust to God's redemptive work for mankind. (2) It will provide an integrating center for the ecumenical doctrines which Methodists and other Protestants have actually regarded as socially significant. (3) Finally, it will build on and develop the major emphasis of the Wesleyan tradition itself. [8]

Thus the doctrines of justification by faith and of sanctification become relevant to the ambiguities of social and historical reality.

Put in terms of the controlling middle axiom of ecumenical social ethics, the idea of "permanent revolution" is expressed as the "responsible society." Although this idea is broader than that of political responsibility, no adequate treatment of this latter is possible without the context of the former. The language of this report to the Amsterdam Assembly, formulated just after the close of World War II, has the vitality of worldwide rapid social change.

Man is created and called to be a free being, responsible to God and his neighbour. Any tendencies in State and society depriving man of the possibility of acting responsibly are a denial of God's intention for man and His work of salvation. [To this definition the following commentary was added by the Amsterdam Assembly:] A responsible society is one where freedom is the freedom of men who acknowledge responsibility to justice and public order, and where those who hold political authority or economic power are responsible for its exercise to God and the people whose welfare is affected by it.

___

[8] Schilling, *Methodism and Society in Theological Perspective*, pp. 209-10.

152

Man must never be made a mere means for political or economic ends. Man is not made for the State, but the State for man. Man is not made for production, but production for man. For a society to be responsible under modern conditions it is required that the people have freedom to control, to criticise and to change their governments, that power be made responsible by law and tradition, and be distributed as widely as possible through the whole community. It is required that economic justice and provision of equality of opportunity be established for all the members of society.[9]

The political sector of culture plays an enormous role in the responsible society. Therefore the state must be truly responsible if the society is to achieve a responsible character. In its relation to society and the state the church must be free to witness to its Lord and his design for the world. The church must combat any denial to man of an opportunity to participate in the shaping of society. The church must condemn any attempt to prevent men from learning and spreading the truth. In no society has responsibility been permanently won. In all societies responsibility must be constantly renewed.

II

Political responsibility is lockstitched into more inclusive duties. But political activity is the key to so much else that happens in society and culture because the state lays down the rules of the game for economics, communications, education, and much else. To the state is given a monopoly over ultimate social coercion. Though Christ cannot be made captive to the state, political government can quite effectively limit the social expression of the church. State, culture, and economic order are generally quite interdependent and mutually interpenetrating. Reform or revolution in one area is hardly effective without corresponding changes in

[9] *The Church and the Disorder of Society*, pp. 200-201.

the other parts of culture. Political revolution is so significant because political responsibility is so comprehensive. In the emerging new nations of Africa and Asia the agenda of political revolution never stands alone. For example, in an Indonesian conference sponsored in 1957 by the National Council of Churches of Indonesia and the World Council of Churches, the findings dealt with "The Social Goals of New Asia" and included resolutions on (1) ethical foundations of government and the political responsibility of Christians; (2) the social goals of economic development; and (3) problems of independence and interdependence and the impact of the West. It also dealt with the role and responsibility of mission boards in the West. In a revolutionary situation political concern has many facets because government is a dimension of all organized social groups.

The situation in newly independent countries is quite different from those situations in the West where, historically, segments of the society have effectively resisted the excessive growth and power of the state and where even the idea of a welfare state is continually under attack. Asian Christians "desire to share more fully in the life of their nation and to contribute their best to it in the light of God's revelation in Christ." This desire is often canalized in terms of an expressive nationalism that permeates the whole social order and places the Christian in an ambiguous position. There is the temptation to limit the universal demands of the Christian social ethic to the political units which themselves stand under judgment.

III

Today the Christian cause is not the major source of social change in the revolutions of Asia, Africa, and South America. Many factors are at work. In some countries revolutionary leaders have no interest in the Christian church. In others the church is not politically significant. In some the church has neither the theological understanding, the leadership, nor the social "know how" to move with significant effectiveness. Historical circumstances and theological insight vary greatly from one continent and nation to another.

Wherever major and rapid social change is taking place the following factors are generally involved: (1) new ideas of social justice with rising hopes among the people for a better day; (2) widespread technological revolution; and (3) the upsurge of nationalism. Nationalism is often, but not always, associated with the idea of national unity based on democratic principles, the rule of law, and is supported by the idea of a universally literate and informed citizenry. The prime movers, as Egbert de Vrics calls them, are new economic forces, technological instruments and know-how, released spiritual forces, social and cultural factors, and political power.[10] These prime movers may have little historical or contemporary connection with the Christian cause or the Christian church.

In these areas of rapid social change Paul Abrecht sees Christians involved in four major ways: As citizens they must help define the goals of new political and social life. They must also participate in thinking about the patterns and structure of the new institutions which must be shaped and developed to fulfill these goals. They must elaborate the conception of man and society needed for these institutions and presupposed in the goals. And Christians must, finally, perform a ministry of love and service amid the new social circumstances.[11]

In assessing the ways in which Christians will relate themselves to the major revolutionary movements we may introduce at this point a recognition of what De Vries calls the carriers of social leadership, the catalytic forces, and the inhibiting factors. The conveyors are in part carried along

---

[10] De Vries, *Man in Rapid Social Change* (Garden City, N.Y.: Doubleday, 1961).

[11] Paul Abrecht, *The Churches and Rapid Social Change* (Garden City, N.Y.: Doubleday, 1960).

by the prime movers but they are also agents with interests and agents in situations affected by the catalytic forces and the inhibiting factors. Stated conversely, the carriers include: (1) the newly emerging educated classes and the whole educational program of the nation; (2) the women in their new roles in work and family and in their women's movements; (3) the teachers who in the new situation play a decisive role in forming ideals, defining goals, and focusing emotional power through ideas; (4) the new industrialists who have such a large stake in the economic developments; and (5) the prophets of new order who are able to appeal to the hungers, needs, enthusiasms, resentments, and aspirations of the people.

These carriers operate in the context of catalytic forces and inhibiting factors. De Vries would include among catalytic agents "status seeking" and the "profit motive" and a general abuse of rewards for efforts to change the old order. They include also the desire among the younger generation to be different from the older generation. In other words, there is tension between the generations. Hence, there is a tendency of the young to denounce old institutions and customs. Psychologically, this means that the white man is oftentimes treated like the "old" man and missionaries may be denounced as "colonial" or old-fashioned.

Other catalytic forces are the cumulative social protest, the moral indignation, and the prophetic fervor which revolt against the old. These may blend into yet other forces like the emotion-laden mass movements with ever accelerating datelines for independence and freedom. Such mass movements may reject reason and even be harmful from an economic and political point of view, but they affect the whole of social life. They may cause a constructive social force to overreach itself and become demonic.

Turning now to the inhibitors of rapid social change we may note the fear of taking risks, including the lack of experience with handling social change. We may note also that in traditional society there is marked perpetuity from generation to generation. Family life, property rights, and vested interests in present social status illustrate three forms of such perpetuity. Moreover, the existing order has always a sacral character. Economic life, as well as family and government, have in Asia and Africa this sacral dimension. There is fear of upsetting the magic or sacral order of social arrangements. If, then, agriculture and medicine are to be improved, there must come about a certain secularization of culture. Christians need to know how to develop a proper Christian secularization along with new Christian vocation.

Another factor inhibiting social change is the traditional rejection of individual deviation in social behavior. Where collective life is highly organic in its tribal heritage, the deviant person is thought often to be crazy. Part of the present revolutionary situation is the need for widespread acceptance of social innovation. The rejection of individual deviation, however, plays into the hands of blind revolution when the carriers of change become highly emotioned mass movements, for the deviant behavior has here no more status than in the traditional culture patterns.

Finally, we must cite the official protectors of the old order. They work, often behind the scenes, in the family, in government, and in the religious sphere. The general conservative role of religion, including the church, must not be overlooked. We can hardly overestimate the religious tendency to associate "eternal" values with the *status* quo in the basic institutions of society. We need only to remember Russia before 1917, Germany before 1914, Franco Spain, the church in South America, the general tenor of papal encyclicals on social questions, and the role of certain Protestant churches in South Africa and the southern states of the United States. Whenever an older society has been deeply integrated and pervaded by religious values and sanctions, political revolution will be accompanied by a major conservative reaction in the religious sphere.

IV

In trying to relate the Christian church to contemporary political responsibility, we cannot overlook the paradoxical character of Christian leadership and institutions in the areas of rapid social change. Besides representing only a tiny minority in many countries the churches have not created the "role expectation" of leadership in political revolution. They were socialized by many forces which made them accommodate both consciously and unconsciously to colonial and imperial powers. This is not to deny the inherent radical character of the gospel, but the missionary movement did not anticipate the age in which a totally new situation has emerged.

The churches have to find a new set of relationships in their respective national environments. M. M. Thomas said in an address at the New Delhi Assembly: "The Church's identification with Western culture and power on the one hand and the Church's pietism and fear of organized group action to change political and social structures, on the other, have been hindrances to the development of a positive responsible relation to the people's struggle for a new life." [12] It is in politics, he adds, that the fear of the world is most marked, inhibiting Asian and African Christians from proper participation.

In the 1930's and 40's Western churches and missions were still providing the main leadership for Christian thinking on social problems in Africa and Asia, and few national church members were expressing themselves on these questions. This situation has been changing, as the conferences of the past decade and a half in Asia and Africa show. But there are inhibiting factors which need correction. There

[12] Thomas, "The Challenge to the Churches in the New Nations of Africa and Asia." (Mimeographed.)

is, first of all, a theological conservatism which does not provide the theological basis for an ethical analysis and criticism of social problems. Abrecht says, "This drag of a theological tradition which is underdeveloped in relation to the life of man in society is clearly one of the major obstacles to the ethical creativity of the younger churches today." [13] Secondly, the old theological formulas do not help sufficiently in social criticism. Many of the applications were developed by Westerners before the present surge of rapid social change, so that now native leaders have to rethink theology in relation to a new social situation. The problem is all the more radical and urgent because the church leaders have to work in a context not only of a fresh theological-ethical formulation but also of scientific studies of social institutions and movements. In very few places are people trained to think at once in theological-ethical and social-scientific terms. Meanwhile the classical and basic doctrinal issues persist and must be understood and mastered.

The problem is not only one of theological formulation but also of adequate ethical leadership. The 1959 International Study Conference on Christian Action in Rapid Social Change reported the critical need "for better training of pastors in Christian social ethics related to the real problems of social change, and they for their part have a responsibility to train the laity for their evangelistic and pastoral work in society." [14]

Another way of stating the problem is that theological education itself does not know how to confront the revolutionary reality and is tempted to substitute simply more intensive biblical thinking for knowledge about, and acquaintance with, the real world. There can be no effective leadership of the church in relation to political responsibility in a revolutionary age when men and women lack the intellec-

---

[13] Abrecht, *The Churches and Rapid Social Change*, p. 49.
[14] *Ibid.*, p. 52.

tual tools for analyzing their fast-moving society. Political intuition based on biblical theology alone may be highly irresponsible.

V

Political responsibility has, then, a close relationship to a revolution in education. This is one of the most serious problems which mankind must face, for educational traditions may resist and reject the principle of "permanent revolution" which we proposed at the beginning of this discussion. A brief excursion into the traditions and motivations of education will bring these issues into sharper focus.

A variety of traditions strongly influence the social purposes of contemporary world education. Historically, some nations started to build the pyramid of education from the top. Spain built universities in Peru and Guatemala in the early sixteenth century, in Manila in 1611, but left its own countryside illiterate. In the Belgian Congo the pyramid of education was built from the bottom upward. Other areas began in the middle, but in every case there is a relation between educational policy and the basic philosoophy of society. Many parts of the world are today paying a heavy price for traditions of education which commit the gifts of youth to serve a class or an elite rather than the responsible interdependence of classes and peoples.

On the other hand, where people see that nations must be lifted from the bottom, countries have known how to combine education and training in fruitful ways. In some European countries primary education has been linked in adolescence with adaptation to techniques in agriculture, home economics, hygiene, cooperatives, and the like. Formal and informal education were seen as a whole.

Of great importance in this connection has been that educational tradition in the agricultural regions of the United States which united public education, both elementary and secondary, with the university, as in Iowa State

University and Michigan State University. They have their shortcomings, but they have shown how farmers and engineers could enter the great educational line of splendor without any sense of inferiority as workers on the land, in the mines, and in the forests. Theirs is a marriage of dirt and dignity which two thirds of mankind desperately needs. Is it any wonder that Michigan State University at East Lansing has a larger number of its American trained faculty doing overseas service as a part of their regular duties than almost any other university in the whole country?

One of the important emphases in Communist countries is the recognition of the need for training local cadres of leadership in government, industry, and society. Let us suppose that in Asia, Africa, and South America at least one local leader is needed for every one hundred families. There are some four hundred to five hundred million families. This means a minimum of four to five million local leaders are needed to fulfill a great variety of functions. And how important are strong, clean, healthy local institutions! In a time of rapid social change the dearth of well-equipped local institutions is a serious threat to society.

It is one of the hardest problems of the present time to turn the talents of the gifted to the lifting of the level of leadership in the local village. For many, rural life is the symbol of poverty and the past, while the city is the bright light that gathers country moths around its dangerous and deadly flame. Even theological education has often been a transmission belt of escape from rural existence rather than a matrix of motivation to serve and save it.

One of the great contributions which some Americans are making to the social and economic revolution in India is the witness of our college-trained agronomists working side by side with less well-trained Indians in the clearing of jungles, the plowing of virgin soil, the planting of fields and orchards, and the general exhibition of the dignity of dirty overalls dedicated to human uplift.

Sociologists have long recognized that in the United States one of the great functions of education has been vertical mobility. By means of education people improve their relative social status. It is a way of climbing up the social ladder. By it class and caste lines are overcome as one moves from lower to middle to upper class standing. Of all the means that men have tried to improve their lot, education, as practiced in the United States, has been generally the most important—up to now. But whom shall the educated serve?

There is no necessary correlation between the overall wealth of a country and its educational level. In Latin America, for example, generally about 40 percent of the population above the age of fifteen is illiterate. Moreover, in countries like Mexico, Guatemala, Ecuador, Peru, and Bolivia large groups of the original Indian population have lived through conquest, colonial periods, and the years of independence without ever becoming completely assimilated in the national life. *The UNESCO Courier* for June, 1961, points out that Costa Rica, a small agricultural country which boasts that its schoolteachers constitute its only army, has a proportion of illiterates as low as most advanced countries on the continent. On the other hand, Venezuela, with the highest per capita income in Latin America (thanks to its huge oil reserves), has a comparatively high percentage of illiteracy. "Education in Latin America is the privilege of a small minority which has access to the various levels of the educational system while the great majority of the population is neither equipped to make an effective contribution to economic development nor able to take a full share in democratic life." [15]

It must be added, in all fairness, that major projects in primary or elementary education are being undertaken in many of the countries and that local and rural education are major objectives. Yet the question remains—after illiteracy

[15] *The UNESCO Courier*, June, 1961, p. 34.

has been abolished—"What are the substantive national goals after the double negatives represented by 'abolishing' and 'illiteracy' have been removed?" At this point the fundamental educational philosophy becomes crucial. Political revolution apart from sound social education is indeed superficial and very dangerous.

In his study of areas of rapid social change De Vries found that there is an urgent need to expand, and at the same time to reorganize, university education. He found that in the Philippines and in India there is a huge number of unemployed persons with B.A. or even M.A. degrees.

Much of the restlessness of Korean youth is traceable to this type of social situation. The root trouble, however, is not only the kind of education which they received but the motivation for education which they possessed. They do not seem to know who they are or whom they should serve. In the competition for jobs thousands find their way to American universities and colleges in the hope that, with an additional degree from the United States, their competitive position for the few available openings will be enhanced. Meanwhile, whole areas of rural life and the local leadership at the base of the social pyramid go begging. Today the military government of Korea has put the whole educational system into something of a straitjacket. All high school graduates are given governmental exams, are sorted as to what kind of higher education they may take, are assigned to specific colleges and universities (thus closing many which are substandard), and are given another government exam before colleges and universities may grant degrees. In the process the civilian point of view is often overlooked. The relationship of political revolution to education is quite apparent, however.

From this evidence of acute areas of rapid social change some observations may be drawn. (1) There is need for a massive strategy of service to the base of the social pyramid. (2) Because of its past heritage of association with rulers, upper classes, nonagricultural and nonmanual labor, most young people in Asia, Africa, and South America tend to link education with privilege and status at the top, rather than with commitment to the whole community and responsibility to those at the base of the social pyramid of class and status. (3) The benefits of education in vertical mobility are so great that the gap widens between the top and the bottom of the pyramid. "To him who has shall be given. From him who has not shall be taken many things he now has." The benefits of science and industry are cumulative. Consequently, the gap between the illiterate and the educated becomes wider; so also the gap between the rural and the urban inhabitants and; finally the gap between the unskilled and the professionals. Unless the educational system has balanced goals, the present values of revolutions in the new nations will be sacrificed to new exploiting classes and power groups.

VI

Does the church have the power or the motivation to accept Christian responsibility for permanent political revolution? If we examine the church in the United States we must give a very cautious and sober answer to this question. America is not in the mood to prosecute much by way of revolution either at home or abroad—and there is a tendency toward consistency between the values of religious institutions and those of the cultural institutions which provide their context, their membership, and their support. In other words, the integrative function of religion tends to make it accommodate heavily with the society in which it is embedded. Integration and conservatism have much in common.

As we compare American life and the integrative role of religion in areas of rapid social change, it may be useful to examine more closely three levels of consensus required for the social integrative function of religion. (1) At the lowest level are the accepted ways of doing things, the norms or prescriptions for daily action. We have already noted that these ways take on a certain sacral character. (2) At an intermediate level are the ideal-values which the norms and prescribed behavior embody or further. These are the ideal ends which make the lowest level of norms seem worthwhile and good. (3) At the highest level are beliefs concerning the nature of man and the world, that is, the ultimate view of reality that makes the ideal-values both viable and rational. If there is unity and coherence among these three levels and harmony with the surrounding culture, there will be little tension or conflict between religion and society, and the force of religion will be essentially protective and conservative as in many traditional societies. A nation tends to socialize its religious institutions in this general integrative direction.

In the United States there is both integration and conflict. At the lowest level of prescriptions American life is full of conflict. For example, there are the Protestant-Catholic conflicts over marriage, family, and education; there is the scandalous controversy over racial segregation and desegregation; there is widespread crime and corruption; and there is doubt as to what norms in daily life are right.

When the prescribed ways of behavior are in conflict, to what are the people committed? Are they committed to the local norms (e.g., segregation and parochial schools), to ideal-values which free them from captivity to worn-out standards, or to ultimate beliefs that release them to reconsider their ideal-values? For example, is segregation or the democratic dream their commitment? What is finally sacred to the people, that is, for what will they finally sacrifice? Where prescriptions of action (daily norms) have become ultimate (like the American way of life), beliefs are their servants and are exploited to support them. On the other hand, unless the beliefs are clearly spelled out so that people know what conduct they mean, opposing values which are concrete tend to win out. A split develops between abstract beliefs and specific behavior. Ideal-values and ultimate beliefs may be short-circuited and the betrayal of these values masked by practices which actually belie them. In time a social deception settles upon people who sense no conflict between Christ and culture.

Whether, and how, the church will serve as a conservative integrator of society or as an innovator depends not only on the level on which commitment is made, but also on the structure of authority in the community. Authority in this context means the ways in which power and decision are legitimated. In government one naturally thinks of legal authority and its sanctions. But there are at least three other important types of authority. These include the social pressures and sanctions of private groups, the transcendent or suprasocial referents (God, Christ, the kingdom of God), and personal integrity or individual conscience. The church has responsibilities to this whole firmament of authority. If the church is tied too closely to race, class, clique, or political pattern, it can quickly lose its moral authority to champion change when these secular norms and customs are challenged. When the Oxford Conference in 1937 said, "Let the Church be the Church!" it affirmed imperatively the church's need to regain authentic authority. From this perspective the churches seem to have lost much of their authority to effect social change. They cannot, however, regain their social authority for change simply by more social action; they have to be renewed in commitment and mission from within.

It would be an error to suppose that the institutionalized churches of the United States are today the most important and powerful integrators of American society. Other value centers may in fact be more "sacred" to most Americans— including the millions in the churches. Today churches may be providing a declining moral consensus in the nation, even while their memberships are growing. The nation's normative local structure shows signs of disintegration. It is conceivable that the church is absorbing more in its institutional life and local behavior from secular society than it is giving to that society by way of standards, motivations, and guidance. Present-day revolutionary movements in the world are not drawing heavily from the *transcendent* beliefs of American or Western Christianity. They are constructing their own secular ideologies which have the appeal of transcendent religious belief. Yet the predominant appeal of the church is harmony—and this emphasis encourages the infiltration of the church by alien elements. Harmony is not the gospel.

One reason that the church is not more of an innovator in American or in world society is that it does not make *explicit* how men ought to behave, for what ends they should live, and for what reasons. The church lacks effective control and criticism of local practices by middle axioms, and of middle axioms by transcendent beliefs. It often operates at such a level of vague abstraction that other social forces fill in the middle axioms and the practical prescriptions. To exercise the ministry of permanent revolution the church must induce specific conflict on issues. Christian reconciliation cannot bypass Christian judgment.

If the church is to be effective in social action there must be unity and not conflict of judgment within the church on which goals are more important or urgent than others. There must be agreement on the action requirements of achieving a goal, once it is chosen. Finally, there must be agreement over which office or institution assumes responsibility. For example, the 1960 General Conference debate over the jurisdictional system illustrates these three dimensions of social action predicaments. There was conflict between the explicit goal of achieving racial justice by eliminating the segregated Central Jurisdiction and the often unstated goal of preventing a split into a northern and a southern church. The second dimension focused on the method, by decisive

167

action by the General Conference or by voluntary and permissive action, church by church, annual conference by annual conference. The third dimension, related to the role of leadership assumed by the church, is relation to society. In what may be a paradigm for some other basic issues The Methodist Church acted as follows: "The General Conference, with frank facing of the conflicts, kept open the dilemma, although it chose temporarily unity over desegregation, permissive over decisive action, and a supportive rather than prophetic role for the church in relation to action by public institutions." [16]

VII

We may bring these several strands of argument into a summary conclusion by suggesting, once again, the dilemma of church leadership in rapid social change and certain guidelines for action.

1. The Western Christian's experience with political revolution has shown a varied pattern of reaction, conservatism, acceptance, and positive concurrence.

2. Whatever Western Christian political experience may have taught the church cannot be applied simply to Africa, Asia, and Latin America. In part, it is misunderstood because of past linkages to colonialism and imperialism, however close or remote; in part, it is misunderstood because leadership must now come from those lands themselves; and in part, because new occasions teach new duties.

3. A major need in areas of rapid social change is thoroughgoing education in theological social ethics. Theology, ethics, and social science need coherent integration in terms of the varying social situations. Sound Christian social ethics is interdisciplinary.

4. The church must recognize that its mission is not to avoid the revolutions of our time, but to seek out the action

[16] Herbert E. Stotts and Paul Deats, Jr., *Methodism and Society: Guidelines for Strategy* (Nashville: Abingdon Press, 1962), pp. 33-34.

of God in them, and to witness to Christ's kingdom with a gospel of inclusive salvation, inclusively expressed.

5. No one pattern of social, economic, or political order may by identified with the gospel of Christ. Since Christ transcends revolution as well as all cultures and social orders, the churches in the new nations must be particularly aware of the universal elements in the gospel. If this dimension is not heeded, they will fall into the same nationalistic limitations which have inhibited the manifestation of the responsible society in Western nations where Christianity is much older.

6. Participation with non-Christians in nation-building is required but it has grave risks, especially when the Christian community is small. This danger is particularly true where Christians have recently lost their privileged status and place as leaders of social service and welfare. Yet participation is of the essence of political responsibility. He who does not participate forfeits the right to criticize political action. The principal rights for which the Christian will contend are those which relate to the fundamental rights of all.

7. It is particularly dangerous for Christians to organize into a Christian political party of their own. The reasons are that the gospel does not provide such a political position, and a Christian political party makes for special concern for narrow communal or churchly interests. The Christian community must strive for freedom, justice, and human dignity for all.

8. Christians will support the idea of a constructive neutral or secular state.

9. The making of new states into political unities in behalf of traditional national religions inhibits the "permanent revolution." Traditional religions tied to traditional politics make for the repudiation of both in an age of revolution and reconstruction. Christians must discriminate between reactionary and constructive appeals to religion.

10. A modern state will have to assume comprehensive

social responsibilities. The social substructure of the political order is of major concern to the Christian, who will attend to the responsible family, responsible education, and responsible agricultural and industrial relations, as well as to the political general welfare.

11. Western parliamentary forms of democracy are not viable unless a suitable social foundation has been provided for them. Democracy is not a mechanism primarily; it is a responsible ethical reality with appropriate pre-political structures and procedures.

12. Christians have a special responsibility to bear witness to the political needs of the whole of mankind. While new nations are being built, the world political order must also be constructed.

13. No greater need in the social witness and service of the churches for Christ exists than that of a renewal of the church, whereby men and women are motivated to lift the social pyramids of their various societies from the bottom.

14. The "permanent revolution" is addressed to every nation.

The Christian and
the New Nationhood

L. Harold DeWolf

Soon after we had read in the papers about certain civil disturbances in the larger cities of Southern Rhodesia, my wife and I received a letter from an African youth about twenty-one years of age for whom we had assumed some responsibilities. He was now working as a lorry driver in Bulawayo. The letter begins as follows:

Dear Father and Mother:

We were all thankful in receiving your letter which you recently wrote to me.

On the first hand I should tell you that here we are not so keepable because Politics have come into fashion with Africans. Now, here I have a question whether what we are fighting in order to gain, what they call Freedom concerns with the Kingdom of God; or we are fighting in order to gain earthly wealth? I haven't join any of the parties fighting for freedom because I don't know why I should join them. Is politics go together with Godly things? I don't know how I should pray true and faithful to my church because each time when I meet people talking about politics I have to drive myself away from them. I would like you to tell me the true about Politics.

The English is not quite capable of conveying the thought adequately. Yet clearly the young man, with a standard six education, writing in a foreign language, has gone straight to the heart of questions which are plaguing many earnest Christians, young and old, throughout Africa and in many other lands as well. The fact that few Americans bother to question the relation between political freedom and God's kingdom, or between politics and godly things, does not indicate that Americans know the answers. At least our young correspondent in Africa was asking the right questions. Most men, both in Africa and in America, are simply swept along by the political tides of their classes and times, without serious thought about their Christian obligations in political life. However, many of the more thoughtful leaders are thinking hard about these matters.

Early in 1956, it was agreed that the Methodist churches of Southern Rhodesia, those promoted by the British and those supported through the Board of Missions in New York, would unite their programs of higher theological education in a new school to be established near Salisbury. We then approached the problem of curriculum. It was agreed that one step to be taken should be to ask all the African pastors at work in our churches what they needed to know that had not been taught in their own theological education. Every man answered first, "politics." Discussion showed this to be meant in a broad sense, including the understanding of new and strange laws, the clash of cultures, the disrupting forces of industrialization, and above all, the Christian attitudes toward various political efforts to gain a more just society.

Both for the proper education of its ministry and for intelligent counsel to its members, the church everywhere needs to face such problems with Christian earnestness and informed political realism. The need is felt with special acuteness in the lands of new or approaching nationhood.

This chapter is in three parts. First, we will look at the claims presented by nationhood and especially the new nationhood today. Secondly, we will seek some Christian understanding of the state, national patriotism, and revolution. Finally, we will attempt to draw out some more concrete, positive directions, or "middle axioms," to guide the action of Christians and churches in these times.

The New Nation-State: Its Nature and Claims

THE NATURE AND FUNCTIONS OF NATION AND STATE

1. *Nationhood and statehood.* The original meaning of the word "nation" includes, as the etymology implies, the notion of common blood ties. The modern nation, however, is not necessarily homogeneous in race, language, religion, or culture. The sense of national unity may be powerful despite wide diversity in all these respects.

The nation, in the modern sense, is a people united under one independent government, or at least believing that it ought to be so united. The grounds of such union or belief are various and sometimes highly complex and subtle.

As Robert M. MacIver says, "The state becomes, or seeks to become the body of nationality." [1] When such embodiment is successful, the nation and the state appear to be almost identical. However, they are not the same, and the difference is important. The nation is the people in all their varied interests and activities and in all the concreteness of personal and social life. The state is the people as ruling and ruled by law.

When we consider the Christian and new nationhood we are mainly concerned with the interest and effort of peoples to develop or to control governments which will embody their rising sense of nationality. Our concern, then, is with newly independent states and the efforts to establish such states as expressions of nationality. In many instances such

[1] MacIver, *The Modern State* (London: Oxford University Press, 1926), p. 133.

173

efforts are aimed—as, for example, in most of the successful liberation movements of Africa—to take over an already established government, remade as an independent instrument of the whole people within the bounds of its legal, geographical limits.

Our subject requires us, then, to think of the new nation-state, its nature, functions, perils, and claims. While our topic speaks of "nationhood," it requires us to think mainly of the striving for and attainment of statehood.

2. *Definition of the state.* In his classic work, *The Modern State,* MacIver arrives at the following definition: The state is an association which, acting through law as promulgated by a government endowed to this end with coercive power, maintains within a community territorially demarcated the universal conditions of social order." [2]

3. *The state contingent and relatively recent.* Some societies have existed and some still exist without any organization into states, even in the broadest sense. The Auca Indians are a contemporary example. But such anarchical peoples are now exceedingly rare. Generally, legal and political institutions grew out of earlier family life and are relatively recent in the total life of human beings on earth. The nation-state, in the strict sense, is a much later development, having risen in Western Europe since the Middle Ages and elsewhere more recently. Such political realities as the Roman Empire were not nation-states, for most of the people living under their rule were not citizens and did not identify themselves as properly belonging within the bounds ruled by the imperial power.

4. *Widening functions of the modern state.* The basic function of the state is simply to maintain social order within its borders despite disruptive internal and external forces. However, this function has tended to broaden continually in response to human needs—which threatened, if unas-

[2] *Ibid.,* p. 22. (All in italics in the original.)

suaged, to induce disorder—in efforts to strengthen the economic base of its military defense, and in response to popular demand enforced through political channels. The typical modern state bears many functions which in former times were borne exclusively by families, religious associations, or individuals and economic organizations. So well established are these wider functions in the modern conception of the state that when peoples aspire to new statehood, they now take for granted that the state should be involved in measures of public health, economic investment and promotion, education, and distribution of land, as well as in the maintaining of internal order and defense against enemies abroad.

5. *Its frequent claims of absolute sovereignty.* The state possesses the dominant coercive force within the area of its rule. This force is an instrument rather than a source of the community of the nation, as MacIver properly insists. However, MacIver is also correct when he says, "It is true that there is no state where there is no overruling force. This is the *differentia* between the state and all other associations." [3]

This possession of overruling force, supported by the expanded functions of the modern nation-state, has encouraged modern states to renew the claim of ancient self-deifying monarchs to absolute sovereignty. No state actually possesses absolute sovereignty. Every state is limited by the loyalties of its people to other associations, by their economic, educational, and moral limits—which can be changed but not ignored nor completely controlled—and by external influences. Indeed, the interdependence of peoples has increased greatly in modern times and has decreased the actual sovereign powers of individual states. However, governments are highly averse to acknowledging limitation by other forces within their own nations and generally refuse

[3] *Ibid.,* p. 230.

to acknowledge any external limitation whatsoever within their claimed bounds of jurisdiction, except as compelled to do so.

CLAIMS AND VALUES OF NEW NATIONAL LOYALTIES

The nationalistic spirit, which has arisen in one country after another recently, is much more than a rising spirit of unity along new lines. Indeed, the nationalism seems in many places to be a product of old injustice and oppression and a means of securing restitution. Everywhere the new nationalism comes with varied claims and offers promise of high values.

1. *Political justice.* The varied injustices against which the new nationalisms have reacted have been rooted mainly in political injustice. The masses of the people have been almost or wholly lacking representation in government. Government, being one-sidedly sensitive to the interests of a few, has tended to serve the many only so far as the privileged settlers or aristocracy desired. The many have been provided education or means of livelihood or protections to health chiefly for the sake of the few they served. Even when government has benevolently gone further, the result has been a degrading paternalism. Condescending charity is no substitute for justice. The replacement of political misrepresentation and injustice with broadened or universal suffrage and some measure of justice is among the most important promises of the revolutionary national movements.

2. *Economic justice.* One of the most serious grievances against the old orders in Asia, Africa, and Latin America is the extreme maldistribution of land. Many times I have been asked by Rhodesian Africans why the European farmers said they could barely make a living for their small families on farms of hundreds or even thousands of acres, while an African farmer, who could not make a good living for his large family with six or eight acres under cultivation and a similar amount of grazing land, was described by the Euro-

peans as an inefficient farmer. Whether the big landowners are foreigners or indigenous aristocrats, the masses of land-poor peasantry have a right to claim a more just distribution of land.

As industrialization advances and increasing numbers of people are employed for wages, the wage scale becomes an increasingly serious bone of contention. When work on the Kariba Dam was halted by a strike, the median wage of the African workers was said to be in the neighborhood of sixpence per day, and the strike was settled by an increase of a penny a day. The low wage scale in many lands enabled white colonials and local aristocrats of moderate income to surround themselves with servants. However, the rising of the masses with nationalistic fervor is rapidly changing this situation. The people do not need Communist agitators to teach them rebellion against such conditions.

3. *Freedom for expression and development of responsibility.* In 1956, during an impromptu but well-attended discussion beside a rural airstrip in Nyasaland, an African schoolteacher asked me if I could tell one good thing about federation.[4] I spoke of certain economic advantages to heavily populated Nyasaland, with its very limited natural resources. The reply was a pointed question: "Sir, would you sell your freedom for more bread?" The negative answer which the African people of Nyasaland and Northern Rhodesia had already given spelled the death of the Federation.

Freedom, with all its perils and temptations, is the price of the responsibility and mature character of any people. Only so far as a people asserts its freedom does it have opportunity to learn the meaning of social choices and, even by its mistakes, develop wisdom and character. Freedom is good and the new nationalisms are affirmations of freedom.

---

[4] "Federation" meant the linking of overwhelmingly black Nyasaland and Northern Rhodesia with colonial-white-dominated Southern Rhodesia in a white-dominated federal union.

4. *Sense of personal identification with government.* Where the masses are denied participation in government, it is often complained that they attach no social opprobrium to arrest and conviction for lawbreaking. It was no accident that when Mayor Hartsfield put four Negroes on the police force of Atlanta, Georgia, the scandalous rate of crime in the Negro neighborhoods abruptly dropped by 50 percent. Even this minor symbolic gesture helped to internalize the law and reinforce the mere fear of penalties with a social conscience. However, the possibilities of real law-abiding citizenship among the Negroes will never be known until they share fully in the processes of legislation, law enforcement, and the judiciary.

Repeatedly, African pastors have expressed to me their bewilderment at the appalling misconduct of their people in the cities of their great continent. Men who had been honest in the country villages take to stealing in the city. Young women of proud chastity in the country quickly and shamelessly bear illegitimate children when they have moved to the city. Why?

The causes are complex. However, one important factor is often overlooked in the attempts at explanation. In the country village the day-to-day relations of the people are governed mostly by native custom and law. The people are ruling themselves. The law is internalized and rules mostly by self-rule. In the city, on the other hand, the laws are the laws of "those white men." Law and order are the responsibilities of other people against whom strong resentments are felt. To be found guilty of transgressing the tribal law in the village is to be humiliated beyond expression. To have served a term in jail for violating Rhodesian law in the city is, in wide circles of African society, to suffer no loss of reputation whatsoever. Indeed, it may bring honor, like the suffering of underground operatives during the Nazi occupation of Western Europe.

The internalizing of law, and hence the acceptance of

responsibility for law and order by the common people of a society, can be accomplished only by processes of such actual or symbolic participation in the law as provide a sense of broad personal identification with the law. The revolutionary efforts to achieve national unity and independence, if successful, may be expected to achieve such a desirable result.

Such, then are some of the more plausible and important claims of the new nationalisms. Before further evaluation and critical comment, we must turn from empirical description to seek some distinctively Christian understanding of the state, of patriotic nationalism, and of revolution.

Christian Understanding of the State, Nationalism, and Revolution

THE STATE

1. *In the Scriptures.* The amount of specific guidance given us by the Bible concerning such modern institutions as the state is severely limited. Reinhold Niebuhr was exaggerating, but he was only exaggerating a truth, when he wrote, "Christianity really had no social ethic until it appropriated the Stoic ethic." [5] For only in the merging of New Testament ethics with the philosophical-ethical synthesis of the Stoics did Christians develop precisely defined general principles which could be applied to a wide variety of political and other social institutions.

In the Old Testament there is much civil and criminal law, it is true, and much of this is still useful in principle. However, it is written for a condition in which the religious and political institutions were indistinguishable, it is pre-Christian, and it is often inapplicable to the radically changed conditions of modern life.

[5] Niebuhr, *An Interpretation of Christian Ethics* (New York: Harper and Brothers, 1935), p. 150.

In the New Testament we have mainly three kinds of teachings concerning the political government and its authority.

First, there are the exhortations to obey. The governing authorities "have been constituted by God" and given authority to "bear the sword" and "execute [God's] wrath on the wrongdoer." These authorities will punish only bad conduct, not good. They should be supported by payment of taxes, by proper respect, and by willing obedience. So Paul argues in Romans 13:1-7. Reinhold Niebuhr is speaking of the opening words in this passage when he says, "No passage of Scripture has had so fateful an influence upon Christian political thought as this word."[6] In this passage, since Paul is writing to the Christians in Rome, he must be writing of the Roman government, pagan, oppressive, and cruel though it was. Jesus is quoted in similar, though much less sweeping, terms as enjoining obedience to the commands of the scribes and Pharisees (Matt. 23:2-3) and as enjoining Peter to pay the temple tax for both of them—though suggesting that it should not be required of them (Matt. 17:24-27).

At the other extreme are many instances of Paul's defiance of commands by the authorities, with consequent punishment, and the repeated declarations in the kerygma that the conviction and crucifixion of Jesus under the government of Pilate, by urging of the Sanhedrin, had been an act against God requiring sober repentance. Peter, in his Pentecost sermon, in this connection speaks of the Roman authorities as "lawless men" (Acts 2:23). To represent this whole class of testimony we may well take the words attributed to Peter and John's defiance of the authorities in Jerusalem: "Whether it is right in the sight of God to listen to you rather than to God, you must judge" (Acts 4:19). We must note also Jesus' contrast between Christian

[6] *Ibid.,* p. 154.

humility and service, on the one hand, and the pride of earthly rulers on the other (Luke 22:25).

Finally, there are the equivocal passages which enjoin some obedience to government but set limits to it. Here would belong Jesus' response to the question about taxes to Caesar: "Render to Caesar the things that are Caesar's, and to God the things that are God's" (Mark 12:27). The principle here is clear and true. We are to obey government so far as obedience is its due. But this does not tell us very much about principles by which we may discriminate between what is due and what is not due.

2. *In Christian tradition.* In the teachings of the church fathers it is generally taken for granted that the proper functions of earthly government are to establish and preserve order, to protect the people against threatening enemies, and to execute justice.

Augustine is particularly emphatic and persuasive in insisting that the mere possession of power is no assurance whatever of rightful authority. His famous words are still relevant: "Justice being taken away, then what are kingdoms but great robberies? For what are robberies themselves, but little kingdoms?" [7]

3. *The new problems of the modern state.* By the older terms of reference the large modern states are international superstates. The Roman Empire was only vaguely comparable because it consisted of a single city-state and many subject peoples, not of one state grown large or formed by union of many states into one state.

Moreover, the modern state has assumed functions far more complex and inclusive than were so much as known in the ancient world. The many provisions for public health, supervision or maintenance of complex means of transportation and communication, provisions for varied education, and the underwriting of economic security represent vast

[7] *City of God,* Book IV, Chap. 4.

extensions of functions only occasionally undertaken in places by the most complex governments in the ancient world. Yet so great are the involvements of modern government in such functions that the basic relations of citizens to government are radically changed, and old guidelines become irrelevant or misleading.

4. *Some positive Christian norms relevant to the national state.* In view of the situation we have reviewed, it is sheer folly to look for Christian *rules* of political action in the Bible. Even in the days of Luther and Calvin such methods were more misleading than helpful. Today they are even worse. Rather we must seek to find the bearing of the most basic Christian principles upon our concrete political problems. Among such principles which will be found relevant are the following:

a) God alone is absolute Sovereign and so alone worthy of absolute obedience.

b) All human beings are his creatures, made in his image, however marred and distorted by sin. All are objects of the Father's love given in Jesus Christ. Hence all must be treated with respect and with concern for their well-being.

c) All men are made for community with one another, under God. For full development they need opportunity for responsible participation in social processes.

d) Human beings are so prone to sin, and especially to pride, that they require greater or lesser external restraints upon their aggressive lust for power and privilege, their careless unconcern for others, and their hostilities.

e) It is the will of God that human beings should not hate, injure, or destroy one another, but should live in love and peace together. Hence we should be seeking always to restrain violence with a minimum of injury and force.

f) God created the earth and its natural resources for the use of all men. All who control such resources are stewards responsible to God for their conservation in order

182

to provide optimum availability to present and future generations.

REEXAMINATION OF VALUES CLAIMED FOR NEW NATIONHOOD

1. *Political justice.* Because all men are made for community and need opportunity for participation in social process, Christians should favor the widest possible extension of the franchise among people prepared to learn its responsible exercise. Such extension is necessary also to secure economic justice and other values. Moreover, such extension makes possible the interiorizing of the law, so that a minimum of injury and force will be required in the maintenance of order.

2. *Economic justice.* Since God made the earth for all and not for a few only, it is required that land be widely and equitably available. The principle of respect and concern for the well-being of all men requires full participation of all workers in the fruits of their labors, whether by adequate wages or otherwise. Moreover, only in conditions of economic justice in fair degree is it possible to maintain public order without excessive repression, force, and injury.

3. *Freedom of expression and development of responsibility.* Only when there is freedom of expression can the suffrage be meaningfully exercised and responsible participation in social process secured. Moreover, only in conditions of free expression can the Christian ministry, including its prophetic critique of injustice, gain maximum effectiveness. Where freedom is denied, it is often difficult or impossible for men responsibly and effectively to preach the gospel in its fullness and to bear one another's burdens in loving concern, as the law of Christ requires.

4. *Sense of personal identification with government.* It must already have been made clear that such identification is necessary to a condition of minimum force in the maintenance of public order and maximum personal growth in social responsibility.

As Christians, then, we are obliged to be positively concerned with the principal values named as espoused and supported by the new nationhoods. If these values were the only consequences of the new nationalisms we should have no basic problem before us. Unfortunately, this is not the case.

PERILS TO CHRISTIAN VALUES

1. *Disorder, violence, and hate.* The Christian conscience of my youthful African correspondent had been especially offended by the hatred and violence of the nationalistic rioters in his city. A new nation can hardly arise without the aggravation of resentments against old injustice, the weakening of old, law-abiding self-restraints, and struggles for power in the new order. Such conditions will predictably increase disorder, violence, and hate for a time, at least.

When years of sabotage and lawlessness occur in a people's resistance to a hated foreign rule, the violence cannot be turned off in a moment when liberation has occurred. Even as late as 1965 much of the violent disorder in the Philippines, especially near the time of elections, was being traced to customs of violence cultivated for resistance to the Japanese occupation twenty years earlier.

Where the revolutionary leaders are men of great wisdom, self-restraint, and abhorrence of violence—men like Mohandas Gandhi or Albert Luthuli or Martin Luther King, Jr., or Kenneth Kaunda—such evils may be minimized. But even when the leaders and their followers teach and practice nonviolence, the foes of the revolution are likely to practice violence, and so injury and hate occur. Moreover, even with violence at a minimum, the orderly ways of government and all the vastly complex system of interdependence by which we live in modern society are likely to be more or less disorganized in a period of transition. Hunger, disease, suffering, and death may result for many, especially in the cities.

2. *Communism.* The naïveté of some revolutionary leaders, their sad experiences of imperialism under the professedly democratic Western powers, and the clever appeals of the Soviet Union and the People's Republic of China—all converge to present a serious peril that any or all of the new revolutionary national movements will be taken over and made part of the Communist system. This would have the effect of plunging some new nations into worse political injustice than they have hitherto suffered, crushing their hopes of freedom, and making them part of a system even more dependent on forceful coercion. Moreover, under Communism the Christian faith would itself be under direct attack by every means devised by its most clever despisers.

3. *Internal misgovernment.* Even without the incursion of Communism, new governments among people of low average education and ill prepared for self-government are peculiarly susceptible to the peril of tyranny at the hands of self-seeking revolutionary leaders. Such tyranny is likely to deprive the people of free participation in government, bring new and acute exploitation of land and natural resources for a favored few, corrupt the courts, and—in the self-righteousness of its revolutionary fervor—resort to unrestrained force and cruelty in suppression of all opposition.

4. *Idolatry of the state.* The claims of absolute sovereignty, so characteristic of the state, though self-deceived, constantly verge on idolatry. Even though there be no strutting monarch to be deified, the state can be, and frequently is, looked upon as the object of highest loyalty and obedience under which all other loyalties are to be subsumed. This is, indeed, idolatry. Given the excitement and enthusiasm of a national uprising, together with the people's identification of their own purposes and dreams with the new nationhood, such idolatry is an especially serious temptation. Moreover, even without full idolatry, the new nationalism tends so to

preoccupy attention, energy, and hope that the church is likely to find the going hard in an atmosphere of national revolution and the enthusiasm of constructing a new state.

In all of North American history, the churches have never confronted such discouraging years as in the decades following the Revolutionary War. In 1962 and 1963 more than one professing Christian among the young men of Rhodesia told me that political activity now left them no time for religion. One of them added, "Politics is the main thing; religion is a subcommittee." It was during the days of his revolutionary activity that Kwame Nkrumah spoke the words later engraved on the base of his statue in front of Government House in Accra: "Seek ye first the political kingdom." Nationalistic fervor can challenge religious devotion itself and so become idolatrous.

5. *Nationalistic division.* Where loyalty to the nation-state is at highest pitch, there is likely to be least concern for the well-being of the world as a whole. A rampant nationalism is always in danger of becoming either isolationist or expansionist. In either case, the people are being led precisely away from Christian concern for all men, and the church is threatened with new division along national lines. The period of revolutionary nationalism presents exactly such conditions and hence tends toward just such perils.

Christian Responsibility in the Midst of Revolution

Having seen the two faces of the new nationhood—one friendly and attractive, the other glowering and ominous— we must now seek to draw some conclusions about Christian responsibility in countries of revolutionary nationalism.

No Confusion of Christian Faith and Nationalism

The Roman Catholic Willi Kreiterling writes in his recent book *Katholische Kirche und Demokratie* that the "central truth of Christianity concerning state and politics" is the *distinction* between politics and religion which is established in the words of Christ: "Give to Caesar what is Caesar's and to God what is God's." [8]

However strong and valid may be one's conviction that as a Christian he is obliged to support a democratic national movement, he must not make the mistake of identifying the political, economic, and social goals of that movement with the kingdom of God. Such identification would lead to unrealistic expectations of the state, to the dilution of the gospel, and to eventual disillusionment with both the political cause and the gospel.

The church must not be subordinated to the state as means to justice and political freedom, nor must the church expect or require the state to serve the spiritual purposes of the church.

As Kreiterling points out—and it is refreshing to read this from an able and devout Roman Catholic—this distinction in principle "frees religion from the domination of the political, just as politics is freed from the hierarchy." [9] It is especially important to remember this distinction when a new nation-state is coming into existence, though it is important to remember it everywhere in this day of rampant nationalism. The church must not try to rule the state, but likewise the church must resist being ruled by the state.

No Escape, but Participation

The Christian is not living in heaven but on earth. While his highest loyalty is to God, he is involved also in the relationships of earth and is obligated to *responsible* involvement. Indeed, this is part of the significance of the incarnation and of the sacraments, that God reveals himself and calls us to obedient service here in the world.

The Christian's neighbors will be deeply affected, for good or ill, by the kind of state which emerges. Hence, if he

[8] (Frankfurt am Main: Europäische Verlaganstalt, 1960), p. 32.
[9] *Ibid.*, p. 34.

loves them in truth and not in mere sentimental self-deception he is responsibly concerned that the state be democratic and just.

For this reason, too, the Christian is obliged to support the nationalistic movement for independence if this movement gives reasonable promise of gaining in significant measure the positive values already described.

MODERATION AND PERSPECTIVE

Christians will rightly participate in the nationalistic movement for independence, and some Christians will be called to make political life in such a movement their main occupation. Yet every Christian must remember to give absolute loyalty and obedience to God alone. This implies that he must think of the well-being of others—even the exploiting imperialists—and not solely of his own exploited people who are his primary responsibility. The effectiveness of Gandhi in India's struggle for independence shows that such universal concerns need not interfere with successful nationalistic leadership; indeed they may lend greater stature to the person and greater stability to the movement and to the new state.

All the while, the Christian must remain loyal to his churchly responsibilities. He will love his neighbor more wisely in politics by continuing steadfastly to love God with heart, mind, soul, and strength.

Even when making his most eloquent pleas for loyalty to the national cause, the Christian's passion must be moderated by remembrance that he has one yet higher loyalty and that obedience to God binds him to all men as brothers. He cannot compete with the fanatical demagogue in wild promises and claims nor in dishonest blaming of the exploiters for all the evils of life. His power must be the power of truth, sobriety, and a passion disciplined by wide perspective. The unprincipled demagogue may be able to win the leadership of the people, it is true. Demagogues, like many other sinners, sometimes have their worldly rewards. The Christian, in political life as in other activities, must recognize quite clearly that he is not bound to win, however eager for victory, but he is bound to be faithful.

Division of Labor in the Church

The church as a whole, within a country swept by a new nationalistic fervor, is obliged to maintain perspective. It will rejoice when some of its able and faithful members enter politics as their specialized field of labor. It will be glad that many others take active part in responsible and promising movements, as volunteer part-time workers. At the same time, it will not permit its pastoral ministry to be downgraded. In time of nationalistic fervor, there is absolutely no task more exalted or more urgently important than the preaching of the Word by sermon, sacraments, and pastoral labors. Only such a ministry, effectively fulfilled, can produce and sustain the kind of Christian political leaders and citizens needed in such critical days. Besides, after the great fervor has passed, when the people settle down to live again in the common light of day, the kingdom of God will still be at hand and not yet fully manifest. The church will still be needed to direct men's eyes from earth to heaven and to bring good news of the Father's forgiving love.

In the time of revolutionary fervor, the church needs also to remind her people that many other tasks need to be faithfully done. Food must be grown and prepared, clothing must be made and sold, the sick must be attended, and children must be cared for and taught. The rise of a new nation-state may make possible more meaningful and fruitful labor, but *labor* will be needed, in full measure and of many kinds. In the state, as in the church, there are many members, and none who perform the work of their sacred callings are to be looked upon as lacking in dignity.

Transcending Tribal and Other Divisions

The church has an especially important service to render the state—whether new or old—simply by being truly the church, transcending and including in its own body the members of various tribes, classes, and parties. In this responsibility the churches in America have dismally failed. The gospel they have preached has helped in many ways, but the form of the life they have practiced has scandalously divided along the most irrational and socially destructive lines of worldly cleavage. Only in the 1960's have the churches in America begun earnestly to grapple with this contradiction. We must work and pray to heal the disease of worldly division in the churches of the United States and to make the church whole in other lands where its form is not yet altogether determined.

In some places, as in many African countries, the tribal divisions are among the most serious barriers to national unity. There the church can render immensely important service by its own intertribal fellowship. Such service is especially demanded in the cities where the people of many tribes are together in one place.

Revolution in Love, Not Hate and Violence

No state or political movement can be a perfect embodiment of Christian love. In most places, the emergence of a properly democratic and just nation-state cannot be accomplished without intense class struggle. Such struggle must not be opposed for the sake of a misguided conception of Christian love. For love must battle against exploitation and injustice.

However, the Christian can use nonviolent methods. Economic pressures by such instruments as the strike and boycott are coercive, it is true, and even at best they bring injury, which may fall on many innocent people. Yet there is a difference between such restrained, self-disciplined, and *relatively* harmless methods and the wild, vengeful fury of riotous mobs or pillaging armies. In revolution, as in the enforcement of law, the Christian must seek to keep violence and injury to a minimum.

The spirit of the Christian revolutionary must, of course, include severe condemnation of injustice. Yet it must exemplify judgment without hate. The Christian revolutionary, like every other Christian, is called upon to love all men, but he is to love without surrender to evil.

JUSTIFICATION BY FAITH

Even after our best thinking has been done, in reverent study and prayer, our choices in many complex situations are still ambiguous, mixed in motives, and uncertain. Recognizing this fact, we must always, and especially in times of intense feeling and momentous decisions, depend much on God's mercy. We are justified by his grace through our faithful reliance upon him. If we were to be judged by the correctness of our decisions or even the purity of our motives, who could stand?

Knowing that salvation is by God's mercy, Christians should be slow to condemn, eager to understand, quick to forgive, and faithful in concern to mend every breach which divides them from their neighbors. Such spirit is critically needed in this revolutionary age to make possible the general will without which there can be no stable state, no concert of nations, and no church of Jesus Christ.

New Thrusts in
the Theology and Life
of the Christian Mission

W. Richey Hogg

The church is the instrument of God's mission in and throughout the world. This affirmation, proclaimed widely by Protestant spokesmen and pastors, now has been solidified into dogma by the Roman Catholic Church in *De Ecclesia* (1964). Theologically, and in its practical implications, this represents a sea change, for it implies not that the church *has* missions, but that in its very life it *is* mission.

This shift mirrors a changed world, a post-Christendom (or "post-Constantinian") age, the ecumenical movement, and on every continent creative response among the churches in obedience to the Spirit's leading.

The thesis here advanced is that around the globe new thrusts in mission find their meaning within the context of a changed and changing world and of the search—increasingly stimulated by the ecumenical movement—for new patterns of responsible corporate Christian witness. In the process a fresh understanding of the church is emerging. This is the century of a new ecclesiology, one grounded in God's mission and in the conviction that mission and unity are inseparably conjoined.

The potential scope suggested by the title of this chapter is staggering. Even a brief catalog of new forms as a basis for meaningful generalization would extend these pages far beyond their limits. The attempt here made is simply to gain a historical and contemporary perspective on major areas of new thrust.

A Century of Councils and a New Ecclesiology

The ecumenical movement is the direct fruit of nearly 175 years of missionary endeavor. Obedience in mission raised the question of unity. That unity and mission are of one piece is now widely accepted, and John 17:21 has become the symbolic scriptural touchstone for this affirmation. Churches, accustomed to separation in the West but encountering one another in common cause in Asia's totally different milieu, suddenly confronted new questions. "Who are we in relation to one another?" "Who are we in relation to God's whole world—to God's men of other faiths?" "In our separation how do we understand ourselves as the people of God's covenant?" The continuing need for answers to these questions has forced the churches to explore the meaning of the church.

That in the ecumenical era they have wrestled with the doctrine of the church is reflected in a century of remarkable councils.

Convened in 1869 and cut short in 1870, the First Vatican Council examined the authority of the church and brought forth the dogma of papal infallibility. A generation later at Edinburgh in 1910, the World Missionary Conference in exploring the Christian mission discovered that implicit in, and essential to, its discussions was the larger question of the whole church in its mission and its unity. "Edinburgh, 1910" dealt with church union—overseas. Despite its ban on discussing matters involving theological disagreement, these arose. They gave birth in the mind of Bishop

Charles H. Brent to the Faith and Order movement.[1]

Another generation later in July, 1948, the Conference of Orthodox Churches, meeting in Moscow and reflecting largely the views of the patriarchate in that city, not only disclosed a problem of authority among the Orthodox churches, but also made pronouncements on Anglican orders, on Rome, and on the World Council of Churches, then soon to be constituted. Other Orthodox assemblies, representative and more important, have met since 1960 to deal with Orthodoxy's understanding of the church and its related response to the Second Vatican Council and the World Council of Churches.

Also in 1948 the constituting First Assembly of the World Council of Churches (WCC) met in Amsterdam. That body stands as a new and unique creation. Anglican, Orthodox, and Protestant churches came together in council and declared, "We intend to stay together." Here was an event, initiating a process, that involves the unity of God's people. In the context of ecclesiology, its full meaning invites, but still eludes, adequate theological understanding.

In 1957 in Prapat, Indonesia, the First Assembly (preparatory) and in 1959 at Kuala Lumpur, Malaya, the Second Assembly (inaugural) of the East Asia Christian Conference (EACC) met. These first major gatherings outside "Christendom" of non-Roman churches from traditionally "non-Christian lands" established a mutually supportive structure. Its purpose: to fulfill a common evangelistic task in Asia. Here was another unprecedented emergent— and one with ecclesiological significance.

Finally, the Second Vatican Council, convened in 1962 and concluded in 1965, enabled the pope to promulgate several major dogmatic formulations, among them those *On Ecumenism*, and *On the Church*. In a totally different

---

[1] On Edinburgh's concern for the church and for church unity see W. Richey Hogg, "Edinburgh, 1910—Ecumenical Keystone," *Religion in Life*, XXIX (1960), 347-50.

world, Vatican II was the fulfillment of Vatican I. Almost inevitably Vatican II's long-range significance will be assessed in terms of its central emphasis upon the church—upon its worship, its mission, and its relation to all those outside the boundaries of Roman Catholicism.

Thus a century of councils, 1869-1965—and this near-century is open-ended—comes into focus. Each council relates strikingly to a growing understanding of the church, its place in the purpose of God, its mission, and its unity. To many these councils may seem unrelated. Yet even now to the eye of faith attempting to discern the signs of the times, the question arises: "In the providence of God, may not these councils and the whole complex of dynamic events they symbolize have a hidden unity?" I believe they do.

Another century of councils comes to mind. Its events have a solid and familiar ring: Nicea, 325; Constantinople, 381; Ephesus, 431; and Chalcedon, 451. When the gospel emerged from the soil of Palestine into the Greco-Roman world, rich in philosophies and religions, Christians had to clarify for themselves and for that world their understanding of God and of him whom they proclaimed as Son of God and Savior. Through those councils in the first century of the Constantinian era, Christianity enunciated its doctrine of the Holy Trinity and of the Person of Jesus Christ.

Some sixteen hundred years later, and in the first century of the post-Constantinian era, Christians are having to clarify for themselves and for the world in which they live their understanding of the church. That process is being accomplished through councils. This is the century of the doctrine of the church—of the church in the world and for the world.

The Demise of Christendom—An Attempt at Perspective

In the first three centuries of its life the church was a tiny minority, illegal and often persecuted, in a pluralistic culture. It knew that it lived its life in mission, in outreach to men everywhere. It planted the faith in cities—centers of commerce and transport, not the industrialized complexes of this century—and watched it spread slowly into the countryside.

With the emergence of Constantine early in the fourth century, the age of the Christian Empire suddenly arrived. Almost overnight the churches were filled. With nearly everyone in the church, what need was there for mission? Congregations of new and nominal Christians lost the dynamic of corporate life lived in outreach and service. Instead, they became established bodies served by a priest. Constantinian Christendom's inversion of the true meaning of the congregation as the apostled *ekklesia* took firm root. The state supported the church and sought the benefits of a Christian society. In the process, the emperor had to convene each of the four great ecumenical councils with the hope that theological agreement would also facilitate political unity.

With the removal of the capital to Constantinople and with the fall of Rome, the church in the West entered a new era of its life. Largely freed from the control of the far-off emperor, the Bishop of Rome became the most powerful figure in the West. The Western church, through its bishops and monks, tutored the barbarians, from the ruins of the empire created a new society, and largely dominated the world. In an agrarian culture, the parish church became the place for worship and for the infusion of grace.

Europe was won to the church through missionary outreach. Sponsored by the pope, supported by the prince, served by the monks, the missions were conducted quite apart from existing parish life. In that "Christian society" parish churches invited men to worship. What lay beyond the edges of their world was the responsibility of the pope and of the monastic orders.

The process by which the church gained supremacy over the state—with its appeal to the doctrine of the "two swords" —begun by Gregory the Great, culminated early in the thirteenth century in the papal theocracy of Innocent III. Even then, the Christian society of Western Europe—Christendom, as commonly used—displayed a unity at the top but was atomized at the bottom.

The actual state of life in the grass-roots parish was such that it usually depresses the honest historian. The Crusades were, so it seemed, a necessary diverting from Christian soil of warlike tendencies.

The Protestant Reformation occurred within European Christendom. The transnational papal theocracy, as seen under Innocent III, had long since collapsed. But in a period of growing nationalism, the Reformation churches maintained one basic notion, among others, of Christendom, namely, that a nation or principality has one church supported by the government. Thus they furthered the rise of national churches.

The Reformation brought a theological revolution. The Word of God as contained in the Scriptures became authoritative for faith, and faith alone sufficed for salvation. The priesthood of all believers and the doctrine of vocation pointed to a new kind of Christian responsibility. The church found embodiment in the congregation in which the Word is rightly preached and the sacraments are duly administered. Congregational life was transformed, but the pre-Constantinian understanding of mission—germinally present in doctrine—was not regained. Reformation congregations were still part of Constantinian Christendom, and they retained the old parish notions. They were part of Europe's Christian society, and outreach was unnecessary. They had *their* needs served by a pastor or priest. The local churches of the Reformation, despite their revitalization, continued to be turned inward and remained largely self-serving.

By the middle of the sixteenth century the Roman Catholic Church had developed extensive missions in the New World and in Asia. Yet in rejecting the papacy and monasticism, Protestantism rejected the known and operating missionary structures of the day. Protestantism did not develop its distinctive missionary thrust and structures until the nineteenth century, after Carey's departure in 1793 for India.

By no means the first Protestant missionary, William Carey nevertheless launched the modern missionary movement. His call for volunteers reverberated through an England transformed by the Evangelical Revival. Recruits came, and there was created the voluntary missionary society, the enabling structure of the modern missionary movement.

In its geographic and demographic survey of the world, Carey's *An Enquiry* made it startlingly clear that Christians in Europe constituted a minority—and it had always been so—among all the world's people. The great majority of mankind had never heard of Jesus Christ. Christendom's minority, the former cobbler declared, bore the obligation to grasp the meaning of sheer numbers and, under God, to penetrate the world bearing the good news. No romantic escapist, Carey recognized the need of multitudes of the unconverted at home. He spoke not once of "foreign missions," but only of the one mission entrusted to the church. His total plan called for a mission in England and, with the remaining funds, for missions overseas.

In Carey's wake the modern missionary enterprise emerged. Its accomplishments are many and are familiar, but four contributions are worth noting here: First, it became the human agency for planting the church among every people and creating a world Christian community. Second, it proclaimed that under God the Christian church, even in Christendom, participates in a mission of worldwide dimension. Third, it demonstrated that each congregation has a direct responsibility for, and is directly involved in, the mission of God. Fourth, by confronting the church in Christendom with accomplished missions, it helped that church to discover mission.

For the purposes of this study the notion of Christendom, so recently buried, requires further probing. Often interpreted to mean that the European masses were Christian, the idea was just as specious and faulty under Innocent III as in Calvin's Geneva, which itself had to pass laws to force people into the churches. In the eighteenth century widespread revulsion at Christendom's wars of religion on the Continent and in Britain reinforced a growing conviction that Christian faith was no longer a claim to fight about or die for. Other and secular values, it was widely thought, held greater worth than religion. What was regarded as Europe's Christian society was being steadily eroded. Then the Industrial Revolution, a growing belief in religious freedom for the individual, and other forces hastened the separation of Europe's industrial working classes and many of the intelligentsia from the churches. But the Constantinian alliance of church and state seemed to hide all this. Even while nineteenth-century foreign missions flourished— and their support came not from the churches but from committed individuals in voluntary societies *outside* official church structures—the shell of Christendom was progressively drained of those it claimed but had never won.

The true inner state of nineteenth-century European Christendom was reflected in the nineteenth century's largest new nation, the United States of America. At its founding many of its states, repeating the Constantinian pattern, had their established churches. But in 1789 the first article in the Bill of Rights declared the separation of church and state, and the several remaining establishments soon disappeared. America was settled by those who had emigrated from European Christendom, but in 1789 only 6 percent of those in the population were church members. Theirs was not a birthright but a voluntary membership, requiring personal commitment and financial contributions. In short, freed from the Constantinian church-state relation, the American churches stood in 1789—numerically and in what their immediate mission was seen to be—in a situation comparable to that in which the European churches awoke to find themselves in 1945, with a "real" or communicating membership numbering only from 5 to 10 percent of the population.

In the 175 years between 1789 and 1964 voluntary church membership (as one measure of Christian commitment) in the United States steadily increased from 6 to 56 percent. Those statistics and their related history suggest several observations on the meaning of the growth of the church in America. (1) In a post-Constantinian setting, it represents largely the fruit of a mission to emigrés from Christendom's heartland. (2) It stands as the "Great Century's" most widespread mass movement, one which also produced the consequent problems of dilution and syncretism. (3) It provides a uniquely instructive example of mission—neither Asian nor European, but more nearly younger church than older church—free minority churches in a pluralistic society.[2] (4) It offers an accurate measure of the unreality of Europe's self-assessment as Christendom even at the time of its nineteenth-century missionary outreach.

In the two decades since the end of World War II, the political configuration of the globe has changed. The world has become physically one, and continues to shrink in size. In the realms of technology, science, history, economics, and politics, mankind has entered the ecumenical era. Universal cultural interpenetration points to the birth of a world civilization. The Christian church, with the ecumenical movement its most notable hallmark, enters this era often speaking itself of "the post-Christian age." That phrase gained currency at the close of World War II, and the realities to which it points were made vividly clear in Hendrik

[2] Cf. K. S. Latourette, *A History of the Expansion of Christianity* (New York: Harper & Brothers, 1941), IV, 9-109, 175 ff. See also Franklin H. Littell, *From State Church to Pluralism* (New York: Doubleday Anchor Books, 1962).

Kraemer's *Christian Message in a Non-Christian World* (1938) and were factually outlined in the Anglican Report, *Towards the Conversion of England* (1945) and Abbé Henri Godin's *France Pagan?* (*La France, Pays de Mission?* 1934).

The notion of the "post-Christian age" (much more precisely but awkwardly, "post-Constantinian" or "post-Christendom") has become entrenched, and the inaccuracy of the phrase plagues much current thought. Christians are seen to be a minority in Europe—as if a new situation had suddenly arisen—and throughout the world. New recognition of an old reality in Europe has led many there and in Asia and Africa to judge that the Christian gospel has been tried and found wanting—an outlook not unlike that held by the old Romans after the fall of Rome and against which Augustine wrote his *City of God*.

The church throughout the world lives today in an environment more nearly like that of its pre-Constantinian period than any it has known for more than sixteen centuries. Everywhere a minority, often persecuted, in some areas illegal, the church—although claiming one third of mankind and being the largest religious community in the world— now sees itself living only on its God-given resources. Yet for the church, the post-Constantinian age differs from the pre-Constantinian in at least two important respects. (1) Then, it was a minority throughout the Mediterranean society; now, it is a minority planted throughout the whole world. (2) Then, it had never been dominant among any people; now, it is widely judged to be a cultural and ethnic religion whose day has passed.

By way of summary: From the perspective of ecumenical history—true world history—mankind still lives in a pre-Christian age. Christians have always been, and continue to be, a minority. Yet, the whole world today is influenced more than ever before by forces which have their ultimate rootage in the gospel. From the perspective of Western history, this is a post-Christendom and post-Constantinian age. State support, favor, and advocacy for the church in the main have vanished and along with it, the church's massive shaping influence in society. From the perspective of contemporary popular understanding, formed by facile images and unexamined slogans, this is in East and West a post-Christian age. Inadequate as that phrase may be, its wide usage and assumed validity confront the church with an important datum for mission. New thrusts in mission thus involve adequately assessing three realities: the pre-Christian, the post-Christendom, and the post-Christian.

Two Contemporary Doctrines of the Church

From the missionary movement of the past 175 years have come the newer churches in Asia, the Pacific, Africa, and Latin America. They, in turn, in recent decades have produced some notable church unions, and in the process have been reformulating the doctrine of the church.

A comparison of the self-understanding of these churches with those that were new in sixteenth-century Europe, produces a striking contrast. The Reformation churches were part of Christendom and saw no biblical or theological warrant for outreach beyond Christendom. Each understood itself chiefly through those elements which differentiated it from the other churches of Christendom. But the new united churches of Asia and Africa have defined themselves primarily by that which is common to all—their mission! And this mission is precisely that which has led to their unity.

1. *The Church of South India* (CSI), formed in 1947, is the best known of these united churches. What is said in its Constitution could be applied also, with minor variations, to the other united churches in the non-Western world:

The Purpose and Nature of the Union. The Church of South India affirms that the purpose of the union by which it has been formed is the carrying out of God's will, as it is expressed in our Lord's prayer—"That they may all be one; . . . that the world may believe that Thou didst send me." (II. 2.)

Therefore the Church of South India purposes ever to be mindful of its missionary calling; and prays that it may not only be greatly used of God for the evangelization of South India, but may also take its due share in the preaching of the Gospel and the building up of Christ's Church in other parts of the world. (II. 3.)

The whole Constitution develops this understanding that the CSI has been called in mission to live its life on behalf of the world.

When, for example, the CSI in its Constitution turns to the ministry, it begins with the ministry entrusted by God to the entire church for the sake of the world and only then moves to the vocation of the ordained ministry.

Enough has been indicated to suggest that in its official theology the CSI projects a new understanding of the church. The essential nature of the church, it affirms, involves mission made meaningful in visible unity.

2. *The Roman Catholic Church.* As one ponders the meaning of this new ecclesiology, there comes the realization that the largest and oldest Christian community in the Western European tradition has just promulgated its first dogmatic decree on the church. The towering importance of this fact—that Rome has formulated its first full-orbed dogma of the church in the contemporary period—must be fully grasped. Forged in the post-Christendom age and in the ecumenical era, it too reflects a new conception. In *De Ecclesia* the Roman Catholic Church has set forth its self-understanding in the context of mission:

Christ is the light of nations. Because this is so, this sacred synod gathered together in the Holy Spirit eagerly desires by proclaiming the Gospel to every creature (cf. Mk. 16:15) to bring the light of Christ to all men. . . . [The Church] desires now to unfold more fully to the faithful of the Church and to the whole world its own inner nature and universal mission. (Par. 1.)

The obligation of spreading the faith is imposed on every disciple of Christ, according to his state, . . . that the entire world may become the People of God. (Par. 17.)

The lay apostolate . . . is a participation in the salvific mission of the Church itself. . . . The laity are called in a special way to make the Church present and operative in those places and circumstances where only through them can it become the salt of the earth. . . . Thus every layman . . . is at the same time a witness and a living instrument of the mission of the Church . . . [and has] the noble duty of working to extend the divine plan of salvation to all men of each epoch and in every land. . . . Even when preoccupied with temporal cares, the laity can and must perform a work of great value for the evangelization of the world. (Pars. 33-35.)

In studying *De Ecclesia*, the Protestant, without affirming the sections on infallibility and on Mary, will understand the reasons for their inclusion. Yet his dominant impression may well be that here is a theological definition of the church basically conceived as God's mission in the world.

For centuries to come, *De Ecclesia* will be theologically determinative for Roman Catholic life, outreach, and experiment in mission.[3] The listing of its chapter titles may indicate further something of its nature and thrust.

I. The Mystery of the Church
II. On the People of God
III. On the Hierarchical Structure . . . And . . . On the Episcopate
IV. The Laity
V. The Universal Call to Holiness in the Church
VI. The Religious
VII. Eschatological Nature of the Pilgrim Church
VIII. The Blessed Virgin Mary, Mother of God, In the Mystery of Christ and the Church

[3] The schema on missions is derived from *De Ecclesia*.

Here are two new formulations of the doctrine of the church. They derive from two bodies totally different in history, size, and outreach. Yet at certain points of basic awareness and orientation, they demonstrate a remarkably similar conviction about the missionary nature of the church. They are included here because all new thrusts in mission spring from response to an understanding of God's purpose for his covenanted people, the church. These two statements exemplify a new and basic theological thrust in mission.

Developments Within the Larger Ecumenical Structures

From this point onward in the survey it becomes difficult to categorize new thrusts. They will be listed in what seems to be their area of most direct applicability.

COUNCILS

Councils constitute a major portion of the ecumenical structure and operate at the local, intermediate, national, regional (international), and world levels. In the degree to which councils do for denominations what denominations cannot do alone, they point to the incompleteness of the denominational church *and* to their own participation, in some measure, in the nature of the church.[4]

Councils have stimulated and launched numerous new thrusts in mission. Moreover, new councils meeting new needs emerge with regularity. One development worth noting is the occasional evolution in title, structure, and function from a basically Protestant and missionary Christian Council to a Council of Churches. This occurred in the Philippines in 1963 and in the Near East in 1964. Each action enlarged the council's constituency to include non-Protestant churches. The Near East Council's current project to produce a Greek-Arabic lexicon and a new translation

---

[4] Cf. *The Ecclesiological Significance of Councils of Churches* (New York: National Council of Churches, 1963).

of the Bible has brought the most diverse groups—from Southern Baptist to Roman Catholic, with varied degrees of relationship—into a sense of common cause.

THE INTEGRATION AT NEW DELHI

The World Council of Churches' integrating of the International Missionary Council (IMC) at the Third Assembly in New Delhi, 1961, must be viewed as one of the important recent events in the theology and life of the Christian mission. Here was embodied acknowledgment by member churches that mission is of the very essence of the church. For the great European churches lacking, with one or two recent exceptions, any integral mission board or agency, the step was of special significance and became another evidence that the Constantinian era's separation of church and mission is theologically and practically indefensible.

Integration has proved meaningful to the Orthodox, and they in turn have contributed to the Commission on World Mission and Evangelism (CWME, formerly IMC). Integration has also simplified and strengthened ecumenical ties in Asia, Africa, and to some degree in Latin America. The new alignment has also helped to clarify the distinguishable but inseparable relationship between mission and service as part of the church's witness.[5] The IMC had been involved in both, and the WCC "formally" only in the latter. The fuller implications of this integration are yet to be unfolded.

Two developments related to all that New Delhi represented for mission require noting:

First, the "six continent view" of mission: The crumbling

[5] An analagous situation is seen in the recent change in structure and name in the former Division of Foreign Missions of the National Council of Churches. Determined to embody and symbolize a unified mission of witness and service, while ridding itself of the word "Foreign," the DFM, integrating Church World Service, since January, 1965, has been the Division of Overseas Ministries of the National Council. See *Annual Report, 1964, Division of Foreign Missions* (New York: National Council of Churches, 1965), pp. 29-30.

of the "Christendom complex," which sees mission almost exclusively as outreach from the Western churches to Asia, Africa, and Latin America (a three continent view), and fresh recognition that the church everywhere is in mission, have given rise to the phrase, "mission to six continents." This slogan points vividly to a new orientation.[6]

Inevitably the size and resources of the Western churches, relative to those elsewhere, preclude dramatic shifts of the kind dear to news reporters. Yet the channeling through the WCC of funds from churches overseas into the Mississippi "Delta Project" provides a salutary and instructive reminder of what is involved. What at the moment may appear less dramatic, but which involves the churches in many more areas, are those experiments in congregational renewal and outreach now seen on every continent. The "six continent view" has already caused the *International Review of Missions* to revise its policy of coverage. The outworking of the implications of this basic reorientation for boards of national and overseas missions will bear watching.

Second, joint action for mission: In its message the Lund Conference, 1952, on Faith and Order pointedly, but modestly in the form of a question, urged the churches "to act together in all matters except those in which deep differences of conviction compel them to act separately." The Third Assembly of the WCC at New Delhi, 1961, in its message urged the churches to "find out the things which in each place we can do together now, and faithfully do them, praying and working always for that fuller unity which Christ wills for his Church."

Whitby's "Partnership in Obedience" (1947), Willingen's "Mobility" (1952), Ghana's "The Christian world mission is Christ's, not ours" (1958), and New Delhi's "All in each

---

[6] Cf. R. K. Orchard, ed., *Witness in Six Continents*. Records of the meeting of the Commission on World Mission and Evangelism of the World Council of Churches held in Mexico City, December 8th to 19th, 1963 (London: Edinburgh House Press, 1964).

place" (1961) lie behind Joint Action for Mission (JAM). That program represents the determination that what the missionary agencies of the churches long have known and been saying for so long shall be made flesh and blood in common action. In referring to IMC policy suggestions and the use made of them, John R. Mott in 1947 said, "Our greatest weakness has been the failure to move from knowledge to action." JAM is an attempt to overcome that criticism by putting existing theory and expressed conviction into creative practice.

JAM is not bare interdenominational action. It represents the determination that in a given geographical area, Christians shall explore together the best approach to their evident task in mission and then proceed to act to meet it as the one people of God in that place. Whether it involves boards, local churches, or both, JAM requires rethinking the witness traditionally given or now needed, willingness to abandon any forms now irrelevant to the need, possible redeployment of resources, and openness to new ventures with no denominational gain.

JAM was enunciated in 1961 at New Delhi and was authorized as a Commission on World Mission and Evangelism policy. Explored in 1963 in three EACC "Situation Conferences" in India, Singapore, and Japan, JAM was re-examined at Mexico City in 1963. Although JAM raises major issues (e.g., church union, denominational conscience, the church home for new converts, etc.), it appears to have the support of many mission boards and of agencies such as the Division of Overseas Ministries.[7] The EACC in its entirety appears to be one possible embodiment of JAM.

[7] W. A. Visser 't Hooft, ed., *The New Delhi Report: The Third Assembly of the World Council of Churches, 1961* (New York: Association Press, 1962), pp. 251-52; *Minutes of the Assembly of the IMC . . . and of the First Meeting of the Commission on World Mission and Evangelism of the WCC, December 7-8, 1961, at New Delhi* (Geneva: Commission on World Mission and Evangelism, 1962), pp. 31-32, 87-89; *Minutes of the Second Meeting of the Commission on World Mission and Evangelism, Mexico*

The London Secretary of the CWME, R. K. Orchard, wrote in the January, 1965, *International Review of Missions* that he knew of no instance of JAM in "full operation"; but in several significant situations steps are being taken for major JAM endeavors. Taiwan is a case in point. There Presbyterians, Anglicans, Methodists, and Lutherans are moving toward JAM in a significant way. Still another example can be seen in Wilmington, Delaware.

MEXICO CITY, 1963

The second meeting of the Commission on World Mission and Evangelism in Mexico City, December, 1963, without attempting to survey the full range of its concerns and responsibilities, nevertheless produced four major Section Reports. Their titles, which point toward new thrusts, are:

I. The Witness of Christians to Men of Other Faiths
II. The Witness of Christians to Men in the Secular World
III. The Witness of the Congregation in Its Neighborhood
IV. The Witness of the Christian Church across National and Confessional Boundaries.

For Mexico City, 1963, "Mission in six continents" undoubtedly will become its symbolic phrase and JAM its distinguishing program policy.[8]

REGIONAL COUNCILS

Since 1957 regional ecumenical bodies have appeared and are growing in importance. At least four new bodies have emerged: the East Asia Christian Conference (EACC,

---

City, December 8-9, 1963 (Geneva: Commission on World Mission and Evangelism, 1964), pp. 58-62; *Reports of Situation Conferences Convened by the East Asia Christian Conference, February-March, 1963* (Distributed by the Commission on World Mission and Evangelism of the World Council of Churches, 475 Riverside Drive, New York, N.Y., 10027); R. K. Orchard, "Joint Action for Mission—Its Aim, Implications, and Method," *International Review of Missions*, LIV, 213 (1965), 81-94.
[8] *Witness in Six Continents*, pp. 144-78.

1957 and constituted in 1959), the All Africa Conference of Churches (AACC, 1958 and constituted in 1963), the Provisional Committee for the Pacific Churches' Conference (resulting from the Samoa Conference, 1961), and the European Conference of Churches (1964). The Near East Council of Churches (1964) grew out of the old Near East Christian Council. In Latin America serious discussion looking toward a council for that region is already underway, and a preliminary draft of a constitution was being explored in late 1965.

The EACC, the most fully developed of these new bodies, has had three assemblies (Prapat, 1957; Kuala Lumpur, 1959; and Bangkok, 1964) and brings together churches within the area bounded by the Karachi-Sydney-Tokyo triangle. Born and continued in the conviction that "the purpose of God for the churches in East Asia is life together in a common obedience to him for the doing of his will in the world," [9] the EACC represents a significant new thrust in mission and unity.

Doing in Asia what neither a national council of churches nor the WCC can do, the EACC meets a new and important need. Among its member churches it has stimulated stewardship and the sending of Asian missionaries. It convenes special consultations on common concerns in mission which range from urban and industrial evangelism to home and family life. Despite the scope of its interests, the conferences it sponsors, and the considerable work it does—(as reflected in the large and substantial contents of its assembly minutes—[10] the EACC is *completely* decentralized. It has

[9] East Asia Christian Conference, Preamble to the Constitution.
[10] The most recent were printed in two parts: *Assembly of the East Asia Christian Conference . . . Bangkok . . . 1964* (Available from U Kyaw Than, 14 Pramauan Road, Bangkok, Thailand), which without including a single speech, details the work of the Assembly in 175 pages; and *The Christian Community Within the Human Community* (Available from M. M. Thomas, 19 Miller Road, Bangalore 6, India) which in 84 pages sets forth the main thrust of the East Asia Christian Conference for the next quadrennium.

no headquarters building. There is no central EACC file. Its secretaries and committee chairmen are found in all parts of Asia. "This," says D. T. Niles, the EACC's general secretary, with a twinkle, "is the Asian way." The chief impact of the EACC to date has been to give the Asian churches a sense of their common responsibility for the Christian mission in Asia.

The All-Africa Church Conference has similar interests and purposes. Despite its youth, it has had to respond vigorously in thought, action, and structure to help shape the response of the African churches to the burgeoning needs and opportunities thrust at them from every part of their revolutionary continent.[11]

PROTESTANT-ROMAN CATHOLIC-ORTHODOX DISCUSSIONS AND RELATIONS

One could fill pages with instances since 1961 of Protestant–Roman Catholic fraternity at the local level. At another level, that of the discussion of specialists, developments thus far are modest but worth noting. For the first time— as one thinks of the CWME representing a continuing line with the old International Missionary Council—Orthodox churchmen were present as members of the CWME at Mexico City in 1963, and Roman Catholics were present as observers. Early in 1965 the WCC created a working group to confer from time to time with representatives of the Vatican's Secretariat for Christian Unity. At the same time the former secretary of the Methodist Board of Missions, Eugene L. Smith, now executive secretary for the WCC's Staff in the United States, prepared a report, "Missionary Developments: WCC Member Churches, 1960-1965," for the first

[11] *The Church in Changing Africa: Report of the All-Africa Church Conference held at Ibadan, January 10-19, 1958* (New York: International Missionary Council, 1958); and *Drumbeats from Kampala: Report of the First Assembly of the All-Africa Conference of Churches held at Kampala, April 20 to April 30, 1963* (London: United Society for Christian Literature, 1963).

meeting on missionary questions between representatives of the Roman Catholic Church and of the WCC. Limited as they are, these initial evidences point toward new developments of future promise.

Developments Related to the Local Church

Several new major thrusts in the theology and life of the Christian mission relate primarily to the local church or to a church within a region. These reflect the new conviction that mission constitutes the church rather than that missions are an activity conducted by one part of the church's organization.

THE REDISCOVERY OF THE LAITY

Out of the experiences of World War II and the remarkable contributions of laymen in making real the witness of the church, the WCC at Amsterdam in 1948 reminded everyone —almost, it seemed, to its own surprise—that the laity constitutes more than 99 percent of the church. In the postwar world the laity has begun to come into focus. Yves Congar's *Lay People in the Church* [12] on the Roman Catholic side and Hendrik Kraemer's *A Theology of the Laity* [13] on the Protestant side marked major stages in this rediscovery. Congar speaks of the laity as always "a subordinate order in the church." But Kraemer insists that the true biblical conception is of the whole church as *laos* (laity, people of God) and "a royal priesthood." For Protestants Kraemer's book is germinal and revolutionary. It raises the fundamental question of whether the church is mission or has missions. For Kraemer the church is the people of God living in mission and service. The WCC's Department of the Laity, Hans-Ruedi Weber's *Salty Christians*,[14] and Paul Löffler's *The*

[12] Trans. by Donald Attwater (Westminster, Md.: Newman Press, 1957), French ed. 1953.
[13] (Philadelphia: The Westminster Press, 1958).
[14] (New York: Seabury Press, 1963).

212

Layman Abroad in the Mission of the Church,[15] all reflect this new thrust in basic missionary understanding. As Kraemer pointedly suggests, the laity must be seen to be of at least equal importance with the clergy in any Faith and Order discussion on the church.

STRUCTURES FOR A MISSIONARY CONGREGATION

Kraemer speaks of the laity as the church's "frozen credits" and points to the need for the radical restructuring of congregations if the people of God are to be able to understand themselves and fulfill their calling to mission and service. From Evanston had come a similar word, and at New Delhi the WCC's Department on Studies in Evangelism was authorized to launch a study on "The Missionary Structure of the Congregation," [16] a theme proposed by D. T. Niles.

Striking experiments from several lands had already underscored the basic need on the local level and suggested the wisdom of a widespread coordinated endeavor. On the Roman Catholic side, for example, Abbé Georges Michonneau's *Revolution in a City Parish* [17] detailed Roman Catholic congregational renewal in an urban-industrial setting, and on the Protestant side the East Harlem Protestant Parish in New York, already well known, found vivid interpretation in George W. Webber's *God's Colony in Man's World.*[18]

This WCC-initiated project is well advanced in many parts

[15] (London: Edinburgh House Press, 1962).

[16] *The New Delhi Report, 1961,* pp. 189-91.

[17] (London: Blackfriars Publications, 1957). Published first in Paris in 1946, the original bore a title more accurately translated *The Parish—a Revolutionary Community.*

[18] (Nashville: Abingdon Press, 1960). See also Webber's *The Congregation in Mission: Emerging Structures for the Church in an Urban Society* (Nashville: Abingdon Press, 1964) and its bibliography which lists some of the many titles in this area. The latest is Wallace E. Fisher's *From Tradition to Mission* (Nashville: Abingdon Press, 1965) which traces the metamorphosis of an old Lutheran city church into a new center of mission vitality.

of the world, and several studies will soon be published. Three already have appeared. Colin Williams, director of the National Council's Department of Evangelism and chairman of the comparable department in the WCC, has written two study books, *Where in the World? Changing Forms of the Church's Witness*[19] and *What In the World?*[20] widely used in American churches. John R. Fleming has edited the EACC's contribution, *Structures for a Missionary Congregation*.[21]

In essence these studies assert that God's purpose for his people must determine the form of their congregational life. Any form or pattern of local church life—no matter how functional it may once have been—which thwarts the outreach of God's people into the social structures that shape the lives of men today negates the apostolate of the church.

New Forms of the Ministry

New forms of ministry and service among laymen, fresh, creative forms of congregational life, and related biblical studies raise certain fundamental questions concerning the ministries of the church. "Is the paid professional ministry the norm by which all other forms of ministry are to be measured?" "Is traditional church order constitutive or essentially functional for the people of God?" "Is the unpaid clergyman who earns his living through secular work a temporary expedient for 'poorer' Asian and African—and even American—churches?" The American Protestant response to this last is almost unanimous until the example of many of the rural Orthodox clergy in Greece is examined and the

[19] (New York: National Council of Churches, 1963).
[20] (New York: National Council of Churches, 1964).
[21] (Singapore: East Asia Christian Conference, 1964). Available from Dr. Fleming at 6 Mt. Sophia Road, Singapore 9.

results of certain recent studies are pursued. "Does ordination confer authority to be the church or to act on behalf of the people of God?" "Are unusual patterns of ministry from the first century acceptable today?" "Is the Holy Spirit free to bring forth new patterns of ministry in our time?"

These questions have their own urgency for congregations in Rio's slums, in India's rural areas, in Chicago's apartment section, or in Los Alamos. They are rising with increasing frequency. A substantial body of data on experience in "experimental forms" of the ministry already exists.[22] Exploration of the present and possible future significance of forms of the ministry quite different from that of the traditional salaried clergyman looms importantly for mission in the immediate future. The possible implications for Faith and Order are exciting to contemplate.

Some Larger Concerns

This section alone could be expanded to book length, but of necessity it must be concentrated. The specific larger concerns which have invited new missionary thrusts are many. Everywhere there are human needs and changed situations that call for new thrusts in mission—the refugees, the world of the university, the population explosion, the revolution in family life around the world, education in an age when nation-states are concerned with the welfare of their citizens and make universal education a prime priority, Christian medical service, mass communications, and theological education.

Other important areas with new thrusts could be cited, but two may be singled out for special mention.

[22] *A Tent-Making Ministry: Towards a More Flexible Form of Ministry* (Geneva: DWME, 1962); David M. Paton, ed., *New Forms of Ministry* (London: Edinburgh House Press, 1965; CWME Research Pamphlets, No. 12).

THE CHRISTIAN INVOLVEMENT IN SOCIETY

The gospel relates to the whole human race, to the created world, and to history. It proclaims God's love and holiness as well as his sovereignty. In God's world today human societies are changing rapidly—everywhere. In the constantly new structures of society the church must be present through the people of God, individually and corporately, making visible in life the meaning of the gospel in the midst of the communities where men live. This involves "the Christian presence" and Christian participation in nation building, community development, industrial life, and in other enterprises.[23]

Obviously, the circumstances of Christian involvement in society are as vast, varied, and complex as the world itself. The possibilities open to Protestants in Spain, to the Orthodox in Russia, and to Christians in China vary markedly from those open to Christians in Brazil, the United States, Nigeria, and India.

In the present emerging world civilization the universal pattern of urbanization and industrialization, with all the attendant upheavals and tensions involved, poses a major challenge to Christian mission. In the United States, in Africa, in India, in Latin America—everywhere urbanization proceeds rapidly. In many Latin American countries, for example, the chief city may hold from 20 to 33 percent of the nation's population. In India and Africa cities of two hundred thousand people are springing up almost overnight wherever a new steel mill or harbor has been built. Men are moving from the land to cities for work and for the experience of a new life. Industrialization also stands out as a prime hallmark of our civilization. Real differences are to be seen as between Detroit and Hong Kong or Durgapur

[23] Cf. P. D. Devanandan and M. M. Thomas, eds., *Christian Participation in Nation Building* (Bangalore, India: National Christian Council of India and the Christian Institute for the Study of Religion and Society, 1960).

and Mombasa, but the basic problem-complex in which industrialization involves the individual and society is everywhere the same.

EACC and AACC conferences on the meaning of Christian mission in urban-industrial centers and the similar probing concern and effort of churches and boards in the West mark the growing urban-industrial complexion of our age as an area for thoughtful, urgent, and massive new thrust. What the Industrial Revolution wrought in and for Europe's Christendom, the universal urban-industrial revolution is repeating in the areas of the traditional non-Christian religions and in Latin America. This challenge to Christian mission is only beginning to be grasped.

Similarly, racial conflict—whether in India, Malaysia, Britain, the United States, East Africa, South Africa or elsewhere—as a concomitant of the present age has often found its context within the larger revolution among the world's peoples. The Christian presence in its constructive and reconciling form (and the converse, one adds sadly) in the racial upheavals of the present day makes a witness watched and weighed in every part of the globe. Forthright and creative relationships amidst this turmoil represent one of the most decisive opportunities for obedient witness open to Christians in their mission.

New thrusts in mission, as indicated above and reflecting the Christian involvement in society, testify that the gospel relates to creation, to the orders of life, and to the structures of society and that *all things* are caught up in, and find their fulfillment in, him, "for God so loved the *world*."

CHRISTIAN ENCOUNTER WITH OTHER RELIGIONS

A most distinctive feature of the emerging world civilization is the encounter among the religions. Still not recognized by many, this encounter will loom steadily larger for as far ahead as man can see. Its challenge to the whole range of Christian faith and its demand for the most fundamental, sensitive, dedicated, and creative thought and life in mission should be obvious.

Much has been written about the resurgence among the traditional religions of mankind,[24] but the question remains, in Max Warren's words, "Resurgence or Renaissance?" Yet in recent times two other great "world religions" have arisen: Communism and secularism, and for both, cases can be made for their being "Christian heresies." These two are seldom mentioned among the resurgent religions, but Communism, with its messianic and missionary zeal, and secularism, universally felt with its subtly quiet shaping of men's world view and ultimate allegiances, are massive participants in the encounter.

Many new thrusts in mission relating to this encounter can be cited. Among them are such creative agencies as the Christian Institute for the Study of Religion and Society in Bangalore, India; the Roman Catholic equivalent in Poona; similar centers in Hong Kong, Japan, and elsewhere; "The Christian Presence Series" (with perhaps the most notable cluster of books being those from Canon Kenneth Cragg, only one of which, strictly speaking, is part of the series); the Lay Academy Movement around the world (admittedly, "encounter of religions" is not the category in which such are usually placed, but for those in Japan the encounter with secularism, Communism, and Buddhism looms large and for those in Germany the encounter is not greatly different); the Islam in Africa Project; and numerous other studies and consultations.

The contemporary world has raised large and troubling questions for those in the church concerning the place of their faith among the world's religions. Moreover, much current theological thought—including the rediscovery that the church is mission, which, with the reception of its

---

[24] Perhaps significantly, almost nothing is said about the serious decline or death of several once important faith systems such as Confucianism, Taoism, Shamanism, certain forms of Buddhism, and African traditional religion.

amazing implications for the congregation's immediate outreach has blinded many to the worldwide dimensions of God's mission—frequently suggests to Christians a view of mission not unlike that of ancient Israel's ingrown "centripetal understanding" of its role. Among Christians, especially in the West, such considerations have created major uncertainty about mission. Indeed, a member of the Vatican's Secretariat for Christian Unity, speaking of the Second Vatican Council and the temper of thinking within the Roman Catholic Church, said in the writer's presence, "There is even some uncertainty that we should be in mission." Such questioning, admittedly, has both positive and negative elements in it.

This is, and will increasingly become, an age of pluralism and of relativity. The meaning of mission, as involving conversion, is a pressing and growing problem. It has produced considerable fuzzy thinking but little study in depth. It demands new attention.

Finally, one is driven to the question asked initially in first-century Palestine: "Who is Jesus Christ?" The most fundamental new thrust in the years ahead must relate directly to ever-new probing into the meaning of God's revelation in Jesus Christ for the people of the covenant and for God's whole creation.

God's Word
and the Aim
of Christian Mission

Everett Tilson

The biblical teaching on mission has been the subject of numerous recent investigations. Such contributions, for the sake of quality[1] as well as quantity,[2] compel me to begin this chapter with an attempt to classify them according to the typical posture of their authors[3] in biblical interpretation. These positions may be characterized, respectively, as the authoritarian, the exemplary, the formal, the functional. Following a description of each of these approaches in terms of its reflection in the writings of important contemporary theologians and biblical scholars, they will be critically evaluated from the standpoint of their relative viability today. I will then employ this evaluation as a basis for outlining several theses in need of careful examination before we go further in pursuit of the aim of Christian mission.

The authoritarian approach grounds the validation of the

[1] Karl Barth, *God in Action*, trans. by E. G. Homrighausen and Karl J. Ernst (Manhasset, N. Y.: Round Table Press, 1936).

[2] *The Theology of the Christian Mission*, Gerald H. Anderson, ed. (New York: McGraw-Hill Book Co., 1961).

[3] Since my chief aim is to make suggestions about methodology, I shall make no effort to provide an exhaustive classification of writers.

missionary enterprise in biblical commandments. The fundamentalists do not, as we might suppose, hold a monopoly on this tendency. It manifests itself, for example, in some of the contributions in the Anderson collection.[4] The essay of Karl Barth is a surprising case in point.[5] If our knowledge of his theory of missions hinged solely on this article, few of us would hesitate to place him in the authoritarian camp. He may be excused from susceptibility to this charge on the ground that he produced this exegesis of Matt. 28:16-20 under assignment. But no matter how extenuating this circumstance, it can hardly do plenary atonement for Barth's single-minded interpretation of this text as a virtual reporter's account of a real "space-and-time" event in the life of the resurrected Jesus[6]—one might add, in sovereign disregard of the testimony of important contemporary New Testament scholars to the contrary.[7]

Barth betrays here a singular determination to find a dominical directive for the theory and practice of Christian missions. A less christocentric theologian might be content with the discovery of such a command anywhere in Scripture, but it would be a mistake to make very much of this difference. Both scope and method of mission would, in any case, still have their common sanction in the words of Scripture.

Although the justification of missions on the basis of this approach has had a long and influential history, its perpetuation has become both a hindrance and an embarrassment,

[4] But one must hasten to add, though, that hardly an essay in this entire volume fails to hint at some of the limitations that beset this approach.

[5] At any rate, his essay in the Anderson symposium, "An Exegetical Study of Matthew 28:16-20," *The Theology of the Christian Mission,* pp. 55-71, reflects a quite different stance from that which the writer came to associate with Barth's name on the basis of some of his other writings.

[6] *Ibid.,* p. 56.

[7] Cf. Johannes Blauw, *The Missionary Nature of the Church* (New York: McGraw-Hill Book Co., 1962), pp. 124-25.

many missionaries feel, in the spread of the gospel.[8]

A closely related but somewhat more flexible method is what may be called the exemplary approach. It is marked by a freer, though still wooden and stultifying, attitude toward Scripture. It demands not proof texts but precedents. But while this precedent may come in the form of action rather than words and from a group, e.g., the church, rather than an individual, the reader is still confronted with a demand for duplication rather than examination. The crucial issue for contemporary Christians is not the *how* but the *fact* of the establishment of the precedent. Its *what* has already been determined.

The pattern itself may have to do primarily with the time, the sphere, or the goal of Christian missions. Cullmann's essay in the Anderson volume[9] illustrates the use of this model with respect to the time of the church's mission. Even while conceding that Paul mistakenly telescoped the end, he works manfully to make room for our performance of the sign of the end, namely the proclamation of the missionary message to all the nations, even though that end, according to Pauline calculation, should have taken place long before we ever arrived on the stage of human history. The really disturbing thing about this analysis is not Cullmann's discovery of a means whereby he can find a place in Pauline chronology for our participation in the missionary task of the church. It is, rather, the subtle, though happily unvoiced, implication that, apart from such a discovery, we might be exempt from all missionary obligation.

Despite certain tendencies in the direction of a dynamic interpretation of the Old Testament as a missiological guide in determination of the sphere of mission, Robert Martin-

---

[8] Lesslie Newbigin, *A Faith for This One World?* (New York: Harper & Brothers, 1961), p. 76, without expressly tracing the problem to its source in bad hermeneutics, laments the fact that "*the prosecution of the Christian world mission has been and still is shot through with legalism.*" (Italics mine.)

[9] "Eschatology and Missions in the New Testament," trans. by Olive Wyon, pp. 42-54.

Achard finally errs toward the exemplary approach. Missionary work in the Old Testament is, he contends, the work of the living God in the life of his obedient witnesses. "Mission has nothing in common," he assures us, "with any sort of political or commerical enterprise; it is entirely dependent on the hidden activity of God within his church." [10]

Since Israel's prophets have a great deal more to say about the intervention of the Holy Spirit to transform Israelite politics and economics than to effect the salvation of the nations, this representation of the Old Testament viewpoint must not go unchallenged.[11] But an even more serious problem, theologically speaking, manifests itself in the author's unexamined assumption of the possibility of defining the task of the church on the basis of Israelite history.

A Finnish pastor, Gustav Kvist, employs this method in his book, *No Other Name: Missions in the Light of the Bible,* to argue for a restricted view of the goal of the missionary enterprise. Just as God protected his heritage from immature syncretism by entry into an exclusive covenant with Israel, he safeguards it in the Christian era by replacing the old Israel with the new Israel. Instead of all the nations falling heir to Israel's place, that place is taken, instead, by the church, the people of God, who are gathered from all

---

[10] *A Light to the Nations,* trans. by J. P. Smith (Edinburgh: Oliver and Boyd, 1962), p. 79. As John Deschner points out in "The Spirit of God and the Christian Witness," *The Christian Mission Today,* ed. Joint Section of Education and Cultivation of the Board of Missions of The Methodist Church (Nashville: Abingdon Press, 1960): "This is a perversion because it suggests that God's activity is the enemy of human freedom, . . . and the more you emphasize God's activity the less you can emphasize man's. . . . The Christian knows that the more he lets God have his way with him, . . . the more he is freed to forgive, love, and serve his neighbor. In the light of the gospel [and the Old Testament!], . . . the more we recognize that the church's mission is God's activity, the more we may properly speak of it as our activity" (p. 40).

[11] See Norman K. Gottwald, *All the Kingdoms of the Earth* (New York: Harper & Row, 1964), who simply explodes the docetizing tendencies of Martin-Achard's interpretation of Israelite religion.

the nations. "It is the *gathering* into the fold of the one Church . . . which is the real task of missions. In obedience to the ascended Lord they can be conducted only by the Church itself. So the whole study logically leads to the last chapter '*Extra ecclesiam*. . . .' This declaration of Cyprian," as seen by Kvist, "is not the expression of a self-satisfied desire to gain clerical power. It is . . . submission to the sovereignty of God, who offers His grace to mankind in the way of salvation which He . . . ordained." [12] Kvist's view of the Bible exaggerates the errors in the approach of Cullmann and Martin-Achard, which by implication, if not otherwise, impugns the Christian character of any church order or missionary activity without direct biblical precedent.

The formal approach, as distinguished from the exemplary, is characterized by a narrower focus. Instead of calling for a wide-ranging duplication of biblical precedents, it extrapolates from the New Testament some particular form or element deemed to be of crucial significance for the spread and practice of Christian faith and turns it into a test of faithful witness. Recent New Testament theology presents us with a case in point in its reiterated stress on the rediscovery of the *kerygma*. John J. Vincent gives us the following severe assessment of the present state of this development:

Even were the *kerygma* idea a wholly watertight theological position in terms of the New Testament evidence, . . . its influence in the field of theology has not been entirely . . . good. . . . It has confirmed our present predisposition to regard correct doctrine as more important than correct behavior. It has led us to believe again that, provided our "message" was right, all other things would be granted unto us. It has not led to political and social

[12] This book, published in the Finnish language, was accessible to me only in the summary of it that appeared in the review by Peter Beyerhaus, *The International Review of Missions*, XLVII (1958), 333-36. Quoted material from p. 335.

involvement. . . . In a word, it has taken the place of Christ and discipleship. It has become itself the new "myth" which needs to be demythologized. [13]

Karl Barth, in his estimate of verbal testimony, gives us an even sharper illustration of the demand for the perpetuation of a particular form, namely the sermon, as the norm of faithful Christian witness. "God communicates with men also by deeds," he writes. But he goes on to say that the Bible, "when it speaks of testimony, . . . means a word spoken by a man to other men." "Where *this* dynamic word of *the* testimony is spoken, there is 'the church.' " [14]

Asked if testimony might not include deeds and suffering as well as words, "I would only remark," Barth answered, "that in the New Testament . . . the word testimony is never used for what martyrs do and suffer. . . . The New Testament reports the death of only one martyr, Stephen. It is his sermon, however, which makes him a witness, and not his suffering." [15]

The New Testament, by Barth's own admission, relates the death of only one martyr. Yet Barth not only turns the failure of the author of Luke-Acts to describe Stephen's suffering and death as "testimony" into a subordination of martyrdom to the sermon; he converts such verbal testimony into a definitive criterion for ascertaining the whereabouts of the church. One can be excused for wondering just what criterion might have taken its place if the *Nazareth Weekly Review* had sent a more competent reporter to cover the story of Stephen's martyrdom.

The functional approach to Scripture, commonly hailed in theory and seldom pursued in practice, may well be on

---

[13] "Christ's Ministry and Our Discipleship," *Biblical Realism Confronts the Nation*, Paul Peachey, ed. (Scottsdale, Pa.: Fellowship Publications, 1963), pp. 186-87.

[14] *God in Action*, pp. 95, 97.

[15] *Ibid.*, p. 131.

the verge of a dramatic breakthrough. Challenges[16] prodding the church in this direction, along with existentialist philosophy[17] and works of the linguistic analysts,[18] include the revitalization of the world's old religions[19] and the growing irrelevance at home[20] and abroad of the traditional evangelistic gimmicks.[21] Under growing pressure from these and other sources, biblical theologians have begun to substitute the bread-and-butter of verbs for the crusts of speculative ontology.[22] Emphasis on status is giving way to stress on function as the key to their interpretation of the biblical message. The contributions of biblical scholars to the Anderson collection marks an impressive and, probably, representative witness to this changing stance. Of the six essays in this volume, at least three, those by G. E. Wright,

[16] See especially Lesslie Newbigin's discussion of the current situation in *One Body, One Gospel, One World* (London: Edinburgh House Press, 1958), pp. 8-13.

[17] As mediated through its influence on current biblical theology, quite often at a distant remove, as would tend to be the case with G. Ernest Wright, "The Old Testament Basis for the Christian Mission," *The Theology of the Christian Mission*, Anderson, ed., pp. 17-30.

[18] The message has got through, at least in theory, to many missiologists, as Geoffrey Allen, *The Theology of Missions* (London: SCM Press, 1943), long since illustrated in deploring "the convention" of calling "non-Christian areas heathen or pagan lands. . . . This language . . . is . . . deeply anachronistic, and false to the realities of the situation today" (p. 29).

[19] See the sharply critical review by L. Elbert Wethington, *The International Review of Missions*, XLVIII (1959), 469-72, of the revival by Edmund Perry of Hendrik Kraemer's older view, in *The Gospel in Dispute*.

[20] While not a native American, Colin Williams in *Where in the World?* and *What in the World?* forms a watershed in the criticism of obsolete evangelism in this country, for in them he goes far beyond a hand-wringing analysis of a depressing situation.

[21] See Alan Walker, *The Whole Gospel for the Whole World* (Nashville: Abingdon Press, 1957), for recognition of the Christian antidote, at once profoundly biblical and vitally relevant, to the now irrelevant evangelism inflicted upon us by nineteenth-century pietistic individualism. More explicitly theological treatments of the problem appear in Julian N. Hartt, *Toward a Theology of Evangelism* (Nashville: Abingdon Press, 1955); Douglas Webster, *What Is Evangelism?* (London: The Highway Press, 1959); Hans J. Margull, *Hope in Action; the Church's Task in the World*, trans. by Eugene Peters (Philadelphia: Muhlenberg Press, 1962).

[22] Wright, "The Old Testament Basis for the Christian Mission," p. 22.

Johannes Blauw, and F. N. Davey,[23] consistently follow a line of interpretation that would put them in this last category. Donald G. Miller makes a few slips in a compromising direction, but the bulk of his article is also marked by vivid reflection of the dynamic concerns peculiar to this method of interpretation.[24] That puts only Barth and Cullmann outside the pale,[25] yet numerous of their writings stamp them as frontline contributors in the movement to replace abstraction with action, concept with conduct, doctrine with decision, status with service, religion with faith.

Nowhere has this method been employed with greater consistency and impact than by certain leading European missiologists. This is apparent in the ecclesiology of such representative writers among them as Johannes Blauw, Georg F. Vicedom and Hans-Ruedi Weber.[26] *The Missionary Nature of the Church*, by Johannes Blauw, may be taken as an outstanding expression of this tendency.

The foundation and motivation for the mission of the church is, Blauw contends, the demolition by the Lord of all history and the God of all creation of every wall of partition in and through Jesus Christ. Thus understood, the mission of the church is both the product of the mission of God in Christ and the instrument for its realization.[27]

Blauw's work has the special merit of setting the history of Israel, old and new, within the parentheses of the divine

---

[23] *Ibid.*; Blauw, "The Biblical View of Man in His Religion," pp. 31-41; and Davey, "The Gospel According to St. John and the Christian Mission," pp. 85-93.

[24] Miller, "Pauline Motives for the Christian Mission," pp. 72-84.

[25] Blauw, *The Missionary Nature of the Church*, cites Barth, *Church Dogmatics*, IV/3, 874-75, where he delineates both the existence and task of the Christian in terms of witness, to refute Bishop Stephen Neill's statement: "As far as I know, no one has yet set to work to think out the theology of the Church in terms of that one thing for which it exists" (p. 169, n. 12). Also see Blauw, p. 158, n. 32.

[26] See Blauw; Vicedom, *The Mission of God*, and Weber, *The Militant Ministry*.

[27] *The Missionary Nature of the Church*, p. 105.

activity of the one God, rather than the other way around. Any belief in the possibility of being the church, as Israelites or Christians, without mission reflects a profound misunderstanding of the biblical notion of election. Election for service in behalf of the one God to all mankind, he concludes, has always been the constituting element for the people of God. [28]

This view carries with it the plain implication that, apart from the self-giving service of the sent in obedience to the Sender, neither Israel nor Christendom nor any other community can justifiably claim the title "people of God" for itself. Hand in hand with this notion goes the corollary idea that membership in this community may be a quite shifting matter. Old members, by refusing to heed the call of the Sender, may be dropped from that body; and former nonmembers, by heeding that call, may be added to that body.[29] Or to employ language suggested by Norman Gottwald's description of the relationship between God and the prophet,[30] we might say of the relationship between God and the church: The church remains a human community but is so caught up into the selfhood of Christ that neither God nor church can be known outside a marvelous unity in mission despite an abiding personal duality. J. C. Hoekendijk has written just the words with which to conclude this discussion of both the functional approach to the Scriptures and the dynamic view of the church which Blauw derives therefrom:

[28] *Ibid.*: "The Church which has been chosen out of the world has been chosen for this end—that she performs for the world the service of giving witness to the Kingdom of God which has come and is coming in Jesus Christ. . . . The triune God who is involved with the world in the *sending* of the prophets, of Jesus Christ, and of the Holy Spirit, also sends the apostles and the Church" (p. 120).

[29] *Ibid.*, Blauw puts it unequivocally: "One of the greatest and haughtiest heresies in the history of the Church is the identification of the institution with this community of the Kingdom" (p. 160, n. 52). Cf. the work of Nils A. Dahl, *Das Volk Gottes* . . . (Oslo: Bybwad, 1941).

[30] *All the Kingdoms of the Earth*, p. 36.

The church *stands* nowhere; she unfolds herself; she happens; she develops as the Gospel of the kingdom is delivered to the world. . . . Therefore the church has no designated place but is a temporary home, a settlement which never really becomes a home, headed outward toward the ends of the world and forward to the ends of time. . . . To bear testimony of the Kingdom to the world is her real work (*opus proprium*); but it is not really *her* work, but the work of the Lord. . . . To the extent that the church has part in this work—the apostolate—she is "the church." [31]

As a reminder of the work of the Lord and, by the same token, the mission of the church, but even more, as a means of facilitating the communion in which this work can be clarified and prosecuted; this is why, in the view of the exponents of the functional approach, the Bible ever came to be written. This is also why, they would likewise insist, it must never cease to be read.

A Comparison and a Choice

Despite virtually unanimous agreement as to the historical character of the Christian faith, the first three of the foregoing approaches to the Bible would hardly incline one to think of it in historical terms. Whether commandment, precedent, or form, all alike find in the Bible a historical guide unhistorically given, henceforth and evermore to be obeyed and treated as the norm of discipleship or mission. As a consequence, the words of Scripture, fundamentally unaltered and unalterable, supplant the Word of God, the threatening and surprising God who joins us to offer comfort when we need it and to stir up trouble when we least expect it. This view can hardly be expected to do justice to man in his twentieth-century setting. It does not even begin to do justice to man in his first-century setting.

Treatment of the Matthean version of the Great Com-

---

[31] Quoted by Vicedom, *The Mission of God*, p. 85.

mission—and the same goes for every other similar passage—as the basis for the mission of the church leaves many questions unanswered. Since Jesus issued this command to the eleven apostles, how can we be sure he intended that we should succeed them in the performance of this mission? How does one make a disciple—by getting him to follow Jesus or obey God? Does he mean that we are to make disciples of all nations or only of some people from all nations? And how shall they be baptized, by pouring, sprinkling, immersion? If by immersion, shall it be face forward or otherwise? Then, what about "the age"? Are we still in it, or did it come to an end, as Luther contended, with the proclamation of the gospel throughout the earth?

This approach to the Bible has yet to yield satisfactory answers to elementary historical questions about the mission of the ancient church. It can hardly be expected to yield adequate solutions to the pressing theological and practical problems concerning the mission of the modern church.

Search of the Bible for precedents leads one, inevitably, to the same sort of frustration. As evidence of this fact, let us consider two oft-asked questions these days: (1) Shall we carry the gospel to the Jews? (2) If other planets turn out to be inhabited, should we seek to evangelize them? The first of these questions takes us straight back to the "Jesus-or-Paul" controversy. At any rate, according to Romans 9–11, the *kairos* for the proclamation of the gospel to the Jews has not dawned.[32] Here to be told to walk in his steps is not enough. One must likewise be told to whom his steps belong, whether Jesus or Paul. The biblical precedents for dealing with our second question provide even less help. As a matter of fact, there are no such precedents. The Bible reports the orbital flights of two or three prophetic astronauts, but any report of their findings, if

---

[32] Taken pretty much at face value by Perry, *The Gospel in Dispute*, p. 221.

made, apparently was confined to members of the heavenly council.

These examples illustrate the futility of turning the Bible into a treasury of examples for contemporary man. It may be easy enough for modern man to understand how the telescoped eschatology of the New Testament drastically curtailed the interest of the early Christians in economic and political institutions. But he can neither understand nor make sense of the expression of a like disinterest in such matters by modern Christians who, paradoxically, insist on a "blood, sweat, and tears" incarnation and, further, have long since abandoned both all hope and all fear of Jesus' return on the clouds of heaven.

The pragmatic test of discipleship implicit in Jesus' words, "You will know them by their fruits," provides a criterion for challenging Barth's elevation of the sermon as the unassailable form of Christian witness par excellence. To contend that the sermon must play *the* crucial role in first-century Christian witness is tantamount to saying twentieth-century Christians must not ride in cars because first-century Christians rode on donkeys. The argument may not sound quite as crass as Billy Graham's magical formula, "The *Bible* says!" but it is no different in principle. If there is one belief to which the New Testament comes close to bearing unanimous witness, it is the divine impatience with all formal straitjackets. God is far more concerned with the reality and integrity of man's witness than he is with its pedigree or form. That awareness moved Jesus, despite a healthy respect for the traditions and forms of the scribes and Pharisees, to scuttle many of those traditions and to forge new forms on the anvil of his own communion with God. We might well ask ourselves whether allegiance to his spirit rather than the letter of the New Testament might not require us to deal similarly with some of our inherited traditions and forms. Might not the same kind of concern for Christian witness that prompted the early Christians to elevate the sermon to top place move us to relegate it to a less prominent position?

The application of Jesus' "fruits" test to the Negro struggle for civil rights hardly justifies the rejection of this possibility out of hand. Martin Luther King, in his 1963 letter from the Birmingham jail, confessed to being "greatly disappointed with the white church and its leadership." He had expected "that . . . white ministers, priests and rabbis . . . would be . . . our strongest allies." [33] Do you know why he was surprised? It was because he did not overhear the question we clergymen kept asking ourselves: "If laymen can listen to our sermons for decades without being changed for the better, why should anybody expect us to take them seriously?"

Before the March on Washington, the sum total of white Protestantism's contribution to the American struggle for civil rights, apart from a few "fools for Christ," consisted of a plethora of "brotherhood" sermons and a vacuum of brotherly deeds. Consequently, some Negro leaders began to call for an end to sermons on brotherhood until we could produce deeds to match. On August 28, 1963, in Washington, D. C., thousands of clergymen began to heed that challenge. That response may not have effected passage of the 1964 Civil Rights Bill but, according to Senator Richard Russell, it did a lot of harm in that direction. Who can forget the witness of the Reverend Bruce Klunder in Cleveland, Ohio? Or that of the Reverend James J. Reeb in Selma, Alabama? Of Mr. Reeb we would have to say, *it was his martyrdom, and not his sermon, that made him a witness.* By the same token, it was the *presence* of Bishop Lord in Selma and of Bishops Golden and Mathews in Jackson, Mississippi, *not their sermons,* that made them witnesses. Ironically, this witness in deed, far from being secondary to witness in

[33] Printed under the title, *Unwise and Untimely* (Nyack, New York: Fellowship of Reconciliation, 1963), pp. 13, 14.

word, may well become the means of restoring the sermon from its present low estate into a position of disturbing relevance and vital power.[34]

Unlike the authoritarian, exemplary, and formal approaches to the Scriptures, the functional approach takes the Bible seriously both as a theological and a historical document. Because it is a historical document, the Bible invites attention both to its points of departure from, and its lines of connection with, its environment. Because it is a theological document, bearing witness to the God who both transcends and invades every time and place, it demands criticism even of its own witness, because it is also historically conditioned, from the perspective of the faith in behalf of whose furtherance it bears that witness. Therefore, in search of biblical guidance in trying to define and implement our Christian mission, to begin with the commandments to engage in missionary activity, the careers and demands of missionaries in the apostolic age, or the correct forms of Christian witness, as these are set forth in the Bible, is to put the cart before the horse. Such questions as the attitude of Jesus toward missions, of Paul toward missions to the Jews, and of Stephen to the place of sermons in the spread of the gospel raise issues of great interest. But these attitudes derive from concern for the will and demand of God, and they are only present, in fact, because of the inescapable conviction that commitment to God compelled decisions in relation to the overriding needs and pressing situations of their day.[35] Their decisions, as they are concretized in the biblical documents, mark the coincidence of the pull of faith and the push of history.

Granted this setting for the Scriptures, we should be greatly surprised to find theological relevance apart from historical relativity; or to put it in terms of our own special

---

[34] So suggests Will D. Campbell, *Race and the Renewal of the Church* (Philadelphia: The Westminster Press, 1962), pp. 73-86.

[35] See Vincent, "Christ's Ministry and Our Discipleship," pp. 188-90.

interest, to read the biblical passages having to do with
missions without, at the same time, hearing a new and
surprising word from God concerning their proper interpretation and contemporary appropriation. Barth has put
it exactly, proving again that the great Swiss theologian is
his own best critic. "We are called," he says, "to hasten to
the place where the prophets and apostles are making
their stand. They are standing face to face with the coming
God. They call us to their own side; not for their own sake
but for the sake of God." [36] Standing there, on the boundary between faith and unbelief, confronted by the God to
whom they and we bear common witness, we can affirm
their relevance without denying their relativity; learn from
their words without equating it with *his* Word; appropriate
God's word to them without mistaking it for God's word
to us; and be faithful to our common mission without
seeking to duplicate the sphere or the form of their labors.

Rehabilitation and Innovation

Martin Buber has written the golden text for the prosecution of the task of seeking a biblical basis for mission in
line with the functional approach to the Scriptures: "Change
and preservation function in the identical current." [37] This
approach demands, as surely as Buber's words imply, both
a deep appreciation of the past and genuine openness to the
future. As evidence of the former, it shall be noted that,
far from compelling dismissal of the passages of Scripture
often employed in line with one of the other methods of
interpretation, it enables us to make sense of them without
turning them into fetishes or, worse, biblical props for
defense of a confined theology and a confining mission.
Then, in support of its demand for openness to the future,
a series of theses shall be suggested that will enable us to give

[36] *God in Action*, pp. 6-7.
[37] *Moses* (Oxford: The University Press, 1944), p. 18.

contemporary shape to our mission without betraying its true and abiding function.

In line with the current tendency to treat all the Evangelists, and not just the author of John, as independent theologians of a dynamic church, Johannes Blauw interprets the Matthean version of the Great Commission, like the universal passages toward the close of the other Gospels, as a creative response to the challenge posed by Paul's evangelization of the world. "Is it too far-fetched to assume," he asks, "that it is also because Paul's apostleship had brought the whole world within their horizon that the authors of the four Gospels (which were all written later than Paul's epistles!) had them culminate in the description of a task that encompasses the whole world? Have they not also come to a better understanding of the import of Jesus' words and work through the expansion of the Church over all of the world that lay within their horizon, the oecumene?" [38]

By allowing themselves to function, as Jesus did, in the service of the mission of God, is it not possible that they discovered in Jesus' formulation of that mission the need for correction and expansion? To reject this possibility out of hand, as an expression of blasphemy, would not only impose arbitrary limits to biblical criticism, but it would likewise betray a supernaturalistic view of the incarnation.

Blauw's devastation of Pauline dispensationalism, according to which the era of the mission to the Jews must await completion of the mission to the Gentiles, leaves Paul no less "the apostle" but something more of a man. He justifies Paul's action in view of the apostle's "Back-to-the-Bible-Hour" scheme of missions without, for one minute, viewing it as a suitable blueprint for contemporary missions. Paul errs here theologically, in Blauw's

[38] *The Missionary Nature of the Church*, p. 125.

view, by "accentuating the *chosenness* instead of the act of divine choosing (election), which election was *for service.*" [39] Psychologically, though, Paul may be excused for concentrating his evangelistic activities among the Gentiles because, Blauw speculates, this was the "only way to continue to do something with his days for an Israel which was for the most part callous." [40] Indeed, the New Testament itself would seem to me to be a source of hopeless embarrassment to the tendency to take Paul's chronology for missionary expansion at face value. Quite apart from the apparent failure of his message to get through to the author of Luke-Acts and Simon Peter, Paul, the convert from Judaism, stands as a monument to the failure of Paul as primitive Christianity's board of missions' schedule-maker.

This Blauwine interpretation of Romans 9–11 commends itself for two reasons. It exempts God of all responsibility for the arbitrary polarization of Jews and Gentiles in the formulation of the Pauline version of Christian mission. Even more important, it deprives us of all excuse for the perpetuation of this division.

A meticulous study of church order in primitive Christianity prompts Eduard Schweizer to relegate the sermon and, with it, all other forms of Christian witness, not just to a secondary, but a dispensable, place in the economy of God. He concedes that the message about Christ with which the church confronts the world is "urgent and final." But "the church that knows this," he hastens to add,

knows at the same time that in its religious phenomena, its ascetic achievement, and its . . . order it is in itself only part of the world, because only the miracle of God's grace, continually repeated in freedom for the sake of God's faithfulness, is its life. *This miracle, however, never becomes the church's own property*

[39] *Ibid.,* p. 167.
[40] *Ibid.,* p. 168.

by *allowing it* either to guarantee the miracle to anyone who complies with the church order or fulfills certain prescribed religious or moral requirements, or *to forget that God can completely bypass the church's organization in calling people to himself.*[41]

By indicating the way the functional approach to the Scriptures might deal with those passages traditionally employed in quest of the biblical basis for mission, I have tried to indicate the shape of our task, looking backward, for compliance with Lesslie Newbigin's demand for a full-orbed theocentric trinitarian basis for Christian missions.[42] I had hoped to be able, looking forward, to be even more explicit and exhaustive in suggesting the shape of things to come. Space precludes the realization of that hope; all that can be done here is to outline four propositions that will indicate the direction in which a program based on the foregoing approach would move.

1. *The God who came and comes, in creation, in Christ, in consummation, neither acknowledges nor wills any limitation to the free and sovereign reign of his reconciling love.* Space and time, far from incarcerating the purpose of God within limits imposed from the outside, are to be seen as channels for the communication of his love. Hence "all the nations" and "the ends of the earth," viewed from the perspective of "the ongoing work of Christ," are not to be regarded as marks of the last dispensation in the evolution of Christian missions. They are to be viewed, rather, as indicators of the absence of every sort of barrier and boundary, geographical or temporal, to the love and therefore the mission of God. They are, by the same token, to be viewed as indicators of the absence of every sort of barrier and

---

[41] *Church Order in the New Testament*, trans. by Frank Clarke (London: SCM Press, 1961), p. 226 (italics mine).

[42] See *Trinitarian Faith and Today's Mission.*

boundary, geographical or temporal, to the love and therefore the mission of the people of God. [43]

If here someone should object to this characterization by appeal to traces of henotheism in Israelite history, let it be admitted that such primitivism does occasionally rear its head in the Bible. But let us not forget this counterbalancing fact: even though certain Israelites may have been practicing henotheists, the Creator who revealed himself in the face of Jesus Christ was not and is not a henotheistic God. [44] And just as all life in every place and time derives its meaning from his purpose, even so must the church in every place and time cut the cloth of its mission on the pattern of his mission.

2. *Life in faith does not depend for its origin or validity on any formulation of the faith.* [45] One would certainly have to contend, on the basis of Christian history, that it is quite the reverse. Every formulation of *the* faith depends on life *in faith* alike for its origin and validity.[46]

Any serious appropriation of this insight, instead of taking the Bible out from under the umbrella of mythology, would establish it there all the more securely. For granted Bultmann's definition of mythology as the presentation of

[43] *Ibid.*: "We are invited to participate in an activity of God which is the central meaning of creation itself. We are invited to become, through the presence of the Holy Spirit, participants in the Son's loving obedience to the Father" (p. 78).

[44] Gerhard von Rad, *Old Testament Theology*, trans. by D.M.G. Stalker (Edinburgh: Oliver & Boyd, 1962), I, 136-65, interprets primeval history in Gen. 1–11 in terms of a cosmic covenant, i.e., with the nations, not Israel, as Yahweh's partner.

[45] Emil Brunner, *Truth as Encounter*, trans. by David Cairns and Amandus Loos (Philadelphia: The Westminster Press, 1964): "It . . . becomes unmistakably clear that what God wills to give us cannot really be given in words, but only in manifestation: Jesus Christ, God himself *in persona* is the real gift" (p. 132).

[46] Brunner, *ibid.*, pp. 196-97, praises Luther for recovering this insight; and he castigates Melanchthon who, in place of faith and obedience, substituted as the marks of the true church "objective criteria, ironclad . . . standards" (pp. 196-97).

the otherworldly in terms of the this-worldly,[47] what we need is not more "demythologizing" but more "remythologizing." Myth thus defined would comprehend not only virgin birth, transfiguration, resurrection, and the like, but all the persons of the Holy Trinity and much else besides— in fact, everything else purporting to describe the action of God in nature or history.

To suppose, therefore, that the future of vital faith hinges on the literal transmission of any theological term, be it the name of Christ or the language of the inherited creeds, would be to reduce Christian faith to a mythology. To suppose that we can say something of Christ that cannot be said, with equal accuracy, of the Lord of mankind, marks an expression, not of full-orbed trinitarianism, but of a unitarianism of the second person of the Trinity. And one might ask, must we not pass similar judgment on the denial of the possibility of salvation for those who, despite their ascription of all the grace of Christ to the Lord of mankind, and their manifestation of discipleship in a life of obedient service to their fellows, nevertheless have an aversion to the address of God under the name of Christ? Not only would I answer this question in the affirmative. I would likewise insist that biblical Christology itself, which is far from either adequately or accurately represented in the exclusive claim uttered in Acts 4:12 by a Pentecostal preacher, would pose no insuperable barrier to the assembly of fellow believers under the name of the Lord of mankind. For as Gregory Dix has well said:

When Christians took to calling Jesus Lord instead of Messiah, the Liberals, wrongly, supposed that they were "heightening the Christology." The point is that Jewish messianism does not yield a Christology of status in metaphysical terms—it yields a

---

[47] Schubert M. Ogden, *Christ Without Myth* (New York: Harper & Row, 1961), p. 24, expresses this polarity in terms of the "unworldly" and "worldly."

J

Christology of function in terms of history. But the function of the Messiah is undoubtedly a divine function, . . . namely his inauguration of God's Kingdom. The Messiah's action in history is God's own action.[48]

The God of our creation is identical with the God of our redemption. Therefore, if and when we identify believers in such a manner as to exclude from the people of God the Redeemer those who belong to the people of God the Creator, we challenge the Christology of the Gospels and the Christian doctrine of the Trinity at their most crucial point. All men share a common humanity, irrespective of whether they presently do, or ever shall, share in common "one faith" or "one baptism" (Eph. 4:5). And they just may share, a fact to which the Bible itself bears telling witness, a common life *in faith* without being able to subscribe to a common formulation of *the* faith.

3. *"Salvation" history differs from "secular" history, not because of preoccupation with a different set of facts, but by reason of its interpretation of a segment of those facts from the perspective of what Tillich calls the "depth" dimension.*[49] The fact that most of the slices of history have been reported as "secular" and not "salvation" history should not be taken as evidence of the absence of God's presence in any slice of history. It only proves, first of all, that the writing of history is the work of man and not God and, second, that God's appearance in human history, even in Jesus Christ, is always partially hidden. If this implies that the secular historian could turn salvation history into secular history, it likewise means that a "full-orbed theocentric, Trinitarian" theologian not only may—he would!—report secular history as salvation history.

---

[48] *Jew and Greek* (Philadelphia: Dacre Press, 1953), p. 79.
[49] Cf. Newbigin, "The Gathering Up of History into Christ," *The Missionary Church in East and West*, Charles C. West and David M. Paton, eds. (London: SCM Press, 1959), pp. 81-90.

4. God is related to all human culture as its ground and goal, its source and hope, its Lord and Judge, yet his reign must never be identified with any human culture. If this implies an end to all thought of an autonomous church or state or economic life, it likewise calls for the acknowledgment in church and state and economic life of the claim of a transcendent reality.[50]

This recognition of the ambiguous character of the divine presence in culture will save us from both the utopian demand for perfect security and the pietistic quest for perfect purity.[51] We will not claim for our culture what belongs to God alone. But on the other hand, we will not seek for our culture anything but what God alone can give. In other words, we will join the dialogue with God in the midst of culture, in pursuit of the hope of transforming it in the image of his will, yet all the while fully aware that he, and he alone, can embody what we seek to make.

Answers to many of the questions implicit in the topic of this chapter have yet to be suggested. But considering my purpose in the preparation of this paper, this should come as no surprise. For it was my goal, not to reduce perplexing problems to neat formulas, but to indicate a viable stance for further reflection on the crucial issues involved in the relationship between the aim of Christian mission and the Word of God.

[50] See Gottwald, "Prophetic Faith and Contemporary International Relations," *Biblical Realism Confronts the Nation*, pp. 72-74, for a penetrating illumination of this paradox.
[51] *Ibid.*, pp. 82-86.

Restating the Aim of Mission

S. Paul Schilling

The Methodist Church defines the aim of missions today in much the same terms as those used by one of its parent bodies in 1928. The present statement, adopted by the Uniting Conference in 1939 and reaffirmed by each succeeding General Conference, is as follows:

The supreme aim of missions is to make the Lord Jesus Christ known to all peoples in all lands as their divine Savior, to persuade them to become his disciples, and to gather these disciples into Christian churches; to enlist them in the building of the kingdom of God; to co-operate with these churches; to promote world Christian fellowship; and to bring to bear on all human life the spirit and principles of Christ. [1]

Actually, this definition represents only a limited revision of the statement of the aim of foreign missions adopted by the Methodist Episcopal General Conference of 1928, and reiterated in 1932 and 1936:

The supreme and controlling aim of Foreign Missions is to make the Lord Jesus Christ known to all men as their Divine

[1] *Doctrines and Discipline of The Methodist Church*, 1964, par. 1176; 1939, par. 931.

Saviour, to persuade them to become his disciples, and to gather these disciples into Christian Churches which shall be, under God, self-propagating, self-supporting, and self-governing; to co-operate so long as necessary with these Churches in the evangelizing of their respective countries, and to bring to bear on all human life the spirit and principles of Christ. [2]

The deletion in 1939 of both the adjective *foreign* and the reference to the countries where new churches are founded was of course necessitated by the fact that the united Methodist Church combined home and foreign missions under one Board of Missions and Church Extension, and the aim needed to be stated broadly enough to embrace all aspects of its work. It would be interesting to investigate the reasons for the other changes made by the Uniting Conference: the elimination of the specific assignment of autonomous responsibility to churches resulting from missionary work; the addition of enlistment in the building of the kingdom; and the inclusion of the promotion of universal Christian fellowship. However, such an inquiry would be outside the scope of the present chapter. But the interested and concerned Methodist can hardly avoid wondering over his church's continued willingness to accept a definition which has remained unchanged since 1939, and in large measure since 1928.

This circumstance may be due to indifference toward formal statements of purpose, to traditional Methodist pragmatism, to unawareness of theological developments, or to a combination of these or other factors. Whatever the cause, the effectiveness of the church's missionary labors is bound to be handicapped if they are carried on without relation

[2] *Doctrines and Discipline of the Methodist Episcopal Church*, 1928, par. 458. The M. E. Church adopted no statement of the aim of missions prior to 1928. The M. E. Church, South, which held its last General Conference in 1938, did not define the aim of its missionary endeavor.

to aims which are biblically and theologically grounded and realistically related to the world of today. During the past four decades new movements have profoundly altered the theological situation, and the world in which the gospel must be proclaimed has undergone radical change. Hence a statement adopted twenty-six years ago and substantially formulated eleven years earlier can hardly be regarded by a living church as an adequate definition of its missionary purpose.

If The Methodist Church is to be a good steward in recruiting, training, and guiding missionaries for service in today's world, it must carefully reexamine the objectives of the mission to which it is called. This chapter undertakes such a reexamination, in a preliminary way, in four stages: (1) a critique of the present formulation; (2) an inquiry into new cultural developments and current theological emphases which might serve as guidelines for a reformulation; (3) suggestions concerning specific biblical and theological affirmations needed in a new definition; and (4) a statement of aims designed to embody these suggestions.

The Present Statement

Our first task is to weigh the adequacy of the present statement of purpose, not for the newly united Methodist Church of 1939, but for today's church in today's world. In this process it may be helpful to see both the statement and our current situation in the light of the chief understandings of the missionary task held by the first Christian community. Seven New Testament passages are particularly relevant, though representative of many others:

The Great Commission (Matt. 28:19-20): "Go therefore and make disciples of all nations, baptizing them in the name of the Father and of the Son and of the Holy Spirit, teaching them to observe all that I have commanded you; and lo, I am with you always, to the close of the age."

The Lucan form of the commission (Acts 1:8): "You shall receive power when the Holy Spirit has come upon you; and you shall be my witnesses in Jerusalem and in all Judea and Samaria and to the end of the earth."

The Johannine commissions: "Peace be with you. As the Father has sent me, even so I send you. . . . Receive the Holy Spirit" (John 20:21-22). "Do you love me? . . . Feed my sheep" (John 21:17).

The eschatological interpretation of the gospel and the kingdom represented by Matt. 24:14: "This gospel of the kingdom will be preached throughout the whole world, as a testimony to all nations; and then the end will come."

The Pauline stress on the ministry of reconciliation: "If any one is in Christ, he is a new creation; the old has passed away, behold, the new has come. All this is from God, who through Christ reconciled us to himself and gave us the ministry of reconciliation; that is, God was in Christ reconciling the world to himself, not counting their trespasses against them, and entrusting to us the message of reconciliation. So we are ambassadors for Christ, God making his appeal through us" (II Cor. 5:17-20).

The conception of the church and its mission in I Pet. 2:9: "You are a chosen race, a royal priesthood, a holy nation, God's own people, that you may declare the wonderful deeds of him who called you out of darkness into his marvelous light."

In important respects the definition of 1939 is clearly in accord with such New Testament conceptions as those cited. (1) It affirms the responsibility of the church to bear witness to Jesus Christ in the entire world. (2) It accepts the goal of winning committed disciples. (3) It recognizes the importance of gathering converts into communities of baptized Christians. (4) It asserts the authority of the teachings of Jesus for the lives of his followers. (5) It reflects concern for the realization of Christian fellowship transcending national and denominational boundaries. (6) It assumes the obligation of every Christian to be an instrument in the coming of the kingdom of God.

However, several features of the declaration, especially certain omissions, make it less than adequate as a formulation of the aim of missionary endeavor for the church today.

Its focus on the plural term *missions* antedates the recognition, recently gained, that specific missionary activities are expressions of one underlying responsibility which permeates the entire life and work of the church. As the recipient of God's gift of himself in Jesus Christ, the church is called or sent to share with all men what it has received. By its very origin and nature the church *is* mission. If we focus attention on the sending, the fact of our being sent, our "sentness" or "commissionedness," we are more likely to keep central our relation to him who sends us, and thus to reach a deeper level of understanding and life. In dealing with basic aims it is therefore sounder to speak of the church's mission as a whole than of its manifold missions.

The definition manifests no clear awareness of the oneness or the wholeness of the church. Drafted before the searching biblical and theological studies of the nature and mission of the church carried out during the past twenty-five years, it envisages gathering new disciples into churches, not into the total Church of Jesus Christ. Moreover, these churches are conceived as sufficiently separate from the sending body that the latter is portrayed as cooperating with them, not as being one with them. The formulation lacks the New Testament conception of the total *ekklesia*, the organic wholeness of the body of Christ, the interdependent identity of the one people of God.

It overestimates the role of man in the coming of the kingdom of God. Though it properly recognizes the need for man's trustful and obedient acceptance of God's rule and his active commitment to the divine will, it does not make sufficiently plain that the kingdom is ultimately a divine gift, depending primarily on the initiative and activity of God. Man's part is actually more like the cultivation of a vineyard than the construction of a building. It is still more appropriately portrayed by Jesus' parable of the sower; men sow the seed and fertilize the soil but God brings his kingdom.

In general, the statement does not emphasize sufficiently the constant dependence of the missionary church on the redemptive, life-giving, transforming activity of God. The mission is first of all his; it is the work of One who acts through men of faith to reconcile the world to himself. The aim of the Great Commission of Matthew, as suggested by its baptismal formula, is that of bringing men into a living relation to the triune God. Similarly, Acts 1:8 roots the witness of the church in the empowerment of the Holy Spirit. The church's mission is of course directed to men in need of salvation, but it originates in, and at every point depends on, the saving action of God.

Lacking in the declaration is any recognition of the eschatological dimension of the Christian mission. It is emphatically and rightly concerned with the fulfillment of the will of God in man's earthly life, but it fails to place this endeavor in the eternal perspective in which it is seen by Christian faith. We need not share the apparent belief of much of the primitive church in the imminent visible return of Christ in order to perceive the profound truth in the New Testament writers' confident expectation of the final consummation of God's rule and the ultimate triumph of his purpose. The gospel proclaimed by the earliest Christian evangelists linked inseparably the action of God in creation, new creation, and final fulfillment. The church's ministry to today's world, threatened as it is by well-nigh total physical destruction, will be sadly incomplete if it omits reference to the accomplishment of God's ends in his everlasting kingdom.

Guidelines for a New Statement

As The Methodist Church or its Board of Missions undertakes to rethink the aim of mission, it should fulfill at least three conditions: (1) It should think in completely ecumenical terms; (2) it must proceed in clear awareness of the present social and cultural situation; and (3) it must take fully into account the contributions made to the understanding of the gospel by recent biblical and theological investigations. The first of these requirements is here taken for granted without discussion, since it should by now be self-evident that the goals of the Christian mission far transcend the interests of The Methodist Church or any particular communion. The other two conditions may be briefly examined.

A Revolutionary World

The Christian mission will fail unless it confronts unflinchingly the revolutionary nature of contemporary society. We live not only in a period of unparalleled and breathtaking scientific development, but also in an era of unprecedented, rapid social change; as hundreds of millions of people, seeking economic, political, intellectual, and personal freedom and dignity are casting off old systems and customs and seeking new ways which promise greater opportunity.

On the one hand, this situation poses grave problems for the church, which has often been woefully handicapped by misunderstanding of the true meaning of the events churning around it, identification with an unjust *status quo*, indifference to the rightful aspirations of underprivileged people, or preoccupation with a dominantly other-worldly conception of the gospel. In any event, the church today faces a cultural environment which, to a startling degree, regards it and its message with indifference, unbelief, or hostility. Much of the world is simply not listening to what the church says or observing with any real interest or approval what it does. Materialistic humanism is in the saddle in both East and West, with Christian standards openly opposed in one case and verbally honored, while subtly rejected or ignored, in the other.

On the other hand, a church true to the good news committed to it is singularly equipped for speaking effectively to our kind of world. As Latourette and Hogg have pointed out, the gospel itself is "revolutionary, and in a more thoroughgoing and constructive sense than is any competitor." [8] It tells of a God who in the Word made flesh has identified himself with the entire range of man's earthly existence. It not only addresses itself to the social ills from which men suffer, but deals radically with the self-centeredness, the lovelessness, the guilt, and the anxiety which lie at the root of social injustice. It calls for drastic change in men's outward circumstances, but offers a still deeper transformation of persons themselves through the forgiving love and renewing power of God. The church must regain an awareness of the radical nature of its own gospel as both gift and demand. Simultaneously, it must be informed and completely realistic regarding the society in which God is already redemptively at work, and to which it is called to minister in his name.

Relevant Theological Emphases

Contemporary Protestant theology exhibits wide diversity and many differing interpretations. Issues occasioning sharp disagreement include such questions as whether priority belongs to the objective givenness of the revelation of God or to man's understanding of existence; the role of reason

[8] Kenneth Scott Latourette and William Richey Hogg, *Tomorrow Is Here* (New York: Friendship Press, 1948), p. 83.

in revelation; the relation of faith and history, especially that between the Christ of faith and the historical Jesus; the problem of hermeneutical method; the relation between law and gospel; the nature and extent of Christian ethical and social responsibility; and the meaning of eschatological existence. Nevertheless, readily discernible are many broad areas of agreement, some of which are directly relevant to the nature and purpose of Christian missionary endeavor. Some major aspects of this consensus may now be indicated.

1. The definitive basis of man's knowledge of God and salvation is God's self-revelation recorded in, and mediated by, the Scriptures. The biblical writings are therefore authoritative in matters of faith. Basically, however, revelation consists in the acts of God by which he discloses himself to men for the purpose of reconciling them to himself. It involves primarily divine-human encounter, not the impartation of eternal truths or propositions.

2. Revelation culminates in the events centering in the coming of Jesus Christ and the continuing witness of the Holy Spirit to his saving power. Therefore, Jesus Christ is central for both Christian faith and Christian theology. The church is commissioned to proclaim his lordship over all of life—a lordship which was demonstrated in his resurrection and will be consummated in his final victory.

3. The depth of man's sinfulness and alienation from God is seen today much more realistically than in the first decades of the twentieth century, though this insight is now balanced by stress on the positive possibilities opened to man by divine grace. Created by God for sonship, man has rebelled, trusting himself instead of God; yet he is "destined for Christ" (Wingren) and enabled through God's reconciling action to become a new creation. Karl Barth still asserts the radical corruption of man, but insists that in the light of the incarnation even sinful man is the being whom

God wills to be his covenant partner; the essential truth about the nature of man is found in Jesus Christ.

4. Salvation is accomplished by divine grace appropriated through faith, not by human works, whether legal, ceremonial, or ethical. Barthians and confessional Lutherans emphasize the sovereignty of the God whose grace calls forth faith. Though Christian existentialists like Bultmann say little of grace *per se*, they stress the absence of all guarantees in saving faith and man's complete dependence for redemption on the God who is not at his disposal and whose favor he cannot deserve or earn. Roman Catholics like Karl Rahner and Yves Congar agree that ultimately man depends utterly on God for salvation. "The grace of God is everything" (Rahner).

5. Some of the main emphases of Protestant existentialists find wide acceptance today. Most theologians include in the province of theology consideration of the objective nature and activity of God himself and the enduring reality of human nature, and are unwilling to limit theological concern to the existential relation of man and God and the faith-events which lead to authentic human existence. However, there is widespread agreement that our fullest knowledge of God is related to the salvation-event in man, that newness of life must be personally or existentially experienced, and that genuine faith comes to focus in the concrete decisions and committed actions of the whole person.

6. The gospel which theology seeks to interpret is kerygmatic in nature; it is proclamation, preaching, or witness addressed to men for the purpose of calling forth their response. This makes it imperative that careful attention be given to problems of communicating the good news, hence to the hermeneutical question. Which method should we employ in interpreting the biblical texts which make known the Word of God to men? What principles should guide our

251

exposition? On what basis may we best understand and communicate to others the biblical message which we are commissioned to proclaim? What language shall we employ? Questions like these elicit sharply divergent answers, but they are being seriously asked by most theologians today, concerned to reach persons where they actually are and lead them to understanding and commitment.

7. Essential to both the propagation of the gospel and growth in the Christian life is the faithful community, the church. At the very time when the institutionalism of the church is being most incisively criticized, the divine foundation and the human necessity of the redemptive community is most emphatically asserted. Widely different views are held regarding the precise nature of the church and its ministry and sacraments, but Protestants, Catholics, and Orthodox agree in affirming its indispensability as the distinctive instrument of God's reconciling activity among men. It is the worshiping, witnessing, teaching, serving fellowship of those who have responded affirmatively to God's redemptive love disclosed in Jesus Christ, and who, in the power of his Holy Spirit, are called to manifest that love and actualize his kingdom.

8. Truly Christian faith involves responsible participation in the life of society and identification with men as they confront the problems of daily existence. In the light of the incarnation, for example, Barth sees humanity as basically fellow-humanity, and calls on Christians to recognize their solidarity with all men. His view is representative of an almost universal assertion by theologians today of the ethical and social responsibility of individual Christians and the church. On all sides are heard pleas for a faith that is relevant to concrete human need, for "worldly Christianity," and for the "secularization" of the gospel. Those who worship the God who in redemptive love has taken on himself the sin, suffering, and hurt of the world are driven to similar

involvement. According to Nikos Nissiotis, eucharistic worship by its very nature thrusts believers out into the world in witness and service; *diakonia* is "the Eucharist *incognito*." This recognition of the secular significance of Christian faith is closely related to a new emphasis on the distinctive ministry or apostolate of the laity, who are the church in the world.

9. Christian theology today is emphatic in declaring the uniqueness of the Christ-event and the salvation which it makes possible. What God has done in Jesus Christ to heal the broken relation between himself and men he has done nowhere else before or since. All men are therefore summoned to accept in trust and obedience the gifts of forgiveness, reconciliation, and renewal of life made available through Jesus Christ. Although sharing this fundamental conviction, theologians take different positions with regard to non-Christian religions. These range all the way from the assertion of a sharp disjunction between religion and faith to the recognition of genuinely Christian elements in the commitment of non-Christians, including even atheists, to causes like justice, truth, brotherhood, and peace which assume absolute value and involve ends which are in fact supernatural. Yet there is widespread recognition, explicit or implicit, that the Holy Spirit is actively seeking to bring all men to his light and truth, and that he is present in their highest strivings whether they are aware of him or not. Methodists will note here a view closely akin to Wesley's doctrine of prevenient grace.

10. Present-day theology is marked by an increasing recognition that the life of the Christian and the church, indeed that of the world as a whole, must be seen in eschatological perspective. Aside from the belief of extreme conservatives in the visible, tangible second coming of Christ, two main views are held. Many theologians interpret the New Testament promise of the return of Christ to mean the event

which will bring the entire temporal process to its ultimate goal, the final consummation of God's purpose to redeem his creation. In contrast, Christian existentialists interpret the end not chronologically, as the terminus of historical time, but qualitatively, as the end of the worldliness of man. The eschatological event is the end of the old world of the individual believer and his entrance into a new and transformed life, in which concern for self and security is replaced by faith working through love. Obviously this second interpretation may be held also by those who take the first position, although the first is rejected by those who hold the second. However, both stress the eschatological dimension of faith as they interpret it, and both see the church as an eschatological community commissioned to call men to repentance and a new existence which faces God's future in faith.

A New Look at the Aims of Mission

The New Testament passages cited above and the theological emphases just summarized, seen in relation to the revolutionary nature of our world, may provide the basis needed for a statement of the aims of mission appropriate to The Methodist Church today. If we reexamine these materials with particular reference to the purpose of Christian missionary endeavor, we find in them the following directives.

In the New Testament passages the followers of Christ are:

1) sent to carry forward among men the ministry of suffering love committed to the crucified and risen Lord himself;

2) commissioned to bear witness to Jesus Christ in places near and far throughout the world;

3) sent forth to win disciples in all nations and to baptize them in the name of the triune God;

4) chosen as the new people of God, and in this capacity called to proclaim his redemptive acts and carry on in his behalf the ministry or ambassadorship of reconciliation;

5) charged with instructing new disciples to observe the teachings of Jesus;

6) counseled to preach the good news of God's kingdom in the expectation that the end of history will disclose the victory of God in judgment and glory; and

7) assured that in all their efforts they will be empowered by the Holy Spirit.

Implicit or explicit in the major emphases of contemporary theology are the following convictions concerning the aims of Christian mission. The church is:

1) responsible for interpreting and communicating the gospel in terms understandable and relevant to men faced by the agonizing problems of life in today's world;

2) called to witness to men everywhere the unique acts by which God in Jesus Christ has revealed himself, as recorded in the Scriptures, in suffering love to sinful men in order to restore their broken relationship with him and each other;

3) commissioned to call on men to accept, in the personal decision of faith, God's gracious gift of forgiveness and newness of life in sonship to him;

4) responsible for leading those who respond affirmatively to full involvement in the worship, witness, and service of the redemptive community which is the body of Christ, and to a ministry of ethical and social responsibility in the world; and

5) charged to live, and to call others to live, in the acknowledgment of the lordship of Christ and in confident expectation of the ultimate fulfillment of God's purpose in his eternal kingdom.

A Suggested Statement

Since contemporary theologians endeavor to interpret the biblical message in relation to the world of today, the extent of the similarity in the two summaries is no occasion for surprise. By synthesizing them, eliminating repetitions, and preserving the distinctive emphases of each, we should be able to draft a statement of aims which is faithful to both the New Testament witness and the insights of present-day Christian thought. The following statement attempts such a synthesis.

The aims of Christian mission are:

1) to witness in all the world, by word and deed, to the unique self-revelation of God in Jesus Christ and to the acts of self-sacrificial love by which he reconciles sinful men to himself;

2) to call men to the personal response of repentance and faith through which, by God's grace, they may find newness of life in righteous, loving relationships with God and their fellow men of all nations and races.

3) to summon men to active participation in the worship, fellowship, and witness of God's servant-community and its reconciling, life-transforming ministry in the world; and

4) to invite men to live in awareness of the presence and life-giving power of God's Holy Spirit, in acknowledgment of his rule over earthly history, and in confident expectation of the ultimate consummation of his purpose.

The conception of the aims of mission here outlined assumes that it is primarily God who calls, summons, and invites, and that it is ultimately he who moves men to respond. At the same time it recognizes that he has entrusted to the church responsibility for proclaiming and living his gospel and preparing men to receive it. As John Wesley declared, "Though it is God only changes hearts, yet He generally doeth it by man." [4] In God's mission we do not presume to do what he alone can do; rather we accept the role he has assigned to us—that of sharing with other men the unsearchable riches of Christ. Paul plants, and Apollos waters, but God gives the growth. Yet Paul and Apollos are "fellow workmen for God," obedient servants of his redemptive purpose. To such responsible servanthood the church is summoned today.

[4] *Wesley's Standard Sermons,* ed. Edward H. Sugden (London: Epworth Press, [1921] 1951), I, 395.

Appendix I

These statistics are taken, with permission, from *Britannica Book of the Year, 1966*. They have been compiled annually since 1951 for *Britannica* by Dr. Charles S. Braden, Professor Emeritus of History and Literature of Religions, Northwestern University, Evanston, Illinois. This same scholar, writing on "The Christian Encounter with World Religions" in *A Journal of Church and State*, Vol. VII, No. 3 (Autumn, 1965), says: "On the basis of the best available statistics, which it must be admitted are little more than educated guesses, here is the picture as it appears now. In India, one of the most intensively cultivated mission fields, there was between 1951 and 1961 a gain of but .01 of one percent in the total Christian population over India's total population growth. In North America and Europe, the major bases of Christian missions to other lands, the percentage of growth of the Christian population over the last decade was 10.87 and 7.4 respectively. But in South America, nominally Christian, the percentage gain in the decade was from 96.21 to 96.61, or but four-tenths of one percent. Thus far, at least, there was a gain. But in Africa, a much cultivated mission field, the percentage of Christians in relation to the total population dropped from 16.8 to 14.6 or a loss of more than two percent. Asia and Australasia combined showed a loss of .41 of one percent. Taking the whole world together, there was a gain on the percentage of Christians in relation to the whole population of .05 of one percent between 1950 and 1960, a wholly negligible gain. Granted that the figures may not be one hundred percent accurate either as to the world or Christian population, it surely points up the importance of the question as to what is to happen to those who have no opportunity even to hear of Christ if there is literally no salvation in any other name" (p. 392).

Estimated Membership of the Principal Religions of the World, 1965

Total world population 3,244,261,000

Total Christian 961,112,000
  Roman Catholic 590,040,000
  Eastern Orthodox 143,402,000
  Protestant[1] 277,670,000

Jewish 13,240,000
Muslim 465,237,000
Zoroastrian 150,000
Shinto 67,762,000
Taoist 52,331,000
Confucian 357,855,000
Buddhist 165,094,000
Hindu 408,679,000
Others, including
  primitive or none 752,801,000

Grand total 3,244,261,000

[1] Since many of the larger Protestant denominations report only "full members" and do not include all baptized persons, as do the Catholic churches, their statistics are not strictly comparable.

Appendix II

Some Statistics on Protestant and Roman Catholic Missionary Personnel [1]

Total Protestant missionaries throughout
the world, sent to lands other
than their own (1963) 42,952

Total Roman Catholic missionaries throughout
the world, sent to lands other than their
own (1966 estimate) 60,000

Total Protestant and Roman Catholic missionaries
throughout the world (approximate) 102,952

Total Protestant missionaries sent from the
U.S.A. and Canada (1960) 27,219

Total Roman Catholic missionaries sent
from the U.S.A. (1966) 9,290

---

[1] This information has been gathered and adapted by the editor from the following sources: *U.S. Catholic Missionary Personnel Overseas 1966* (Washington, D.C.: Mission Secretariat, 1966); Frank W. Price and Clara E. Orr, "North American Protestant Foreign Missions in 1960," *Occasional Bulletin* from the Missionary Research Library, XI, 9 (1960); Harold Lindsell, "Faith Missions Since 1938," in *Frontiers of the Christian World Mission*

In 1911 only one third of the 21,000 Protestant foreign missionaries scattered around the world came from North America. By 1925 there were over 29,000 Protestant missionaries, and approximately half of them came from North America. Of the 42,250 Protestant missionaries in 1960, nearly 65 percent came from North America. Thus in fifty years the North American percentage of the total Protestant missionary task force was reversed. Whereas in 1911 about two thirds of the Protestant foreign missionaries came from outside North America, in 1960 it was the other way around.

A breakdown of the affiliation of North American Protestant missionaries shows that:

37 percent are sent out by mission boards and agencies related to the Division of Overseas Ministries of the National Council of Churches;

44 percent are sent out by mission boards and agencies related to the three conservative evangelical associations (21 percent by the Evangelical Foreign Missions Association; 19.5 percent by the Interdenominational Foreign Mission Association; and 3.5 percent by the Associated Missions of the American Council of Christian Churches);

19 percent are sent out by unaffiliated and independent boards and agencies.

It is estimated that approximately one third of the North American Protestant missionaries today come from so-called faith mission sources.

Since 1938, ed. by Wilber C. Harr (New York: Harper & Brothers, 1962), pp. 189-230; Harold Lindsell, "An Appraisal of Agencies Not Co-operating With the International Missionary Council Grouping," *International Review of Missions*, XLVII (1958), 202; *Christianity Today*, January 29, 1965, and April 29, 1966; *Map of the World's Religions and Missions*, ed. by Martin Schlunk and Horst Quiring (4th ed.; Stuttgart: Evang. Missionsverlag, 1966).

Bibliography

Compiled and Annotated by Gerald H. Anderson

Bibliographies

Anderson, Gerald H. *Bibliography of the Theology of Missions in the Twentieth Century.* 3rd ed. revised and enlarged. New York: Missionary Research Library, 1966.

A classified bibliography, with annotations, of 1,500 references in four sections: (1) biblical studies, (2) historical studies, (3) Christianity and other faiths, (4) theory of missions. Three indexes.

Jackson, Herbert C., ed. *A Select Bibliography on Judaism, Jewish-Christian Relations, and the Christian Mission to the Jew.* New York: Missionary Research Library, 1966.

More than 1,500 references, arranged by title in the following categories: (1) biblical studies related to an understanding of and work among the Jews, (2) history of the Jews, (3) contemporary Judaism and Jewish social and cultural life, (4) Jewish-Christian relations, (5) miscellaneous. Author index.

Maps

C.S.M.C. World Mission Map, 1966. Harold J. Spaeth, ed. Cincinnati: Catholic Students' Mission Crusade, 1966.
>A wall map, published annually, with the latest available statistics on the Catholic population in all areas of the world.

Map of the World's Religions and Missions. Martin Schlunk and Horst Quiring, eds. 4th ed. Stuttgart: Evang. Missionsverlag, 1966.
>A colored wall map, giving statistics and showing the location of Christian missionary work and the major world religions.

Books and Articles

Althouse, LaVonne, *When Jew and Christian Meet.* With an Afterword by Rabbi Balfour Brickner and Dr. David R. Hunter. New York: Friendship Press, 1966.
>An introductory study, especially useful for youth and young adults, which includes rules and guides for setting up a dialogue.

Andersen, Wilhelm. *Towards a Theology of Mission: A Study of the Encounter Between the Missionary Enterprise and the Church and Its Theology.* (IMC Research Pamphlets, No. 2.) London: SCM Press, 1955.
>The most important single item one could read for a succinct survey of developments from Edinburgh, 1910, through Willingen, 1952, emphasizing a trinitarian-centered approach and suggesting further possible lines of development.

Anderson, Gerald H., ed. *The Theology of the Christian Mission.* New York: McGraw-Hill Book Company, 1961.
>The views of twenty-five scholars from America, Europe, Asia, and Africa; representing diverse theological viewpoints. Includes 21 pages of annotated bibliography.

————, ed. *Sermons to Men of Other Faiths and Traditions.* Nashville: Abingdon Press, 1966.
>Sermons from D. T. Niles, Walter G. Muelder, Franklin

H. Littell, Martin Marty, Kenneth Cragg, David G. Moses, and others, to the Buddhist, the Muslim, the Secularist, the Hindu, the Shintoist, the Jew, etc.

Bates, M. Searle and Pauck, Wilhelm, eds. *The Prospects of Christianity Throughout the World.* New York: Charles Scribner's Sons, 1964.
Excellent for a concise, critical, and authoritative non-Roman Catholic survey of the state of Christianity around the world.

Beaver, R. Pierce. *From Missions to Mission: Protestant World Mission Today and Tomorrow.* New York: Association Press, 1964.
Concise and reliable introduction to recent developments and new patterns.

Blauw, Johannes. *The Missionary Nature of the Church. A Survey of the Biblical Theology of Mission.* New York: McGraw-Hill Book Company, 1962.
This study, commissioned by the WCC, sets forth the results of the most important theological research of the last thirty years concerning the basis and purpose, the place and meaning of missions, from a biblical perspective.

Bockmühl, Klaus. *Die neuere Missionstheologie. Eine Erinnerung an die Aufgabe der Kirche.* (Arbeiten zur Theologie, I. Reihe, Heft 16.) Stuttgart: Calwer Verlag, 1964.
A study of developments in Continental mission theology.

Bouquet, A. C. *The Christian Faith and Non-Christian Religions.* New York: Harper & Brothers, 1958.
By an Anglican scholar who has a preference for the larger view of revelation "supported by Söderblom and William Temple, as against the opinions of Witte and Kraemer" (p. 425).

Bridston, Keith R. *Mission Myth and Reality.* New York: Friendship Press, 1965.
A very penetrating and provocative study; the myths discussed are classified as geographical, cultural, ecclesiological, and vocational.

Campbell, Robert E., ed. *The Church in Mission*. Maryknoll, N.Y.: Maryknoll Publications, 1965.
Eleven essays by representative Catholic scholars on major themes of mission theology.

Carpenter, George W. *Encounter of the Faiths*. New York: Friendship Press, 1967.
The Christian attitude and approach to men of other faiths.

The Christian Mission Today, ed. by the Joint Section of Education and Cultivation of the Board of Missions of The Methodist Church. Nashville: Abingdon Press, 1960.
Essays by twenty-one leaders who consider: (1) motives for the Christian mission, (2) the church in America, (3) Methodism and the mission overseas, (4) the mission faces a world of change, (5) the task of minister and people.

The Church and Society, 4 vols. Prepared for the World Conference on the Church in the Modern World, held in Geneva, 1966. New York: Association Press, 1966.
Christian Social Ethics in a Changing World. John C. Bennett, ed.
Responsible Government in a Revolutionary Age. Z. K. Matthews, ed.
Economic Growth in World Perspective. Denys Munby, ed.
Man in Community. Egbert de Vries, ed.

Cooke, Gerald. *As Christians Face Rival Religions. An Interreligious Strategy for Community Without Compromise*. New York: Association Press, 1962.
The author seeks a creative and constructive solution to the problems of rival claims among the world's religions.

Danielou, Jean. *The Advent of Salvation*. Trans. Rosemary Sheed. New York: Paulist Press, 1962.
One Protestant scholar has said that "no present-day writer should essay to write on the theology of missions without first making a careful study of this book" by the noted French Roman Catholic theologian.

Dewick, E. C. *The Christian Attitude to Other Religions.* New York: Cambridge University Press, 1953.
The best presentation of the case for "continuity."

The Documents of Vatican II. Walter M. Abbott, S.J., ed. New York: Guild Press–America Press–Association Press, 1966.
All sixteen Vatican II Documents in English, together with introduction and commentaries by noted Roman Catholic bishops and council experts and essays by Protestant and Orthodox clergy and scholars.

Dodge, Ralph E. *The Unpopular Missionary.* Westwood, N. J.: Fleming H. Revell Company, 1964.
An American Methodist bishop in Africa, with long missionary experience, writes perceptively concerning the challenge of the new situation in Africa.

Eckardt, A. Roy. *Christianity and the Children of Israel.* New York: King's Crown Press, 1948.
A scholarly survey of the Christian relationship to the children of Israel and a suggested theological basis for a Christian approach to the Jewish people. Extensive bibliographical references.

Ferré, Nels F. S. *The Finality of Faith, and Christianity Among the World Religions.* New York: Harper & Row, 1963.
This noted American theologian says, "Jesus is not unique but final, because he is the universal relation between God and man."

Fife, Eric S., and Glasser, Arthur F. *Missions in Crisis: Rethinking Missionary Strategy.* Chicago: Inter-Varsity Press, 1961.
Conservative evangelical rethinking.

Gensichen, Hans-Werner. *Living Mission: The Test of Faith.* Philadelphia: Fortress Press, 1966.
In five brief chapters treating the crisis in missions, the basis, aim, and work of the mission enterprise, the author, who is professor of missions at the University of Heidelberg, develops the thesis that there must be a dynamic relationship between theology and missiology.

Gilkey, Langdon. *How the Church Can Minister to the World Without Losing Itself.* New York: Harper & Row, 1964.
A professor of theology at the University of Chicago asking, "How is the actual life of our churches related to the culture in which we live?"

Goodall, Norman. *Christian Missions and Social Ferment.* (The Beckly Social Service Lecture, 1964.) London: Epworth Press, 1964.
Relates the work of the missionary movement to the social implications of the gospel.

Hahn, Ferdinand. *Mission in the New Testament.* (Studies in Biblical Theology, No. 47.) London: SCM Press, 1965.
The most comprehensive study of its kind in recent years; well documented.

Hedenquist, Göte, ed. *The Church and the Jewish People.* London: Edinburgh House Press, 1954.
Essays by Christians and Jews, prepared under the auspices of the IMC to impress upon Christians their continuing responsibility in relation to the Jewish people today.

Henry, A. M. *A Mission Theology.* Notre Dame: Fides Publishers, 1962.
A French Dominican, applying the "six-continent" concept of missionary obligation to the Roman Catholic Church.

History's Lessons for Tomorrow's Mission. Milestones in the History of Missionary Thinking. Geneva: World's Student Christian Federation, 1960.
Essays by Latourette, Hogg, Margull, Gensichen, Neill, and others. Includes extensive annotated bibliography.

Hocking, William Ernest. *Living Religions and a World Faith.* New York: The Macmillan Company, 1940.
Developing further the basic position in *Re-Thinking Missions* (1932), Dr. Hocking suggests the way toward a world faith, not by means of "radical displacement," but by "synthesis" leading to "reconception."

————. *The Coming World Civilization*. New York: Harper & Brothers, 1956.

A philosopher's approach to history, in which he gives attention to the character and future role of Christianity among the religions of the world.

Hoekendijk, Johannes C. *The Church Inside Out*. Philadelphia: The Westminster Press, 1966.

Selected essays by a creative and controversial Dutch theologian who is now professor of missions at Union Theological Seminary in New York City.

Hogg, W. Richey. *One World, One Mission*. New York: Friendship Press, 1960.

An interdenominational study book on the theme "Into all the world together," which gives a substantial introduction to the foundations, the history, and the problems of the Christian mission; includes bibliography.

————. *Pages from an African Journal* (The Purdy Lectures at Hartford Seminary Foundation, 1962-1963). Special issue of *The Hartford Quarterly*, III (Spring, 1963).

Observations on the life and growth of the church in revolutionary Africa.

Horner, Norman A. *Cross and Crucifix in Mission. A Comparison of Protestant-Roman Catholic Missionary Strategy*. Nashville: Abingdon Press, 1965.

An introductory study by a Presbyterian missions scholar with ecumenical experience and sympathies.

Jarrett-Kerr, Martin. *Christ and the New Nations*. London: SPCK, 1966.

The author describes the impact, or, as in many cases, the lack of impact, made by the Christian faith on the new Afro-Asian nations. A candid appraisal.

Jones, Tracey K., Jr. *Our Mission Today*. New York: World Outlook Press, 1963.

As one missionary era ends and a new era begins, an

executive of the Methodist Board of Missions discusses the complex and critical issues involved.

————. *The Missionary Intruder. A Brief Examination of the Contemporary Missionary Role.* Nashville: Scarritt College, 1966.

The Journal of Bible and Religion, "Symposium on the Contemporary Jewish-Christian Encounter," XXXIII, 2 (April, 1965).

Kirkpatrick, Dow, ed. *The Doctrine of the Church.* Nashville: Abingdon Press, 1964.
Scholarly papers from the Third (1962) Oxford Institute on Methodist Theological Studies.

————, ed. *The Finality of Christ.* Nashville: Abingdon Press, 1966.
Papers from the Fourth (1965) Oxford Institute, by noted Methodist scholars from America, Britain, Europe, and Asia.

Knight, George A. F., ed. *Jews and Christians: Preparation for Dialogue.* Philadelphia: The Westminster Press, 1965.
Well-known scholars seek to help Christians understand the common ground and the differences between the two faiths, and to encourage honest, searching dialogue.

Kraemer, Hendrik. *The Christian Message in a Non-Christian World.* Published for the International Missionary Council. New York: Harper & Brothers, 1938. Reprinted; Grand Rapids: Kregel Publications, 1961.
One of the most important books in the evolution of mission theology among Protestants in the twentieth century, this was written for the IMC meeting at Tambaram, Madras, in 1938, and emphasized "biblical realism" and "discontinuity."

————. *Religion and the Christian Faith.* Philadelphia: The Westminster Press, 1957.
The approach and material are new, the author's exegetical

study of the biblical data is especially valuable, but his position is basically unchanged from that in his earlier book.

———. *A Theology of the Laity.* Philadelphia: The Westminster Press, 1959.
The pioneering Protestant study in this whole field.

———. *Why Christianity of All Religions?* Philadelphia: The Westminster Press, 1962.

Lacy, Creighton, ed. *Christianity amid Rising Men and Nations.* New York: Association Press, 1965.
Nine specialists in world affairs and religions discuss the present problems and future potentials revealed in the confrontation of the church with social revolution in newly developing nations.

Lindsell, Harold, ed. *The Church's Worldwide Mission.* Waco, Texas: Word Books, 1966.
The proceedings of an important conservative evangelical missions conference at Wheaton, Illinois, in April, 1966.

Löffler, Paul. *The Layman Abroad in the Mission of the Church. A Decade of Discussion and Experience.* (World Council of Churches, Commission on World Mission and Evangelism, Research Pamphlets, No. 10.) New York: Friendship Press, 1962.
A careful study of the rediscovery of the active role of the laity in the life and mission of the church.

Lutheran World (Publication of the Lutheran World Federation, Geneva, quarterly). The following two numbers were devoted entirely to issues related to the Jewish-Christian encounter:
X, 4 (October, 1963), "Symposium on the Church and the Jews."
XI, 3 (July, 1964), "Symposium on Christians, Jews and the the Mission of the Church."

McGavran, Donald Anderson, ed. *Church Growth and Christian Mission.* New York: Harper & Row, 1965.
Studies in the theological and practical factors that affect

the strategy and success of church growth in the Christian mission.

Margull, Hans Jochen. *Hope in Action. The Church's Task in the World.* Philadelphia: Muhlenberg Press, 1962.
The theology of missions as an ecumenical problem in the twentieth century, by a German scholar.

Marsch, Wolf-Dieter, and Thieme, Karl, eds. *Christen und Juden: Ihr Gegenüber vom Apostelkonzil bis heute.* Mainz: Matthias-Grünewald-Verlag, 1961.
An indispensable symposium of scholarly essays, with valuable bibliography.

Mathews, James K. *To the End of the Earth. A Study in Luke-Acts on the Life and Mission of the Church.* Nashville: Methodist Student Movement, 1959.
A biblical study by the Methodist bishop of the Boston area who was formerly a missionary in India.

Methodism and Society, 4 vols., ed. by the Board of Social and Economic Relations of The Methodist Church. Nashville: Abingdon Press, 1960-62.

    I. *Methodism and Society in Historical Perspective,* Richard M. Cameron.

    II. *Methodism and Society in the Twentieth Century,* Walter G. Muelder.

    III. *Methodism and Society in Theological Perspective,* S. Paul Schilling.

    IV. *Methodism and Society: Guidelines for Strategy,* Herbert E. Stotts and Paul Deats, Jr.

These volumes constitute a major contribution toward helping Methodism "to ponder the lessons of its heritage, to redefine its social motivations and ideals, to assess its present activities and resources, and to project adequate strategies for more vigorous advance."

Michalson, Carl. "What Doth the Lord Require of Us?" *International Review of Missions,* XLV (April, 1956), 145-54.

————. *The Hinge of History.* New York: Charles Scribner's Sons, 1959. See especially Chap. X, "The Mission of the Church."

————. *Worldly Theology. The Hermeneutical Focus of an Historical Faith.* New York: Charles Scribner's Sons, 1967.

Muelder, Walter G. *Foundations of the Responsible Society.* Nashville: Abingdon Press, 1959.
Ethical foundations of social responsibility from the Christian perspective.

Neill, Stephen. *A History of Christian Missions. (Pelican History of the Church,* Vol. VI.) Grand Rapids: Wm. B. Eerdmans Publishing Co., 1965.
The best one-volume study of its kind, ecumenical and comprehensive.

————. *The Unfinished Task.* London: Edinburgh House Press, 1957.
A critical reappraisal of the Christian mission by a distinguished Anglican missiologist.

————. *Creative Tension.* London: Edinburgh House Press, 1959.
Carries forward the discussion of issues from the previous book.

————. *Christian Faith and Other Faiths.* New York: Oxford University Press, 1961.
One of the most helpful studies of its kind in recent years.

————. *Colonialism and Christian Missions.* New York: McGraw-Hill Book Company, 1966.
A much-needed critical study from the historical perspective.

Nelson, J. Robert. *Criterion for the Church.* Nashville: Abingdon Press, 1963.
The author seeks a criterion that is "both consistent with the life and pattern of the earliest Christian community and yet vitally effective today."

Newbigin, Lesslie. *A Faith for This One World?* New York: Harper & Brothers, 1961.
In lectures at Harvard University this ecumenical statesman

studies the claim of Christianity to be the faith for our world in the situation of today and in light of the arguments of men such as Radhakrishnan, Toynbee, and Hocking.

———. *Trinitarian Faith and Today's Mission.* Richmond: John Knox Press, 1963.
Exceedingly valuable statement on the theology of mission.

Niles, D. T. *The Preacher's Task and the Stone of Stumbling.* (The Lyman Beecher Lectures for 1957.) New York: Harper & Brothers, 1958.
An ecumenical leader from Ceylon asks: "What is the nature of the existence of the Christian message in a non-Christian world?"

———. *Upon the Earth. The Mission of God and the Missionary Enterprise of the Churches.* New York: McGraw-Hill Book Company, 1962.
Deals with the question: "What does it mean in theological terms and in practice in this ecumenical era for the church to discharge its mission to all the nations?"

———. *The Message and Its Messengers. Missions Today and Tomorrow.* Nashville: Abingdon Press, 1966.
The author looks at the church and asks questions about its faith, its mission, its structure, and its direction for the future.

Ohm, Thomas. *Machet zu Jüngern alle Völker: Theorie der Mission.* Frieburg im Breisgau: Wewel Verlag, 1962.
A monumental study by the late Catholic missiologist at Münster.

Orchard, Ronald K. *Out of Every Nation. A Discussion of the Internationalization of Missions.* (IMC Research Pamphlets, No. 7.) New York: Friendship Press, 1959.

———. *Missions in a Time of Testing: Thought and Practice in Contemporary Missions.* Philadelphia: The Westminster Press, 1965.
"Attempts to discern some of the things which may be

learned from the main thrust of the biblical message about the next steps in missionary action" (p. 13).

————, ed. *Witness in Six Continents: Records of the Meeting of the Commission on World Mission and Evangelism of the WCC Held in Mexico City, December 8th to 19th, 1963*. New York: Friendship Press, 1964.

Addresses, reports, and statements from the first fully representative meeting of the Commission on World Mission and Evangelism of the World Council of Churches since the integration of the IMC with the WCC.

Outler, Albert C. *That the World May Believe*. New York: Joint Commission on Education and Cultivation, Board of Missions of The Methodist Church, 1966.

A study of Christian unity and what it means for Methodists, by a respected theologian at Southern Methodist University.

Panikkar, Raymond. *The Unknown Christ of Hinduism*. London: Darton, Longman & Todd, 1964.

Written by a Catholic priest, this is the most radical approach and attitude to men of another faith in recent years. The author speaks of "a living Presence of Christ in Hinduism," of Hinduism as "a vestibule of Christianity" or as "a kind of Christianity in potency, because it has already a Christian seed."

Parrinder, Geoffrey. *The Christian Debate: Light from the East*. Garden City: Doubleday & Company, 1966.

The author believes that Christians can learn from the great Oriental faiths; that "the impact of eastern religious ideas upon the West amounts to a third Reformation or Revolution."

Perry, Edmund. *The Gospel in Dispute. The Relation of Christian Faith to Other Missionary Religions*. Garden City: Doubleday & Company, 1958.

This American Methodist scholar says that all non-Christian faiths "not only are unable to bring men to God, they actually lead men away from God and hold them captive from God."

Pickett, J. Waskom. *The Dynamics of Church Growth.* Nashville: Abingdon Press, 1963.

From an authority on Christian group movements who was a missionary bishop in India and believes that the opportunity is now ripe and the church is equipped for a major advance in rapid growth.

Ranson, Charles W. *That the World May Know.* New York: Friendship Press, 1953.

The dean of the Theological School at Drew University interpreting the life and task of the church in the world.

Re-Thinking the Church's Mission. Karl Rahner, S.J., ed. (Vol. 13 in *Concilium, Theology in the Age of Renewal.*) New York: Paulist Press, 1966.

A scholarly Roman Catholic symposium inspired by Vatican II; includes a major essay on the concept of mission by Eugene Hillman, C.S.Sp., whose basic thesis is that mission among non-Christian peoples and pastoral care of the Christian people (even though largely dechristianized) are two wholly different tasks of the church. This concept was affirmed by the Vatican Council in its "Decree on the Church's Missionary Activity." The book also contains a valuable bibliographical survey article.

Retif, Louis, and Retif, André. *The Church's Mission in the World.* Trans. from the French by Reginald F. Tervett. (Vol. 102 of the *Twentieth Century Encyclopedia of Catholicism.*) New York: Hawthorne Books, 1962.

Perceptive Roman Catholic analysis of the new missionary situation of the church.

Scherer, James A. *Missionary, Go Home! A Reappraisal of the Christian World Mission.* Englewood Cliffs: Prentice-Hall, 1964.

An American Lutheran scholar summarizes the major issues and thinking in Protestant mission theory today.

Schlette, Heinz Robert. *Towards a Theology of Religions.* New York: Herder and Herder, 1966.

A radical approach by a German Catholic scholar who says that "it is possible to describe the way of the non-Christian religions as the ordinary, and the way of the Church as the extraordinary, way of salvation" (p. 81).

Schmidt, Martin. *The Young Wesley: Missionary and Theologian of Missions*. London: Epworth Press, 1958.
"Methodism . . . was formed under the banner of foreign missions," according to this German scholar (p. 24).

Slater, Robert Lawson. *World Religions and World Community*. New York: Columbia University Press, 1963.
This Christian scholar says that "the prospect of One World —One Religion [is] a very remote prospect" and "a pattern of coexistence . . . seems to be all that can be expected" (pp. 225-26).

Smart, Ninian. *A Dialogue of Religions*. (The Library of Philosophy and Theology.) London: SCM Press, 1960.
A hypothetical, but instructive, dialogue between a Christian, a Jew, a Hindu, a Muslim, and two Buddhists (from Ceylon and Japan), in order to show the kinds of consideration which are relevant in interfaith discussion.

Smith, Eugene L. *God's Mission—and Ours*. Nashville: Abingdon Press, 1961.
The nature and meaning of the Christian mission.

Soper, Edmund Davison. *The Philosophy of the Christian World Mission*. New York and Nashville: Abingdon-Cokesbury Press, 1943.
Midway between Hocking and Kraemer, this writer's position is still representative of much American thinking on the subject.

Springer, Charles R. *Christianity and Rival Religions*. Philadelphia: Fortress Press, 1966.
Brief and elementary introduction to the basic issues and alternatives.

Stewart, James S. *Thine Is the Kingdom: The Church's Mission in Our Time*. New York: Charles Scribner's Sons, 1957.
Lectures on the missionary aim and motive by a noted Scottish theologian.

Stockwell, Eugene L. *Claimed by God for Mission. The Congregation Seeks New Forms.* New York: World Outlook Press, 1965.

The author considers some present congregational structures as heretical, but sees the local congregations as a source of hope "provided mission is central to their life."

Stowe, David. *When Faith Meets Faith.* New York: Friendship Press, 1963.

This noted Protestant missionary leader seeks sympathetic understanding and serious dialogue with men of other faiths, as we move toward one world culture and technological unification.

Street, T. Watson. *On the Growing Edge of the Church: New Dimensions in World Missions.* Richmond: John Knox Press, 1965.

Examines the place of missions within the total mission of the church.

Sundkler, Bengt. *The World of Mission.* Trans. from the Swedish by Eric J. Sharpe. Grand Rapids: Wm. B. Eerdmans Publishing Co., 1966.

The theology, history, and present situation of the missionary church, by a noted Swedish Lutheran missions scholar.

Taylor, John V. *For All the World. The Christian Mission in the Modern Age.* (Christian Foundations, No. 12.) London: Hodder and Stoughton, 1966.

An admirable introduction to the basic issues of missionary theology in this new era, by the general secretary of the Church Missionary Society in London.

Tillich, Paul. *Christianity and the Encounter of World Religions.* New York: Columbia University Press, 1963.

Discusses "the emphasis on and the characterization of the quasi-religions, the elaboration of the universalist element in Christianity, the suggestion of a dynamic typology of the religions, the dialogical character of the encounter of high religions, and the judgment of Christianity against itself as a religion and its ensuing openness for criticism" (Pref.).

————. *The Future of Religions*. New York: Harper & Row, 1966.
Tillich's last essays, including "The Effects of Space Exploration on Man's Condition" and "The Significance of the History of Religions for the Systematic Theologican."

Van Dusen, Henry P. *One Great Ground of Hope. Christian Missions and Christian Unity*. Philadelphia: The Westminster Press, 1961.
Discusses the intimate and inevitable relationship of the movements for mission and unity.

Van Leeuwen, Arend Th. *Christianity in World History: The Meeting of the Faiths of East and West*. New York: Charles Scribner's Sons, 1966.
A momumental study which interprets history, with God's action in Israel and in Jesus Christ as its clue, in terms of the breaking down of all "ontocratic" structures of culture in favor of the dynamic freedom which God offers to all peoples.

Vicedom, Georg F. *The Mission of God: An Introduction to a Theology of Mission*. Trans. by G. A. Thiele and Dennis Hilgendorf. St. Louis: Concordia Publishing House, 1965.
Emphasizes a theocentric approach to the Christian mission, and responds to Hoekendijk's critique of German mission theory.

————. *The Challenge of the World Religions*. Philadelphia Fortress Press, 1963.
The new challenge of resurgent religions to the Christian gospel and mission.

Vincent, John J. *Christ and Methodism. Towards a New Christianity for a New Age*. Nashville: Abingdon Press, 1965.
This British Methodist minister maintains that the distinctive word for this generation is not Christ as Savior but Christ as Lord; that we must be prepared to part company with "orthodoxy."

Visser 't Hooft, Willem A. *No Other Name: The Choice Between Syncretism and Christian Universalism*. Philadelphia: The Westminster Press, 1964.
Strongly rebuts the view that there is no unique revelation

in history, analyzing the differing forms of syncretism in the West as well as the East, and facing the challenge posed through the development of a "world culture."

Walker, Alan. *The Whole Gospel for the Whole World*. With an Introduction by E. G. Homrighausen. Nashville: Abingdon Press, 1957.
Written by an Australian Methodist with ecumenical perspective, this book challenges contemporary concepts of evangelism.

————. *A Ringing Call to Mission*. Nashville: Abingdon Press, 1966.
The mission to metropolis, based on a theology of change.

Warren, Max. *Perspective in Mission*. New York: Seabury Press, 1964.
Reflections on mission theology by a British Anglican missiologist.

Webber, George W. *God's Colony in Man's World*. Nashville: Abingdon Press, 1960.
The life and mission of the church as experienced in the East Harlem Protestant Parish, New York City.

————. *The Congregation in Mission: Emerging Structures for the Church in an Urban Society*. Nashville: Abingdon Press, 1964.
The author asks, "Do these suggested structures provide a means by which the gospel will confront the reality of modern urban life, gain a genuine hearing, and provide a way through which men may discover their true humanity?"

Weber, Hans-Ruedi, *Salty Christians*. New York: Seabury Press, 1963.

————. *The Militant Ministry*. Philadelphia: Fortress Press, 1963.

Webster, Douglas. *Unchanging Mission: Biblical and Contemporary*. Philadelphia: Fortress Press, 1966.
A theological approach to the question "What is the mission of the church in the 1960's?"

————. *Local Church and World Mission*. New York: Seabury Press, 1964.
The author examines what mission is in the world today,

the church as the instrument of mission, the Bible as its basis, and worship as its continuing inspiration.

————. *Yes to Mission.* New York: Seabury Press, 1966.

West, Charles C., and Paton, David M., eds. *The Missionary Church in East and West.* (Studies in Ministry and Worship, No. 13.) London: SCM Press, 1959.
Studies that aim to erase the boundary line which divides "mission" from "ecclesiology," and ask the basic question, "What does it mean to believe that the church itself is a missionary body?"

Wiedenmann, Ludwig. *Mission und Eschatologie. Eine analyse der neueren Deutschen evangelischen Missionstheologie.* Paderborn: Verlag Bonifacius, 1965.
A thorough study of twentieth-century German mission theology, by a Jesuit.

Wieser, Thomas, ed. *Planning for Mission. Working Papers on the New Quest for Missionary Communities.* New York: The U.S. Conference for the World Council of Churches, 1966.
Solid studies by reliable scholars on "The Missionary Structure of the Congregation."

Williams, Colin W. *What in the World?* New York: National Council of Churches, 1964.

————. *Where in the World? Changing Forms of the Church's Witness.* New York: National Council of Churches, 1963.
Both of these small books discuss the question, "Is the present form of church life a major hindrance to the work of evangelism?"

———•———

Audio-Visual Resources [1]

MOTION PICTURES (16mm)

Beyond the Night. 28-minutes, b&w. Produced by the Commission on Ecumenical Mission and Relations, United Presbyterian Church in the U.S.A., 1960.

[1] Compiled with the assistance of Herbert F. Lowe and David W. Briddell,

A thief in Brazil encounters a Protestant church and receives its witness in various ways. As his feeling of personal guilt grows, he is attracted to the Christian way of life and decides to make a fresh start with their help. The film emphasizes the interrelationship of Christian understanding of the gospel, the methods of witness, and the missionary activity of the church. The storyline is one which viewers can envision happening anywhere in the world, perhaps even in their own community.

The Day Geography Got Lost. 30-minutes, b&w. Produced by TRAFCO for the Methodist Youth Fund, 1965.

An MYF group in Richland, Illinois, decides to give a special offering to an MYF group in Sarawak. The unexpected response from Sarawak results in a reexamination of their concept of giving and of mission.

Four Religions. 54-minutes, b&w. Produced by the National Film Board of Canada, 1962. Also available as two 30-minute films. Part I, Hinduism and Buddhism; Part II, Islam and Christianity.

Basic origins and beliefs of the four major religions are presented through live action, artwork, architecture, and literature. Each presentation of the four faiths becomes a "festival" of religious arts with special attention given to architecture and music. Arnold Toynbee is featured as content specialist.

Harambee. 28-minutes, color guide. Produced by the Broadcasting and Film Commission, National Council of Churches, 1964.

The title means "forward together," and the film demonstrates the vitality and talent of young future leaders in new

---

Department of Visual Education, Board of Missions of The Methodist Church. Film descriptions and evaluations are taken, for the most part, from *Audio-Visual Resource Guide,* ed. Alva I. Cox, Jr. and Janet Isbell (7th ed.; New York: National Council of Churches, 1965); and *A Comprehensive List of Audio-Visual Materials,* recommended by the general boards and agencies for use in Methodist churches, published by *The Methodist Story* (Fall, 1965). Address all orders and inquiries for purchases or rental of audio-visual resources to denominational film libraries. When writing to secure a film, request that a guide for using the film be included, if available.

nations (Malaysia, Lebanon, Kenya, and Tanganyika). Except for a brief opening statement, there is no narration—only sound effects and small portions of live dialogue. It is different! Good for an unadulterated look at other cultures and talented, vital youth of other countries.

Household of Faith. 28-minutes, color or b&w. Produced by the Broadcasting and Film Commission, National Council of Churches, 1960.
A documentary film, stressing ecumenicity in mission, the need for all churches to be "sending" and "receiving" churches. Photographed in India, Africa, and Thailand.

Major Religions of the World. 20-minutes, color or b&w., guide. Produced by Encyclopedia Britannica Films, 1954.
Man's quest for a relationship with the Divine is traced through the ages as Hinduism, Buddhism, Islam, Judaism, and Christianity are described in outline. Maps of the world areas in which the religions originated are included, also rituals and major beliefs of each.

Peter Mahadeo's Quest. 29-minutes, color. Produced by the United Church of Canada, 1964.
A young lad's concern for the true meaning and practice of the Christian life. The revealed weaknesses of formal Christianity stir his search for meaning. Filmed in Trinidad.

View from the Cross. 24-minutes, b&w. Produced by the Division of Evangelism, United Presbyterian Church in the U.S.A., 1963.
Shows what some churches are doing to proclaim the gospel in the light of community needs, of reaching "outside the camp" in witness in such unconventional spots as a church-based narcotics clinic, an apartment-house ministry, a legal aid clinic, work with unwed mothers, and a coffee house in which church members are the waiters and take time for conversation with those who come in out of the night. Raises the question: What is motivating the church to witness through these new forms?

Work and the Word. 28-minutes, color. Produced by the Commission on Ecumenical Mission and Relations, United Presbyterian Church in the U.S.A., 1960.

The problems of change from a rural to an industrial economy in Japan; the depersonalization of the individual which results in a new challenge to the church in seeking to make the Word relevant to men.

FILMSTRIPS

After the Flag. 67-frames (11 min.), color, script, guide, 33 1/3 rpm record. Produced by the Woman's Division, Board of Missions of The Methodist Church, 1964.

The problems of the new nations and the responsibility of Christians in understanding these problems.

Counterfeit. 68-frames (11 min.), color, script, guide, 33 1/3 rpm record. Produced by the Board of Missions of The Methodist Church, 1962.

Senior high church group studies needs faced by people in Korea, Hong Kong, Pakistan, and India. The film explores the motives of giving, but stresses that giving money is not enough. Love, concern, and understanding must be given or the money is "counterfeit."

The Factors That Confront Us. 78-frames (15 min.), color, script, 33 1/3 record. Produced by the Board of Missions of The Methodist Church, 1962.

Seven major factors confronting the Christian mission are portrayed: population explosion, technological revolution, rising expectations in underdeveloped countries, rising nationalisms, the end of Christian predominance, the emergence of a world church, and the weapons revolution. Methodist-produced, but not denominationally slanted.

The Faith That Compels Us. Set of four filmstrips, color, script, guide, one 33 1/3 record. Produced by the Board of Missions of The Methodist Church, 1963.

The Gospel, 95 frames (10 min.). Starts with questions which people have about missions and seeks to answer the basic question, "What is the gospel?"

The Mission, 68 frames (10 min.). Discusses missions and culture, missions and the world, missions and history, and the church and missions.

The Younger Churches, 76 frames (10 min.). Describes the establishment of the Christian church in virtually every country of the world as "the great new fact of our time."

The Missionary, 79 frames (10 min.). Attempts to help viewers understand the close relationship between their idea of what a missionary is and what their own personal faith is.

The Frontiers That Call Us. 64-frames (13 min.), color, script, 33 1/3 record. Produced by the Board of Missions of The Methodist Church, 1963.

Presents the new mission frontiers in a changing world where frontiers are no longer simply geographical; describes new situations in American society (suburbia, labor, etc.) as well as the contemporary world scene.

Mission Perspective. 65 frames (9 min.), color, script, guide, 33 1/3 record. Produced by the Board of Missions of The Methodist Church, 1965.

Related to the study theme on the missionary structure of the congregation, this film emphasizes the role of the congregation in affirming the activity of God both within the institutional church and in the "marketplace."

New Nations Challenge Christianity. 77-frames (12 min.), color, script, 33 1/3 record. Produced by the Board of Missions of The Methodist Church, 1964.

Considers several contemporary challenges which new nations of Asia and Africa present to the Christian church. A study map, illustrated question frames for discussion, and visual responsive reading are included as optional frames.

One Traveller. 75-frames (15 min.), color, script, guide, 33 1/3 record. Produced by Church World Service, 1963.

Describes the work of Church World Service throughout the world and the agencies which support it and through which it works. Describes man's responsibility to his fellowmen; demonstrates the self-help aspects of CWS programs as well as the wide range of other help given.

Two Faces of Faith. 70-frames (10 min.), color, reading script. Produced by Friendship Press, 1965.

Explores the two ways in which Christians express their mission: through participation in the worship, nature, and fellowship of the church; and in their response to situations in daily lives.

You Are the Builders. 102-frames (13 min.), color, script, guide, 33 1/3 record. Produced by the Board of Foreign Missions of the Lutheran Church in America, 1961.

The world situation as it relates to the task of Christian missions: religious, political, and economic aspects of core world problems today, which include the population explosion, the rise of nationalism, revival of non-Christian religions, and the means of mass communication. The responsibility of the Christian church and actual measures taken to deal with these problems are shown.